D1262482

Other Books by Muriel Beadle

THE LANGUAGE OF LIFE *(with George W. Beadle)*

THESE RUINS ARE INHABITED

A CHILD'S MIND

A CHILD'S MIND

How Children Learn During the Critical Years
From Birth to Age Five

MURIEL BEADLE

Illustrated by
E. John Pfiffner

LONDON
METHUEN & CO LTD

First published 1970 in the USA by
Doubleday & Company, Inc.

© Muriel Beadle 1970

First published in Great Britain 1971 by
MacGibbon and Kee Ltd

First published as a University Paperback 1972 by
Methuen & Co Ltd
11 New Fetter Lane, London EC4P 4EE
Reprinted 1976 and 1977

ISBN 0 416 70040 3

Printed in Great Britain by
Fletcher & Son Ltd, Norwich

This paperback edition is sold subject to the
condition that it shall not, by way of trade or
otherwise, be lent, resold, hired out, or otherwise
circulated without the publisher's prior consent in
any form of binding or cover other than that in
which it is published and without a similar
condition including this condition being imposed
on the subsequent purchaser.

To My Mother
and
in Memory of My Father,
with Thanks

ACKNOWLEDGMENTS

Several members of the faculty at the University of Chicago have been helpful in the creation of this book. My greatest thanks go to Eckhard Hess, Professor of Psychology, who started me off by providing background material, read the entire manuscript and made many valuable suggestions, and at all stages cheered me on.

I am also grateful to those at Chicago who criticized individual chapters or suggested additional source material: Jacob W. Getzels, Professor in the departments of Education and Psychology; Wilbur A. Hass, Assistant Professor in the departments of Psychology and Linguistics; Robert McCleary, Professor of Psychology; Helen M. Robinson, Professor Emeritus in Education; and F. Howell Wright, Professor of Pediatrics.

If errors remain, however, the fault is mine, not theirs.

Assistance was also given by people at other universities: Marie Clay, Senior Lecturer in Education, University of Auckland; Eleanor J. Gibson, Professor of Psychology, Cornell University; Benson E. Ginsburg, Professor of Biology, University of Connecticut; Arthur R. Jensen, Professor of Educational Psychology, and Curt Stern, Professor of Zoology, both at the University of California at Berkeley; and Roger J. Williams, Professor of Chemistry, University of Texas.

About half the illustrations are the wholly original work of E.

John Pfiffner, the kind of artist every author hopes to find. A consummate craftsman, he is as careful about relating a sketch to the text as he is about the composition and rendering of the sketch itself.

For those illustrations which he adapted from photos or drawings in other published works, I thank the following: Allyn and Bacon (Figure 5); American Orthopsychiatric Association (Figure 23); The Journal Press (Figure 32); Liveright Publishing Corporation (Figure 28); and, *Scientific American* (Figures 1, 2, 7).

In addition, permission was kindly given to reproduce directly from test materials distributed by the Harvard University Press (Figure 20) and The Psychological Corporation (Figure 21); and from a children's reader published by Lothrop, Lee & Shepard (Figure 29).

It is customary, in books of this sort, to include among the Acknowledgments a word of thanks to the typist. I did not use one, and therefore owe a special debt of gratitude to Doubleday's Lawrence P. Ashmead, who had to edit several hundred pages of manuscript typed by my loving hands at home. About this and other trials that authors inflict on editors he has been unfailingly cheerful, however, and I appreciate his help and that of his staff.

Finally, a special note of gratitude is due my husband. In addition to his forbearance on days when the writing was going badly, he helped also by reading the manuscript in both first and final draft. Sometimes his role was that of the intelligent layman for whom the book was written, and sometimes—especially in sections dealing with his scientific specialty, genetics—his role was that of scholarly adviser. I thank him twice, therefore: once as spouse and once as mentor.

M. B.

CONTENTS

PREFACE AND PREVIEW

This book is not in itself a scholarly work; it is a review of certain scholarly work which has been published within the past twenty-five or so years, thereby providing for man a huge reservoir of new information about himself. The part that I have extracted deals in general with the mental development of children, and in particular with the course that learning takes during the earliest years of life—*before* children go to school.

My reason for attempting such a review is simple, evangelical, and, probably, naïve. It seems to me that twenty-five years is much too long a time—nowadays—for knowledge that could help to solve pressing social problems, or at the least to improve the social milieu, to remain largely unused. This has not been true of discoveries made during the same period about the physical universe. They have traveled at breakneck pace from scientific laboratory to technological application to public usage. Those of us in our fifties, for example, can recall our reactions to Lindbergh's solo flight to Paris while waiting to watch a TV broadcast from a manned moon rocket. And despite our having been blasted into the space age at supersonic speed, we have accommodated ourselves with seeming ease to those changes in our physical environment which have accompanied the technological advances of the past quarter century.

Much of our social behavior, however, continues to be guided by beliefs which are as outmoded as the biplane and the horse-drawn buggy. Most of us, for just one example, support a public school system which has not changed fundamentally in philosophy, organization, or curriculum for at least forty years—and in consequence is failing to educate large numbers of American youth.

Although it is convenient to blame "the professional educators" for this failure, in truth it is we the public who are more at fault. It is we who shape the schools, not they us; and it is we who do not know, or have ignored, long-available information that could have been put to use to keep our school systems viable. We have considered ourselves up-to-date when we have provided such products of educational technology as teaching machines, language laboratories, and classroom TV; but they have turned out to be ameliorative rather than curative, and what do we do now? In my opinion, the solution to these school difficulties lies in wide application of what is known about why and how children learn.

That, then, is the main purpose of this book: to speed the rate at which psychological and related research has been filtering out of the professional journals and into the public domain. Perhaps, stripped of jargon and collected in one volume, the information here assembled will come to the attention of more laymen than has so far been its fate. I am not foolish enough to think that great reforms will follow; but on the other hand I don't see why *some* people might not enlarge their understanding of children's mental development or even modify their attitudes toward their part in such development, as a result of my effort. It was, at any rate, worth the try.

To explain how I happened to undertake this project, an autobiographical note is necessary. For many years after my 1936 graduation from college, I was engaged in activities far removed from academic life; and not until 1953, when I married a university professor who later became a university president, did I return to a college campus. During those intervening years, my knowledge of what the professional students of man were learning about him was limited to what I read in the popular periodicals. And this, I promptly discovered, had been neither very much nor very good.

I understand why, since I once worked for a newspaper myself. It is a rare editor who will allow a reporter enough time to acquire the background knowledge that is required if he is to comprehend the research he is asked to report. And it is an even rarer editor who will allocate space for the explanatory material that must, for the sake of accuracy, accompany any account of a "scientific discovery." The articles that *do* see print therefore tend to be oversimplified. Lost en route are the paragraphs that might have explained the relationship of the findings to what was already known in the field in question, or their import for the future. Here are some examples:

I doubt that many people know why the general practice of welfare agencies is to shift abandoned babies into foster or adoptive homes as soon as possible after birth—beyond a vague awareness that "it's better for the baby."

I doubt too that large numbers of people really know what "cultural deprivation" is, and in what respects "enrichment" programs can help children thus deprived. *I* certainly didn't have adequate background for assessing activities of this sort until I made a systematic search for the studies that provide the rationale for such programs.

I also doubt that many people question the great American belief that human beings have limitless ability to change their ways "if only they'd take advantage of their opportunities." The fact, I have learned, is that behavioral change is virtually impossible if opportunity presents itself at the wrong time—an important bit of knowledge for people whose tax money is maintaining welfare programs or whose first-born sons are being nagged through school with a parentally set goal of admission to an Ivy League college on the far horizon.

Yet this, and the research underlying the other examples I've just given, should have become common knowledge at least ten years ago.

In collecting material for this book, I began about where I left off in 1936. Do readers of my college generation remember 1930-style man as I do? His mind, as I recall him, was somehow different from his brain; the one (including how he learned) was the province of the psychologists, whereas the other (including how it functioned) was the concern of the neurologists. The source of his emotions, similarly, varied according to whether the psychiatrists or the endocrinologists were discussing his behavior. A few people in the biological or social sciences wondered what "consciousness" was, but they left it to the philosophers or theologians to decide whether it was the same as "soul." And none of these specialists talked very often to each other.

I learned in college that man was motivated largely by a desire to escape from primitive or painful internal drives. "Behavior" meant the way that he—or his stand-in, the laboratory rat—responded to a specific stimulus. Certain of his skills were the product of heredity, and developed as inexorably as the seasons turned. Yet others of his traits were infinitely plastic, and like soft clay were molded by influences in the environment.

In short, 1930-style man was a mass of semiclosed systems. He didn't seem too difficult to understand because you could look into each of the separate compartments enclosing one aspect or another of his being and convince yourself that if you understood the parts you understood the whole.

In contrast, 1970-style man is far less compartmentalized (and far less easy to understand). One of the most important developments of recent years has been the creation of Early Education Research Institutes, Centers for Cognitive Study, Committees on Human Development, and similar composites; they exist at every major university. They are staffed by people whose individual specialties differ but whose interest jointly focuses on some specific aspect of human behavior. This kind of interdisciplinary contact has been supplemented by the birth of such new specialties as psychobiology, which concerns itself with the relationship of brain function to other biological processes; behavioral genetics, which concentrates on the inheritance of action patterns and traits of temperament; and psycholinguistics, which studies how we learn our language, use it, and are shaped by it.

Of course, not all neurologists and all psychologists yet understand each others' shop talk, and very few scientists and philosophers or theologians communicate at all—but 1970-style man has nevertheless emerged as a whole being (at least among the professionals). His recollections of what he sees or hears and how he feels about his experiences are stored as specialized molecules or perhaps within self-perpetuating electrical circuits in his brain; whatever the details turn out to be, the essential fact is that the product of his learning and the use to which he puts it center in an organ which is nourished by the same blood stream that nourishes the rest of him and is subject to the same laws of function.

To describe him so, without a split between "mind" and "body," has been a primary objective in the organization of this book.

A second change in man's view of man has had to do with the

factors that cause him to learn. Among psychologists, there are still many behaviorists—either those who infer from a change of behavior that a child (or a rat) *has* learned, and let it go at that; or those who probe more deeply, and hypothesize as to the neural networks underlying the observed changes in behavior. Both types see man as essentially a reactive organism, one who responds rather than initiates, one whose behavior is predictable from his past history.

I would guess that the literate public tends to accept this notion of development—not only because it had solid support in the 1920s and 1930s (when much of today's literate public was, like me, being educated) but also because its basic philosophy is so strongly reinforced by psychiatric thought. The initial and continuing impact of Freudian theory needs no elaboration here; it is so pervasive in American society that one needn't even be literate to be familiar with it.

Recently, however, this view of man has been challenged. In the late 1940s and early 1950s, new and persuasive theorists emerged. As a group, they say that human beings are more complicated, that our brains have greater capability and work in more subtle ways than the behaviorists believe. Members of this new school of psychologists view man as an initiator as well as a responder, a seeker after pleasure as well as an escaper from pain. They assert that he actively participates in his own development; that he is less of an inheritor of his past, more an architect of his future.

In the following pages, I have tried to present both points of view. I realize, however, that belligerents do not see neutrals as neutrals see themselves, and am prepared for volleys from either camp.

The nature-nurture controversy of the early decades of this century has quieted. To state it in "either-or" fashion was always silly, for as one scientist has said, "The dichotomy, carried to its logical conclusion, would define innate behavior as that which appears in the absence of environment, and learned behavior as that which requires no organism." In recent years, however, new understanding of the *relationship* between the two influences has occurred; for example, that hereditary and environmental factors can interact in highly individualized ways. Many of the solid foundations of yesteryear have therefore become plastic. It is not at all certain any more that children will develop in certain ways just because their cells carry a genetic blueprint that specifies how their bodies should mature.

Those of my generation who are parents almost certainly raised their children according to the gospel of that great developmentalist Arnold Gesell. Partly because he assured us that there are wide variations of behavior within the limits of normalcy, but mostly because of his firm belief in both the orderliness and inevitability of maturational stages, Gesell calmed us when we suddenly realized that every year-old infant in the neighborhood was walking or talking or toilet-trained—except ours.

It is still true, of course, that most American middle class children develop physically according to much the same timetable. What is new, and sobering, is the realization that they do so because a good many environmental factors are held constant: the mother's nutrition during pregnancy and lactation, the quality of care she offers the newborn child, the amount of visual and verbal stimulation she provides, the amount of freedom she allows him. In child populations where American middle class standards do not prevail, maturation can follow a different course. And in all populations, the direction of both physical and mental development can be altered not by heredity or environment alone but also by the dynamics and timing of their interaction. The throwing of a chemical monkey wrench into a cell at a certain critical period of growth can profoundly affect development. So can the absence of social interaction at a time when the genetic blueprint of that particular individual requires it.

You will find examples of such interaction in a number of the chapters of this book.

Also significant is the recent discovery that much mental retardation and some personality disorders are caused by genetic diseases—for example, by gene-enzyme failures which interfere with normal body chemistry and thus with the development and functioning of the brain—or by chromosome aberrations which occur during cell division. The thought has inevitably occurred to some scientists: How much behavior that we have for years ascribed to environmental influences may in fact have its source in heredity?

The outcome of one such query is Bernard Rimland's *Infantile Autism*, a monograph that is cited here instead of later in the book because Rimland's viewpoint so well exemplifies the new interest in biological bases of behavior. Autistic children seem to withdraw completely from the world; they become mute, or speak a highly private and incomprehensible language; are abnormally detached, aloof, and self-sufficient—seemingly out of contact with the here-and-now and without interest in it.

Autism is generally believed to be an acute disorder of personality, psychosocial in origin. The majority of autistic children have exceptionally intelligent, perfectionist, coldly objective, and unemotional parents; and it is thought that dutiful but joyless mothering—without warmth, interest, or responsiveness to the baby—convinces the child that he is powerless to act upon the environment in his own behalf, so he just gives up the effort.

But, Rimland asks, if autism results from bad mothering, why is it that many autistic children have normal brothers and sisters? Why is autism so resistant to psychiatric therapy? Why not at least consider the possibility that the condition is inherited?

"When dark-haired and dark-eyed parents produce a dark-complexioned child," he says, "we all are quick to agree, 'Mendel was right!' But when introverted parents produce a child who similarly shows little interest in socialization, the refrain inexplicably changes to 'Aha! Freud was right!'"

Assuming that a certain combination of genes are responsible for the personality traits evident in each of the parents—genes that if inherited in double dose could produce a super-introvert—the extremely withdrawn behavior of autistic children could be explained genetically.

Alternatively, Rimland says, how does anybody know that the autistic child's refusal to speak *is* a refusal—a rejection of his parents or a deliberate withdrawal from the world? Maybe he was never really *in* the world. Perhaps he suffered neurological damage that has grossly impaired his ability to relate new information to remembered experience; such inability would prevent his development and use of concepts, symbols, or abstractions.

Autistic children who speak intelligibly tend to mimic what they hear. Having been asked, "Do you want milk?" they indicate that they want it by saying, "Do you want milk?" They also often memorize incredibly long lists of words or numbers. Rimland suggests that maybe they have done all they can with language: repeat it rather than understand it. He thinks that the autistic child's brain may function "as though it were operated by a clerk rather than a chemist; raw material comes and goes, but the parcels are never opened and their contents are never mixed to form any useful compound."

Rimland's full case cannot be presented here, and he admits himself that it becomes highly speculative before he is done. The point of mentioning it is simply that the old dogmas of the behavioral sciences are being questioned and the scholarly climate is such that skepticism is welcomed: Rimland's book got a prize because of its thought-provoking and original character.

(If you decide to read it, however, you had better read Bruno Bettelheim's *The Empty Fortress*, also. He has an opposite viewpoint, and writes more eloquently than Rimland.)

Yet another change that has occurred in scholarly thought about child development in the course of the past few decades is a new awareness of the importance of the very early years of life. It is not new to say, "Train up a child in the way he should go and when he is old he will not depart from it." But today the proverb could be amended to read ". . . and when he is old he will be *unable* to depart from it."

Perhaps the most impressive of all the works I have read in the course of writing this one is *Stability and Change in Human Characteristics*, by the University of Chicago's Benjamin S. Bloom. It is difficult reading for one not trained in statistics, but the effort is worth making—especially if one has never seriously questioned the "implicit assumption running through our culture that change in behavior and personality can take place at any age or stage and that the developments at any one age or stage are no more significant than those which take place at another."

This is simply not so, Bloom says, after having compared the findings of a great many longitudinal studies (the kind in which the progress of the same individuals is recorded over a period of many years*). A central finding of his book is that for five selected

---

* Such studies are difficult and costly, if only because Americans are so mobile. Marie Skodak and Harold Skeels, for example, started in 1934 to keep records on 180 children who had been adopted by families living in the vicinity of Ames, Iowa; by 1937 could find only 152 of them; by 1940, only 139; and by 1946, the sample was down to 100. To visit these 100 for interviews and testing required over twelve thousand miles of driving, so widely had the families scattered.

For another example, Dolores Durkin recently attempted to follow two groups of early readers through their first few years at school. One group, 49 children who lived in Oakland, California, when they started school, had by

human characteristics—height, general intelligence, general school achievement, aggressiveness in males, dependence in females—the growth rate starts fast and then progressively slows, *on the average reaching its midpoint before children are five years old.*

► Boys gain 54 percent of their mature height between conception and age three, another 32 percent between ages three and twelve, and the final 14 percent between ages twelve and eighteen.

► Of general intelligence (as measured at age seventeen, for both boys and girls), about 50 percent of development takes place between conception and age four, about 30 percent between ages four and eight, and about 20 percent between the ages of eight and seventeen.

► As for vocabulary development, reading comprehension, and general school achievement, 33 percent of whatever academic skills children have attained at age eighteen develops between birth and age six, 42 percent between ages six and thirteen, and 25 percent between ages thirteen and eighteen.

► In the area of personality, there is no scale for determining the amount of aggressiveness, say, that the average person exhibits at maturity. However, if one compares individuals on a relative scale at one age and relates these results to those obtained on another relative scale at a different age, one finds that 50 percent of the aggressiveness that males show at age eighteen or twenty has developed by age three and that 50 percent of the passivity that females exhibit at age eighteen or twenty has developed by age four.

I hate to belabor the obvious, but maybe the meaning of "stability" isn't obvious to everyone. Bloom says, "One basic finding of this work is that less and less change is likely in a group or

---

sixth grade been in fourteen different school systems. The other group, 156 New York City school children, had by third grade dispersed so that one child was living in Toronto, one was in Tokyo, twenty were in public schools in cities other than New York, nine were in private schools in New York, and only 125 remained in that city's public schools.

Miss Durkin speaks for all psychologists who undertake similar studies when she says, with more than a hint of weariness, "Longitudinal research requires the persistence of a sleuth as much as it needs the skills of a researcher."

individual as the curve of development of a characteristic reaches a virtual plateau . . . It is possible that very powerful environmental and/or therapeutic forces may overcome and alter the most stable of characteristices—but this is yet to be demonstrated."

That's a gloomy conclusion; but before you throw up your hands and write off the possibility that your particular Johnny or Janey will be a "late bloomer," I must stress that Bloom is talking about *statistical probabilities.* Human beings are both resilient and unpredictable, and some few always beat the odds.

Nevertheless, for children in general, the time to worry about academic failure in high school is not when they are in eighth grade—for by then they have developed 75 percent of whatever skills they will, in the normal course, have. The time to provide remedial help is prior to and during the first grade, because at age six some 66 percent of final achievement is still available to be influenced.

If this is the only fact that remains in a reader's mind when he closes this book, I shall be satisfied. Too many people still believe that the high school dropout problem will be solved if children are forced to stay longer in school. The emphasis on correcting failure should shift to the other end of the age scale, with provision for the acquisition of intellectual skills at a time of life when children can best use the opportunity—that is, between the ages of two and six. The Head Start programs are the merest beginning.

Now, a few words about my choice of material.

Although the content of this book is mostly drawn from the work of psychologists and psychiatrists, I have dipped to varying degrees into the published works of sociologists, anthropologists, and educators both theoretical and practicing. There is information here from the research of geneticists, zoologists, biochemists, and those in other subspecialties of biology. Among men of medicine, pediatricians, physiologists, neurologists, and endocrinologists are represented. There are even some bits from physics and engineering, in sections that have to do with computers and communications theory. How could such a book be other than superficial? (However, there is a list of references at the back of the book for those who want to read the original papers from which I have quoted.)

Some readers will undoubtedly find that I have skimmed some topics too fast for their taste, or have spent too much time on others. Some topics that another chronicler of the same subject might consider essential are not included at all. That's because I have abstracted, from the mass of reports and reviews I have read, the material which interested *me*. Inasmuch as I consider myself to be the "intelligent layman" for whom this book is intended to provide updated information about children's mental development, I can only hope that I am typical.

MURIEL BEADLE

Chicago, Illinois
August 1969

A CHILD'S MIND

CHAPTER 1

NEVER TOO YOUNG TO LEARN

There he lies in his mother's arms: five days old, a healthy, normal infant—and only the eyes of love could view him as other than a provisional member of the human species. His eyes are small and squinty, his nose is flat, his head wobbles. His body is oddly proportioned: his head accounts for a full quarter of his length, his shoulders are narrow, his abdomen bulges. His arms are only a fourth and his legs a fifth as long as they will be at maturity, and both are characteristically flexed instead of extended. His movements are spasmodic, his respirations are shallow, his heartbeat is fast and variable; in fact, none of his internal processes are fully regulated or coordinated.

Yet even in five days he has come a long way.

The first and biggest job he had to accomplish was to survive the cataclysmic experience of his own birth. For forty weeks he had occupied a benign and sheltering environment, one which made virtually no demands on him. His mother's metabolic machinery served his needs as well as her own; he was protected from pain, pressure, or infection; and his buoyant suspension in liquid gave him considerable freedom of movement.

Then suddenly he was expelled—suddenly but not swiftly, for his birth journey took many hours and was attended by a host of insults to his body. No part took so severe a beating as his head. The various bony parts of the skull often overrode each other as they were forced, by the contractions of his mother's uterus, to adapt to the shape of the funnel that is her pelvis; and at the end of this journey, his exit was finally accomplished by forceps clamped to his head.

Nor was this the last of stress and shock. Silver nitrate was dropped into his eyes. His mouth and nose were wiped to clear them of matter that might impede breathing. The cord linking him to his mother was surgically cut. He was layered in fabric that was mildly abrasive to his very thin skin, and laid in a bassinet within which the weight of his own body on a solid surface kept him practically immobile. There, despite such physical handicaps as an at-birth drop in temperature to 96 degrees and an invasion of his alimentary tract by bacteria within ten hours of delivery, he nevertheless began to cope successfully with many do-it-or-die problems.

One major problem was mechanical. During fetal life, his blood had drawn its oxygen from the placenta in his mother's womb, via his own umbilical cord. Now he had to redirect the flow so that the blood would become oxygenated in the lungs; start the muscles working that cause the lungs to expand; and expel the fluid in the tiny sacs that enable the lungs to hold air. In addition, he had to adjust to as much of a change in oxygen concentration as a climber upon descending from Mount Everest to Katmandu.

Another problem was to accommodate his metabolic processes to a different kind of nourishment, a different method of intake, and a different system of excretion. To solve this problem requires monstrous readjustments in every part of a newborn baby's body, adjustments that range—to name only a few—from the mastery of sucking and swallowing to the establishment of digestive rhythms to the regulation of water balance in the tissues.

A third problem was one of adjusting to extremes: to an environment whose temperature was more variable than he had known before, where sounds were no longer muted, where dark was newly offset by light. New, too, was the experience of being touched, turned, lifted, and left—an on-again, off-again sensation in sharp contrast to a past in which he was in constant physical contact with his mother.

By this, his fifth postnatal day, the infant has by no means fully solved the problems presented by his birth, but he is already doing a very creditable job of assimilating food, digesting it, and eliminating waste products. He clearly responds to a touch. He can hear, although he cannot yet identify the source of a sound. He squints or sneezes if the light is too bright. His eyes may follow, though sluggishly, a moving object. When he cries, he quiets if held; perhaps he has already begun to associate his mother's presence with the satisfaction of his needs. (*She,* at any rate, believes that he does.)

But he is still so immature that it is difficult to see in him the rational human being he will some day become. His behavior is so disorganized, his responses are so gross and generalized, and his eyes have such a curious glassy opaqueness that it's hard to believe he has a working brain inside that still-soft skull. It is not unusual, in medical journals especially, to see him described as "essentially decorticate"; that is, lacking a functioning cortex, the part of the brain to which is ascribed the organization of those traits which make us human.

In 1890, describing the birth experience, William James said, "The baby, assailed by eyes, ears, nose, skin, and entrails at once, feels it all as one great blooming buzzing confusion." Is that a poetic or a scientific observation? *Can* a newborn baby feel anything, in the sense of being aware of his emotions? Does he "know" that a light is shining in his eyes, or is his reflex blink his sole reaction? So much newborn response is automatic that it is easy for observers to believe that *all* newborn response is automatic; that the baby, though animate, is psychologically a nonentity.

There is no easy way to find out. Babies have exceedingly limited ability to respond to stimuli in ways that are meaningful to the observer—and, besides, they are notoriously uncooperative in test situations. One psychologist reported in a footnote to a test résumé that a particularly alert baby had spotted his eye at a peephole and consistently watched the watcher instead of the crib toy that was supposed to engage the attention of the babies in the experiment. Another investigator recorded 71 instances out of 168 trials during which his young subjects were fretting, crying, or too sleepy for him to be sure what their reaction to his test situation was. Another investigator, similarly frustrated, let his exasperation creep into a scholarly paper; he ended it by saying that one child "was so restless that he was completely useless."

In recent years, however, a number of ingenious methods for studying newborns have been developed. As a result, a body of evidence is being amassed which indicates that the human infant is more than an automaton. Many studies show that babies take *selective* notice of their surroundings right from birth; further, that their responses to "sensory input" can be changed right from birth. This means—as I will explain in more detail shortly—that babies can learn right from birth.

In fact, they can learn *before* birth.

The psychologists Jack Bernard and Lester W. Sontag once tested fetal response to sound by placing a loudspeaker close to the mother's abdomen (but not in contact with it, to assure that sound waves would travel through air). They found that the broadcast sound caused the rate of fetal heartbeat to increase sharply. This didn't prove, of course, that the unborn baby was hearing—only that it was sensitive to sound stimulus.

Something a little more ambitious was then attempted by David K. Spelt (who, like Jack Bernard and a number of other psychologists mentioned in these pages, started out in academic life but shifted to consultive work for business). Spelt's experiment was to use sound in "conditioning" unborn babies; that is, he decided that he would try to teach them to transfer to stimulus B a response originally elicited by stimulus A.

(The conditioned response was discovered and named, in the 1920s, by the Russian physiologist Ivan Pavlov. While doing experiments on digestion and salivation in dogs, he noticed that the animals, as the experiment went along, began to salivate before food was presented to them—first on sight of the dish it was served in and then upon hearing the food bearer's steps. Pavlov then checked this observation by presenting food in combination with the sound of a bell; shortly, the dogs salivated when they heard the bell, whether food was present or not.)

Spelt's version of this kind of experiment began by securing the cooperation of sixteen pregnant women who were past the seventh calendar month of gestation. He divided them into several groups. With one group, he ascertained that a vibrator applied to a maternal abdomen would not disturb the fetus sufficiently to cause movement. Experience with another group showed that a loud noise just outside the mother's body (an oak clapper hitting a pine box) *would* cause fetal movement. Then, using a third group, Spelt combined the vibrator and the sound—timing them so that there was a few seconds' lag after he started the vibrator and before he loosed the clapper.

After 15–20 pairings of the vibrator-plus-sound, the fetuses began to move in response to the vibrator alone. In two cases, the experiment was interrupted for more than two weeks, yet when the expectant mothers returned to Spelt's laboratory, their unborn babies "remembered" the experience and again moved in response to the vibrator alone.

Such experiments are not as bizarre as they might at first seem to a layman. After all, those babies were at the same stage of development as many another child whose luck it is to be born during the eighth or ninth month of gestation. And premature babies, although they are weaker and slower than infants who are born at term, nevertheless forge right ahead once they *are* born. (In responsiveness, a two-months-premature baby will be ahead of his equal-age cousin, a full-term but newborn infant.) Birth is really only one point in developmental time, one event in a continuum of existence—the beginning of which has a special aura of mystery because it is hidden.

Once a baby is over the threshold of birth, however, it is possible to observe and measure his behavior with some objectivity. A group of investigators at Brown University, notably a young man named Lewis P. Lipsitt, have run a variety of experiments in which they have conditioned two- and three-day-old infants to turn their heads in response to a sound, after first pairing the sound with a gentle stroking of the baby's cheek and the presentation of a bottle of sweetened water. One of the most dramatic of these experiments involved sixteen babies, aged two to five days, who learned to turn their heads to the right at the sound of a tone but not at the sound of a buzzer; and then learned to reverse their response, turning for the buzzer but not the tone.

Lipsitt consequently said, "The magnitude of the effect, induced experimentally in the first few days of life and with a relatively short period of training, lends credibility to the proposition that the human newborn is not only a learning organism but may be remarkably sensitive to environmental events."

Another indication that something more than automatic responses are involved in behavior is an individual's ability to discriminate between or among sensory stimuli. Lipsitt and a colleague, Trygg Engen, have also shown that newborns can distinguish between odors—a feat requiring more higher nervous system functioning than tiny babies are ordinarily credited with having.

To do this the two psychologists took advantage of the well-known fact that repetition of an initially strong sensory stimulus will cause a progressively weaker response. You are familiar with this phenomenon: if you enter a house filled with the aroma of freshly baked chocolate cookies, you are aware of it for only a few minutes and then sensitivity diminishes. Babies react to sensory stimuli in the same fashion. A loud-ticking clock, for example, will initially disrupt their sucking, but in a matter of minutes they will cease to respond to it and sucking will resume. So too with odor. Lipsitt and Engen discovered that newborns respond with a startle response to presentations (under their noses, on swabs) of banana oil or another pungent oil called heptanal, but quickly and progressively become less sensitive to these odors.

However, if one introduces two odorants alternatively, habituation to the second one makes the organism again responsive to the first one (although not so responsive as when both odorants were completely novel). Lipsitt and Engen found that this "recovery of response" phenomenon is as true of babies as of adults, which in turn made them wonder whether newborns could discriminate one odor from another. Therefore they combined banana oil (33 percent) and heptanal (17 percent) with a non-odorous carrier, and habituated the babies to the mixture. Then they administered the pure odors alone; and found that recovery of response occurred just as it would have if the components of the mixture had been presented separately. In fact, the vigor of the response recovery was proportional to the amount of each odorant in the mixture. Finally, the same test was given to adults. It revealed the same levels of response recovery—although the adults *told* the investigators whether or not they could smell the pure odors after having become habituated to the mixture, whereas the babies' response was in terms of body movement, heartbeat, and changes in respiration.

Robert L. Fantz of Western Reserve University undertook another fascinating group of experiments, this time on visual perception in newborns. Disputing "the standard textbook knowledge that the young infant cannot see objects or patterns," Fantz not only demonstrated that newborns prefer pattern over color, but also that they have definite preferences in patterns.

When eighteen infants under five days of age were given various choices of what to look at—a schematically drawn face, a bull's-eye pattern, a section of newsprint, a plain white circle, a fluorescent yellow circle, or a red circle—eleven of them looked longest at the

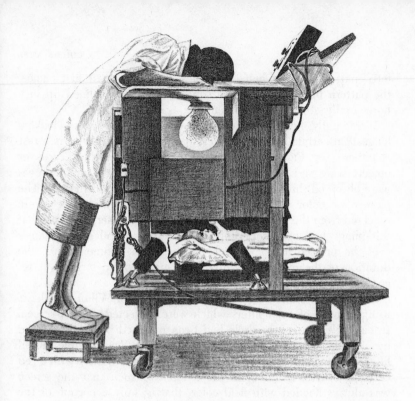

FIGURE 1

Robert L. Fantz used this apparatus to test very young infants'
visual discrimination. Patterned cards or (as above) three-
dimensional shapes were slid into slots above the baby's head
and the duration of his interest in different patterns or forms
was recorded. (Adapted from a photograph by David Linton.
Copyright © 1961 by *Scientific American*. Reproduced by permission of David Linton and *Scientific American*.)

face pattern, five at the bull's-eye, and two at the newsprint. None
looked longest at the plain colors. The same pattern preference was
shown by babies less than twenty-four hours old, most of whom
consistently looked at the face pattern.

Fantz has also shown that very young babies can discriminate
among quite similar patterns. To thirty-five infants under two weeks
of age, he showed five different arrangements of small black squares
on a white background. Some of these small squares were organized
into stripes, others into a checkerboard, others in a random "con-

fetti" pattern. Almost half the babies picked, as their first choice, the pattern in which the small squares were neatly lined up in a horizontally striped arrangement.

Incidentally, how did Fantz know that the babies were "looking longest" at certain patterns? He cradled his young subjects in a test chamber (see FIGURE 1) at the top of which various cards or objects were slid into an illuminated slot; then the infant's eyes were observed through a small hole just to one side of the slot. The pattern or color on the card or the shape of the object were reflected from the baby's cornea, and when the observer noted that this image had been superimposed on either pupil of the baby's eyes, he pressed a microswitch connected to a timer. Thus, the duration of the infant's attention to a given visual target was recorded.*

Still another study involving vision was that of Wilton P. Chase, using a series of color filters which were projected upon a screen. In each filter, a center circle had been punched out and replaced by a circle punched from a different filter. (For example, a red filter with a yellow-green center and a yellow-green filter with a red center.) Magnification upon projection was such that the screen was always flooded with field color; that is, only a portion of the filter was used, and even if one moved it back and forth in the projector the viewer would get no sense of movement because the field color never went off the screen. Such movement would only be apparent relative to the center spot, and then only if the viewer could discriminate one color from another.

One can see why a man capable of designing as ingenious an apparatus as this might wind up, as Chase has, at TRW Systems in California, which specializes in space-age engineering; but then he was a young academician at the University of North Carolina. His subjects were twenty-four infants from fifteen to seventy days old, and he decided that the babies could be considered to be seeing the movement of the central spot if their eyes followed the movement at the same rate that the investigator was moving the filter in the projector. Each infant, Chase noted, seemed to have a rate at which he could best follow, and the rate of movement was therefore adjusted to each baby's ability. The result of this experi-

---

* It should be mentioned here that initial preferences for pattern give way, around three months of age, to preferences for solid objects or textured surfaces.

ment was that all babies discriminated between most of the colors combined in the filters; the only combination to which some didn't respond was yellow-green with a green spot in the center.

Having offered these several studies as evidence of my earlier statement that "babies can learn right from birth," I come now to a discussion of what learning *is*.

Laymen tend to define it as the simple acquisition of knowledge. Psychologists once defined it that way too; but in the early years of this century a majority of psychologists switched to a more activist definition. Learning, most textbooks now say, is "a process which brings about a lasting change in an individual's behavior as a result of contact with the environment." Lipsitt's babies, for example, showed an ability to learn because they first associated a sound with feeding and then transferred their head-turning response to the sound alone. Thus, behavior was observably modified by contact with the environment; by experience.

But some psychologists are now broadening this definition to include, once more, the older one. Robert Fantz has said, "A person may read a book or watch a moving picture without giving any indication of what has been learned, either in immediate responses or in lasting changes of behavior, and yet it would be rash to claim that the person has learned nothing." He points out that acquisition and ordering of information about the environment is basic to control of one's actions within that environment, and thus speaks for many other contemporary psychologists in postulating that learning is not necessarily measured by observable changes in behavior. The fact that newborns seem to do no more than attend to certain aspects of their surroundings does not prove that they are not as a result experiencing internal changes which can properly be called learning.

Quite the contrary, in fact, if the animal studies on "latent learning" can be extrapolated to human beings. Here are two examples:

Cornell University's Eleanor Gibson and George Washington University's Richard D. Walk raised two groups of litter-mate rats under the same circumstances except that the side walls of one cage were plain and the walls of the other cage were decorated with metal cutouts of a circle and a triangle. Nothing was done to call the rats' attention to these forms; they were just there. Later, when both groups of rats were trained in solving problems that involved discrimination of geometric forms, the group that had been raised in the cage with the metal cutouts learned faster and made fewer errors. *Something* unobservable but lasting had obviously occurred in the brains of the rats that performed better.

E. Roy John and several colleagues at New York Medical College's Brain Research Laboratories have recently reported that cats learn by observation too. Using standard conditioning techniques, they taught a number of cats to press levers, the reward being food. At the same time, they placed an "observer" cat in a cage close to the training apparatus. No special efforts were made to assure that the observer cat watched the learner cat, but feline curiosity seems to have matched its reputation. When the observers were later set the same problem, they learned faster and made fewer errors than the first group of cats. In fact, several performed correctly on their first try; they didn't have to puzzle out the job, using the trial and error methods that typify the early stages of training in experiments of this sort.

John and his collaborators therefore conclude that "the impressive speed and efficiency of observational learning, contrasted with the slowness and need for repetition which often characterize conventional conditioning, suggest that the latter may well utilize relatively unnatural mechanisms. Observational learning may be the primary method of acquiring language, ideas, and social habits in man . . ."

However one defines or studies it, learning is the process by which babies become humanized. Ours is a species in which relatively little adult behavior is built in by nature, and instead must be learned. This is another way of saying that environment has a profo·nd effect upon human development. But it is *not* another way of saying that environment is all. In fact, if one today weighs the twin influences of nature and nurture, an exercise which in the recent past tipped the scales rather heavily in favor of environment, one notes that the balance is swinging more toward heredity. As we shall see in subsequent chapters, nature seems to have laid out a precise and not-too-broad path which must be followed if the child is to learn the kind of behavior which will fit him for human society.

CHAPTER 2

BIOLOGICAL BASES OF BEHAVIOR

Man is unique, but many of his parts and most of his basic processes are not. The growth and functioning of these are determined by his biological inheritance—an inheritance that goes back well over a billion years, makes him kin in greater or less degree to every creature that ever lived, and lays down certain inviolable rules of development and behavior.

Like all other living organisms, for one example, he matures from the top down and from the center outward. Mothers who keep regular entries in their copy of "Our Baby's First Seven Years" will record a sequence in which eye and mouth movements come under control first, then those of head and neck, later those of trunk and arms, still later those of the hands and lower trunk, and finally those of pelvis, legs, and fingers. There are, therefore, physical limits to what a child can do at any given time: though he has legs and from birth can make walking movements if properly held, he cannot actually walk until the musculature of his back and pelvis and the structures of the brain that maintain balance have matured sufficiently to permit him to stand up and stay up.

Also like other living organisms, he progresses from "the whole to the part, from the random to the orderly, from the general to the specific." As a newborn, he reacts to a stimulus with his whole body; then he is able to direct his hand to what he wants without moving his torso; finally, he can coordinate eyes, arm, hand, and fingers and use them in an integrated action such as picking up a crayon and drawing with it. A corollary of this gradual specialization is that young organisms experience more widespread effects, if normal developmental processes are interfered with, than if damage occurs after individual parts have begun to function more independently.

At all stages of development and in adult life, furthermore, living things are organized so that changes in one part trigger compensatory changes by other parts. This process, which is called homeostasis, maintains the whole organism in a steady state. For example, if there is an oversupply of sugar in the blood, the pancreas releases insulin, which helps to burn up the extra sugar and restore the blood to its normal chemical composition. The object of this, and the thousands of other internal balancing acts, is to preserve the organism's functional equilibrium.

General sequences of physical maturation such as I have just described, and the chemical reactions upon which life itself depends, are initiated and regulated by one's genes; that is, such activity is *innate*, part of the physical structure of the organism at birth. But "innate" does not necessarily mean "inflexible" or "unchangeable"; in fact, the circumstances in which a particular organism finds itself can and often do modify its genetically determined activity. Lack of Vitamin D in a diet, for instance, can permanently deform the skeleton of a child whose innate capability for forming bone is the same as that of a child who gets Vitamin D and consequently has healthy bone. Nature's scheme for the maturation of other parts of the body can similarly be subverted if the environment fails to provide some necessary ingredient for growth.

And the same is true for behavior.

Arthur R. Jensen of the University of California at Berkeley makes the point well when he says that it is a common misconception "that inherited characteristics are immutable while environmentally acquired characteristics are easily changed. According to that view, to say that a trait is hereditary is tantamount to fatalism. This is incorrect . . . Determination of the heritability of a behavior trait tells us the sources of the influences—biological or psychological—to which the trait is most susceptible, rather than the degree of immutability of the trait."

The following chapter will discuss the relationship of environment to heredity in much more detail. The important point that needs making now is that human babies are not passive receivers of experience, blank pages upon which environment can write at will. It is true that they are much more immature at birth than the young of any other species, and therefore are more malleable, but that is not the same thing as saying that they are lumps of dough which can be shaped any which way. They are active participants in their own development simply because they are *alive;* because certain capabilities and predilections underlying behavior are built into their cells.

Furthermore, these capabilities and predilections are now known to be more numerous than has been believed in the recent past. The early learning capacities of infants, as mentioned in the preceding chapter, are a case in point. Here is another example, from the work of a young Scottish psychologist, T. G. R. Bower, who is now at Harvard:

Bower's young subjects are about eight weeks old, and he tests them to measure performance on quite complex perceptual problems. In one test, for instance, he conditioned babies to recognize a white cube; then, in order to see whether the size of the cube as originally registered on the retina determines the infant's later recognition of the object, he displayed cubes of different sizes at different distances from the baby's eyes. A majority of babies identified the original cube—which indicates that they perceived the true size of this object even when they saw it at a distance. This in turn means that they could process the kind of information dependent upon both binocular and motion parallax (the process by which two eyes, seeing the same object from a very slightly different point, combine the images).

Another of Bower's tests involves conditioning babies to respond to a wire triangle with a bar across it, then showing them four similarly shaped objects. (See FIGURE 2.) Of the four, those numbered 1 and 2 are more like the original shape—*if* one perceives the original as a single unit in one plane. If the original is seen as a shape composed of two elements—a triangle and a bar—the shapes numbered 3 and 4 are most similar. Bower's babies picked the plain triangle (3). This indicates that they had "seen through the bar" as adults do, and had perceived the shape of the original triangle despite the interruption of line created by the superimposed bar.

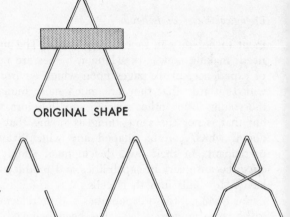

ORIGINAL SHAPE

1   2   3   4

FIGURE 2

Most people—even very young infants, according to T. G. R.
Bower—"see through the bar" superimposed on the triangle
above, and choose as most like it either of the two shapes at
the right of the sketch. (Adapted from a drawing from "The
Visual World of Infants," T. G. R. Bower. December 1966 issue
of *Scientific American*. Copyright © 1966 by Scientific American,
Inc. All rights reserved.)

Commenting on this and the space-constancy test, Bower has
said, "What the experiments seem to show is that evolution has
tuned the human perceptual system to register not the low-grade
information in momentary retinal images but rather the high-fidelity
information in sequences of images or in simultaneous complexes
of images."

Another test involved the babies' ability to perceive constancy of
shape despite the alteration of orientation that occurs when one
slants a rectangular object so that one end is closer to the viewer
than the other end. On this test, Bower's young subjects could
register shape *or* orientation, but not both at once.

He says, "The most plausible hypothesis is to assume that their
perceptual systems can handle simultaneously only a fraction of
the information they can register. They may be able to process
only one of these variables even when both are present and registered . . .

"The theory emerging from our studies and [those of] others is based on evidence that infants can in fact register most of the information an adult can register but can handle less of the information than adults can. Through maturation they presumably develop the requisite information-processing capacity."

An interesting footnote to Bower's work is that he expected to show that infants' visual perception is entirely learned; instead of which, he showed the reverse. Thus, he joins the ranks of other investigators—mostly young men, Fantz being forty-five, Lipsitt, forty-one, and Bower, twenty-nine—who now believe that our inborn capabilities are much greater than earlier generations of psychologists and physiologists had suspected.

There is also good reason to believe that human infants are genetically structured to learn specific kinds of things.

In a famous experiment, Keith and Catherine Hayes (who were then at the Yerkes Laboratory in Orange Park, Florida) "adopted" a newborn chimpanzee and for some five years raised her as if she were a human child. Her abilities developed in the same sequence and her general behavior was comparable to that of human children of the same age—except for two things.

Her play was much more athletic than a child's; that is, she spent a larger part of the day running, climbing, and jumping. And she was much less vocal. She babbled a little early on, but became silent at about five months of age. Inasmuch as the variety of sounds she had initially made indicated that her vocal organs were capable of producing satisfactory approximations of human speech, the Hayeses began a speech-training program.

It took Viki five months to learn to produce—with much grimacing and straining—a hoarse staccato grunt. Eventually (at the age of fourteen months), she learned to say "Mama," "Papa," and "cup," and to use them appropriately—most of the time. But that achievement exhausted her ability. Nor was it a very significant achievement: Viki, intelligent enough on other tests suitable for her age-group, failed those based on verbal intelligence.

The Hayeses therefore said, "Our results strongly suggest that the two species are much more alike, psychologically, than has been supposed. They suggest, in fact, that man's superior ability to use language may be his only important *genetic* advantage. This one genetic advantage makes further advantages possible, however, since language is a means of sharing knowledge.

"Intelligence depends upon three factors: the individual's innate capacity, his personal experience, and the experience he acquires second hand, through communication with others. This last factor, while unimportant to most species, makes man less dependent upon individual abilities by providing him with a more effective 'group intelligence.'"

To a genetically determined capacity to perform specific activities one should add a genetically determined sensitivity to specific aspects of the environment, a sensitivity that waxes and wanes according to a specific timetable. During such periods, organisms are highly susceptible to modification (for better or worse) by external factors that do not affect them at other developmental periods. Many examples of critical periods will be given in a later chapter, but here is one from an experiment that is typical of the many "deprivation" studies that have been made on animals:

Robert L. Fantz, whose work with human babies was described in the previous chapter, placed rhesus monkeys in a dark room within several days of birth (first with their mothers; later, alone). They remained in lightless surroundings for periods ranging from one week to sixteen weeks, except for a daily five-minute test period when they could peek through a hole into an illuminated chamber. There, the choices of things to look at were similar to those that Fantz had offered to human newborns—checkerboard squares, bull's-eye circles, horizontal stripes, plain colors of varying brightness, flat or textured objects.

The monkeys' visual development paralleled that of human infants, an initial preference for patterns being followed by increased attentiveness to solid objects—but only if the monkey was transferred to a lighted nursery at about the eighth week of the experiment. If kept in the dark beyond that point, monkeys subsequently lost interest in patterns and did not develop normal interest in solid objects. They experienced anatomical degeneration of certain structures of the eye and neural degeneration of certain brain cells related to vision. Furthermore, these effects were lasting: when the same monkeys were retested at the age of fifteen months, those who had been deprived of visual experience beyond the eight-week point (even though deprivation had ceased at sixteen weeks) were only half as good at visual discrimination problems as those that had been brought into the light at eight weeks or sooner.

There also appear to be genetically based variances in human temperament—a statement that will warm the hearts of people who have never been wholly persuaded by twentieth-century scientists that a hot temper isn't inherited along with red hair. For that belief, I hasten to add, there is still no proof—but other aspects of behavior or traits of personality have lately been found to have their source in the genes or chromosomes.

That there are temperamental breed differences among animals has, of course, long been known and exploited. Ask any dog fancier or pet shop owner. ("Young children in the house? I'd advise a beagle rather than a terrier. They're not so excitable.") Or consult psychologists who use animals for laboratory research. Rats and mice have long been as intensively bred for behavioral characteristics as for susceptibility or resistance to certain diseases.

A typical venture of this type was that of C. S. Hall, who now heads the Institute for Dream Research in Santa Cruz, California. But in the 1930s, when he was at Western Reserve University and "rat psychology" was in its heyday, he exposed a group of rats to a mildly stressful situation in which their reactions could be quantitatively measured; inbred the animals whose reaction to stress fell at either extreme; tested their offspring as he had the parents; and inbred those who reacted similarly. For six more generations this program of selective inbreeding was followed. It resulted in the isolation of two distinct strains—one very susceptible to stress and the other very resistant.

It has not been possible until quite recently, however, to pinpoint the physiological site of any inherited behavior pattern, and even now the findings are scant. What made a beginning possible was a series of discoveries by biochemists, dating from the 1940s. They found that the physical basis of life is the nucleic acid packed into one's chromosomes; that the nucleic acids of various species differ only in the sequential arrangement of their four component sub-units, the nucleotides; and that it is this arrangement —essentially a molecular code—which directs the growth and functioning of the organism through regulation of its chemical processes.

With understanding of the mechanisms of inheritance it has been possible in a few instances to link particular aspects of behavior to particular conglomerations of nucleic acid. In the fruit fly, for example, the specific gene (genes are segments of nucleic acid) which controls a specific wing-beat pattern has now been located. But fruit flies have only eight chromosomes, whereas human beings have forty-six and are correspondingly more complicated; and all evidence discourages the assumption that there is any one-to-one relationship between specific genes and any gross behavioral pattern in humans.

At the cellular level, however, the behavioral consequences of certain gene defects have now been well documented. There are a number of inherited diseases characterized by broken links in gene-controlled sequences of metabolic reactions, breakages which allow toxic substances to build up in the body. Perhaps the best known of these diseases is the one abbreviated as PKU. If diagnosed soon after birth and the baby's diet adjusted to reduce his intake of the substance that he cannot metabolize, the condition can be ameliorated. If not treated in time, brain damage occurs; and PKU children become feeble-minded.

Another "inborn error of metabolism" is the adrenogenital syndrome ("syndrome" means a *group* of effects), whose victims produce inadequate amounts of the growth-regulating hormone cortisone and experience abnormally rapid development of the sexual organs. This condition is not always identifiable at birth, and in fact is often not treated until the affected individual is well into childhood; then, cortisone therapy normalizes growth.

But there is an interesting behavioral corollary to this disease. John Money and Viola Lewis (two of a group of Johns Hopkins investigators who have been studying hormonal disorders) have noted that the adrenogenital syndrome is associated with an above-average IQ. Further, the cortisone therapy that brings physical growth back into line does not reduce the IQ. They theorize, therefore, that *if* a deficiency of cortisone is responsible for the elevated IQ it must have its effect during the prenatal or immediately postnatal period. (Parents reading this will think wistfully that it would be nice if a child could experience one effect without the other.)

Yet another inborn error of metabolism is believed to cause hereditary choreoathetosis, in which affected children have neurological malfunctioning of the sort that characterizes spastics who experienced brain injury or lack of oxygen at birth. Dick Hoefnagel and several colleagues at Dartmouth's Medical School have found that the uric acid secretion of choreoathetosic children is very high compared to normal controls—a common clue to a gene-caused breakdown in metabolism.

The behavioral aspect of this disease is as sad to witness as the inability of the child to control his limbs. As soon as afflicted youngsters acquire their permanent teeth, they begin to chew their fingers and lips in a compulsive manner and otherwise wound or bruise themselves by banging their foreheads and noses against hard objects. As they grow older, they become very belligerent toward others: they spit, bite, pinch, hit, and use obscene language.

In the above examples, specific gene defects are at fault. There are also a number of aberrant physical conditions which are caused by the inheritance of the wrong number of chromosomes, and some of these have clear-cut behavioral effects. Among them is Mongolism, more correctly called Down's syndrome. This condition is caused by a child's inheritance of three chromosomes of a given kind instead of the two it should inherit. Presumably by changing the intensity of normal chemical reactions (just as an oversupply of baking powder affects a cake), the extra amount of genetic material causes a cluster of effects, the most notable of which are the mongoloid slant of the eyes and severe mental retardation. It was only recently that scientists noted that children with this affliction also have uncommonly cheerful, friendly, and loving dispositions. This trait is too consistently associated with the other effects of Down's syndrome not to have the same origin.

And then there are the studies that are finding a genetic component in aggressiveness.

All normal human beings have two sex chromosomes: females, XX; males, XY. But sometimes, during fertilization and subsequent cell division, the parental chromosomes do not sort themselves out by twos and the fertilized cell ends up with one or three sex chromosomes. Then, as in Down's syndrome, they alter normal development and functioning of the individual who develops from that cell.

Among the most interesting of recent studies of sex chromosome aberrations are those under way in England, the subjects being XYY males who are inmates of state hospitals for the criminally insane. Why seek them in such a setting? Because, as the University of Sheffield geneticist M. D. Casey discovered, the double Y constitution occurs in only .2 percent of the newborn male population but in a population of those institutionalized because they are mentally

subnormal and persistently violent the percentage rises to 2.2 percent.

Patricia Jacobs of Western General Hospital in Edinburgh studied
the chromosomes of almost two hundred inmates of such hospitals,
and found that the XYYs had an average height that was an inch
over six feet, whereas the average height of the XYs in the same
prison population was five feet seven inches. Colleagues of hers,
W. H. Price and P. B. Whatmore, checked the backgrounds of
criminals who were also XYYs, found that the majority had IQ's
in the 60–80 range, no known history of brain damage, epilepsy,
or psychosis, no family history of criminal behavior or mental illness.
Yet "all suffer from a severe degree of personality disorder. They
are extremely unstable, have little depth of affection for others,
display an impaired awareness of their environment, and cannot
tolerate the mildest frustration." They are atypical criminals in two
respects: they were first convicted at much earlier ages than was
true of the XY criminals in the same hospital (some as early as nine
years old); and they had been much less likely than "normal"
lawbreakers to commit crimes against the person.

The "double Y syndrome" that is emerging from this work includes both physical and psychological traits: excessive height,
seriously disorganized personality, and intelligence of such low level
that it cannot control (in Price's and Whatmore's words) "the dis-
ordered drives leading to criminal behavior." Commenting upon the
English studies, the University of California (at Berkeley) geneticist
Curt Stern has said, "These observations suggest that the double Y
condition predisposes to aggressiveness. It is tempting to extrapolate
from here and speculate that the female sex owes its gentleness to
the absence of a Y chromosome and the normal male his moderate
aggressiveness to a single Y."

Another abnormal condition resulting from a chromosomal aber-
ration is Turner's syndrome. This one affects females and results
from a deficiency of genetic material rather than from the excess
present in Down's syndrome or the XYY condition in males. Girls
or women with Turner's syndrome lack the normal female complement of two X chromosomes, having XO or a mixture of XO and
XX cells. They are abnormally short and may not mature sexually.
Unlike the XYY male, whose IQ is almost always extremely low,
the XO female is in the normal range but has diminished ability
in certain special areas of mental function. According to a report

by John Money and his colleague Duane Alexander, girls with Turner's syndrome "do all right on verbal memory and reasoning, but they possess a specific cognitive defect in space-form perception; have a hard time with numerical manipulations; and have difficulty mobilizing attention and memory."

And, for a final example, there is the curious inheritance discovered in a family studied by three Philadelphia investigators headed by P. S. Moorhead of the Wistar Institute. The father's chromosomal count is normal, and so is that of one of the six children. But the mother has only forty-five chromosomes, parts of two having apparently fused into one, and four of the children have the same anomaly. Her verbal behavior is within the normal range but the four children have varying degrees of mental retardation, of which the most striking feature is a failure of speech development. It seems logical to assume that the mother possesses some genetic factor or factors that enable her to override the deficiency; factors that she did not pass on to the children and that they did not get from their father, either. In addition, the sixth child in the family is mongoloid. All of which indicates the presence in the mother of some condition or predilection that interferes with the process by which forty-six chromosomes normally pair, and thus assort themselves evenly in the fertilized egg cell.

It is much too early to make sweeping statements about the inheritance of temperament or traits of personality. But discoveries such as those just cited plus research on the biochemistry of certain mental diseases which in the past have been assumed to be largely environmental in origin are together establishing for certain "psychological" traits of individuals a much firmer biological base than they have had heretofore.

And what of the social behavior of man as a species? Here too some remarkable changes of opinion have recently occurred.

During the past twenty years there has been a great renaissance of scientific interest in animal behavior, led by such European ethologists as Konrad Lorenz and Nikko Tinbergen. (An ethologist is interested in *phylogenetic* traits, those characteristic of a species rather than of any individual member of that species. For example, ethologists see the baring of teeth and hunching of shoulders, when enraged, as an ancient inherited behavior pattern. Both men and apes do it.) This work has yielded a wealth of information about

the genetically programmed nature of much social behavior among
animals.

In particular, it has been learned that many animals do not
respond to other animals per se but to a series of signs ("social
releasers"), each of which fits into a set sequence and is dependent
for activation upon the appearance of the immediately preceding
sign in a set. An example given by the University of Connecticut
geneticist Benson Ginsburg, in a paper on the relationship of heredity to personality, describes such "releasers" in the mothering behavior of goats:

When a kid is born, it bleats. Under the influence of placental
hormones (whose effect lasts for only some four hours—here is another example of a critical period), the mother goat orients herself
toward the kid's head and begins to lick it. This massaging action
stimulates the kid to stand. It automatically flicks its tail, a sign
stimulus which causes the mother goat to orient to the tail. This
move on her part puts the kid in position to nurse. If the kid doesn't
find an udder, sooner or later it again bleats; and this starts the
whole sequence all over again. The mother goat orients to the kid's
head, licks it, its tail flicks, she turns herself around, thus putting
the kid in position to nurse; and so on, until the kid has successfully
made contact with the teat.

During the same years that the animal behaviorists have been
documenting the automatic character of responses that were once
thought to be spontaneous, the anthropologists have made a discovery that has caused a fundamental reversal in the theory of
human evolution. Many ancient remains have now been found of
tool-using primates who did not have the big brains that used to
be credited with man's learning to make and use tools. In consequence, it is now believed that we developed our big brains in
order to use tools better. An equivalent way of expressing the same
idea is to say that man is the primate who found a unique niche
in the world by specializing in intellectual development—just as
other primates specialized in swinging from branch to branch in
order to tap a unique food source available in the treetops.

Natural selection exerts no pressure for change upon attributes
which make no particular contribution to an organism's survival,
hence the thought has occurred to many more investigators than
Keith and Catherine Hayes that man may not differ much in general
from his closest animal kin, but only in his adaptive specialty. Some

are now saying, therefore, that he may have as sizable a genetic component in his social behavior as other animals are known to have. And if he does, this may be the reason that he is no longer as well adapted to his environment as he needs to be in order to survive as a species. This last, a chilling thought, is based upon knowledge of the slowness of evolutionary processes. *Homo sapiens* hasn't changed physically to any marked degree in thirty thousand years, and if social behavior is also under genetic control there isn't any likelihood that *it* will change swiftly.

There was no advantage to man, even five thousand years ago, in developing the social behavior necessary to survival in a world without elbow room. Nor did an ability to plan ahead—a century into the future, say—have any value to the species; it was enough of an accomplishment to live out the year. Today, however, these abilities—essential because of environmental changes created by man's own intellectual accomplishments—are critically important. And they are little in evidence.

Could it be, some anthropologists, ethologists, and behavioral geneticists are asking each other over the coffee cups, that mankind is stuck (perhaps fatally stuck) with genetically determined patterns of social behavior that were no handicap to a nomadic and technologically immature species and therefore have been transmitted across generations like the useless but potentially dangerous appendix?

The ethologist Irenäus Eibl-Eibesfeldt has said, "Our social reactions may be less controlled by reason than we believe . . . How can we otherwise explain the fact that we have failed, up until now, to solve our many social problems, whereas we have solved the most extraordinary technical problems, including flight to the moon? Lorenz actually takes this paradox as proof that man, in his social reactions, reacts in a programmed way, whereas in his intellectual reactions he is free.

"Man often becomes strongly emotionally involved when he approaches social problems, and we know that problem-solving is handicapped by strong emotions. A dog will not make a detour around a fence if a piece of meat is presented immediately in front of him [but behind the mesh or grillwork of the fence]. If the meat is placed farther back, tension is reduced and the dog finds the solution.

"Similarly, Köhler's chimpanzee Sultan* failed to discover that he could make a longer stick by putting two sticks together until he left the task. As long as the chimpanzee tried to get to the banana just out of reach, he did not find the solution. When he relaxed and started to play with the sticks, he hit upon the solution and immediately returned to the task.

"Strong emotional reactions govern our social relations to an increasing degree and, since we are not fully aware of the tensions and their consequences, we fail to step back and detach ourselves —a prerequisite for finding an intellectual solution. Insight into the mechanisms that govern behavior may help. We know much too little about the extent and ways in which phylogenetic adaptations control our behavior."

If human social behavior *is* part of our biological inheritance, we could attempt social therapy analogous to the medical therapy that is now brought to bear on genetic diseases. But the first step is to show that man is constitutionally unable—not merely unwilling— to prevent the wholesale pollution of his planet's waters or to limit the self-destructive proliferation of his peoples; and all that sustains the argument at this point is the speculation of a handful of behavioral scientists.

Nevertheless, the new interest in the role of innate factors in behavior is not only encouraging more research but also, as a kind of bonus, is beginning to put "mind" into the same conceptual package as "body." What divided the two in the first place was excessive stress by the professionals on the importance of environment in the development of behavior. Once it is generally appreciated that there are biological determinants of behavior as well as of physical structure, and that environment is a dynamic partner in the development of the organic whole that is the child, the popular image of the human organism will more closely match the functional reality.

* The German psychologist Wolfgang Köhler, a pioneer in research on the learning process, studied apes living on Tenerife in the Canary Islands, and showed that they are capable of reasoning. His observations of the chimp he called Sultan have given that animal a permanent place in psychology's family album.

CHAPTER 3

HOW INHERITED BEHAVIOR CAN BE MODIFIED

As living creatures ascend the evolutionary ladder, the amount of their behavior that is controlled by fixed—that is, inherited *and* unmodifiable—action patterns is broken down into smaller and smaller units. This allows the organism, whether mouse, monkey, or man, an increasing amount of freedom to modify its behavior as a result of learning.

One example of a fixed action pattern is the ability of tadpoles to swim. When Leonard Carmichael was a young assistant professor at Princeton—he has since been the president of Tufts and is now the National Geographic Society's vice-president for research and exploration—he performed the following, and classic, experiment:

He anesthetized a batch of frogs' eggs, using a chemical that allows physical growth but prevents response to stimuli, and at the same time allowed a control group to develop normally. When the controls were ready to swim, the experimental group was removed from its anesthetic bath. Tadpoles in each group swam with equal facility.

Yet frogs also have to learn to do certain things. Newly metamorphosed frogs instinctively snap at anything small and moving but must learn to distinguish between small moving things that are palatable and those that are not. The same kind of refinement from the general to the specific is true of ducks and geese: during a short period after hatching they instinctively respond to rhythmical sounds or movement by following the source. That's a fixed action pattern. But they then *learn* the specific properties of whatever it was they followed—usually the mother duck or goose, to whom they thereafter stay attached.

Irenäus Eibl-Eibesfeldt, the ethologist, has closely studied the inherited versus the learned behavior of red squirrels. Even if one raises them on a liquid diet in wire mesh cages and deprives them for two months of a chance to handle solid objects, they still know what to do with nuts. As soon as they first get one, they go through the entire burying routine—even though they may lack soil to dig in and there are no trees at whose base the nuts can be buried. Eibl-Eibesfeldt's young squirrels homed in on any vertical object in his laboratory, went through the motions of digging and sweeping earth over the nonexistent hole they had just tried to dig. This behavior, obviously, is innate.

But a red squirrel's technique for opening nuts is learned. He is born with an interest in nuts and with the ability to gnaw and split them. However, young squirrels who had never seen a nut until they were four to six months old had a hard time opening the first ones they were given, made quantities of mistakes, and took fifteen to twenty minutes at the beginning of the effort to do what experienced squirrels do in two or three minutes. Obviously, learning makes the difference.

Among the innate action patterns of human beings is the sucking response to tactual stimulation of the lips—but this too can be quickly modified by experience. Lewis Lipsitt and H. Kaye observed the nursing responses of thirty babies who were two to four days old —ten of whom were started off on rubber nipples, ten of whom had to suck through rubber tubing, and ten of whom were fed alternately by one method or the other. Those who were fed by tube sucked at half the rate of those who were fed by nipple, a rate that held steady throughout the period of observation. But those in the alternated group progressively diminished their rate of sucking whenever fed by tube and progressively increased their rate of sucking on the nipple. Experience clearly taught them to prefer the method of feeding that delivers food faster.

Smiling also appears to be a fixed action pattern. A recent report by the Harvard Medical School psychiatrist Peter H. Wolff suggests that those "gastric smiles" of the newborn baby are an involuntary reaction to changing intensities of sensory stimulation; they often occur, he has observed, just as a well-fed infant drowses off, thereby shutting out of his consciousness the sights and sounds of the world around him. They can be elicited by external stimuli, however, within the first week of life—by stroking the cheeks, for example.

Within two to eight weeks after birth, the "social smile" begins to evolve from this initially involuntary action. The stimulus, at first, is auditory: a human voice elicits a smile better than any other sound and more readily than a visual stimulus. (Blind babies, at this stage, smile as much as those with sight.) A bit later, human faces become the great smile-producers, and babies will smile at them even if they do not smile in return.

This fact was dramatically demonstrated by René Spitz and K. M. Wolf, who showed that it is the configurational pattern of the human face rather than the emotion expressed by that face which elicits the smile from three- to six-month-old babies. Motion is important too—that is, movement of the head or any of its parts; but not the particular set of features which adults interpret as cheerfulness or anger.

In one experiment, for example, the two investigators correlated the smiling response of babies with the presentation to them of a smiling or nodding human face in full face or in profile, and discovered that the babies' smiles were turned off like a light the moment the observer turned sideways. It was apparent that one eye, one ear, and the lips in profile—even when motion continued—were no substitute for the full-face configuration as an elicitor of smiles.

Then the observers put on masks whose expression was like that of those used in Japanese No drama or in the ancient Greco-Roman theater, the kind calculated to inspire terror. "No grown-up would be inclined, even for a moment, to mistake this expression for one of friendliness," say Spitz and Wolf. "Its savagery is unmistakable." (See Figure 3.)

But the babies saw nothing menacing in these masks, and continued to smile at their wearers—until they turned sideways, and then the babies stopped smiling, or cried. The two psychologists conclude, "Whether smiling, speaking, nodding in a friendly manner, or baring its fangs in an expression of savage rage, the human

face as seen 'en face' and in motion remained for the child the signal
of a human partner and was reacted to with a smile."

But this undiscriminating behavior ceases during the fifth or sixth
month. Then a baby begins to smile selectively, favoring his mother
with a gleeful grin of recognition and informing strangers by a wail
of distress that he can now identify unfamiliar faces. He has learned,
in short, to associate a particular configurational pattern and particular facial expressions with specific human beings.

Older psychologists believe that social smiling is a conditioned
response; that it is wholly learned through interaction with the people in one's environment. It is the viewpoint of younger psychologists that is presented above: that smiling is innate, and is then
modified by the experiences of the child. (Incidentally, I will
have more to say about its behavioral role in child development in
Chapter 6.)

Much innate behavior thus seems to be nature's way of giving
the organism a start, a pattern of action upon which change can
capitalize. Nor is that pattern necessarily observable at birth. As
the organism matures, action patterns appear which are relevant
to the particular stage of development which has then been reached.
These may be modifiable by the environment, or they may be fixed.

In animals which depend a great deal on visual cues to guide behavior, an innate action pattern which helps to prevent falling is
not triggered until the animal is mobile enough to fall into a hole
and its visual development is such that the eyes can warn of danger. The onset of this behavior has been demonstrated in a series of
elegant studies—but before I summarize them let me tell you how
they happened to be undertaken.

Eleanor Jack Gibson, who is known to her friends as Jackie, is a
distinguished psychologist who is married to a distinguished psychologist, James Gibson. When their daughter was about two years
old they were vacationing in Arizona and decided to picnic in the
Grand Canyon area. Mrs. Gibson was uneasy about the site her
husband had chosen because it was so close to the rim, and she
feared for the safety of their toddler. James Gibson, an expert on
depth perception, assured his wife that the little girl would be all
right because she could see the depth of the drop-off as well as an
adult. And indeed she could, as the following paragraphs will report—but even today Mrs. Gibson's maternal self remains dominant

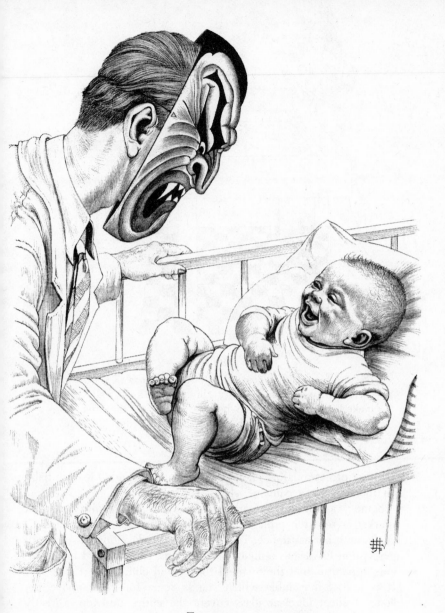

FIGURE 3

Older youngsters would be frightened of this hideously masked man, but René Spitz and K. M. Wolf discovered that babies three to six months old smile joyously at any human face, regardless of the expression it wears.

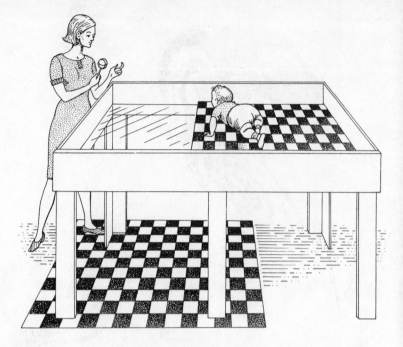

FIGURE 4

Despite his mother's coaxing and the presence of a safe glass surface between him and her, this six-month-old baby cannot make himself crawl to her—because he can see the drop below him. Richard Walk and Eleanor Gibson call this apparatus a "visual cliff."

over her professional-psychologist self. "I still wouldn't leave a baby on the edge of a canyon," she says.

Some years after that particular incident, her recollection of it sparked a research project carried on by her student Richard D. Walk, with her assistance. To investigate the development of depth perception in various animals and humans, they created an ingenious apparatus that they named the "visual cliff." (See FIGURE 4.) It is a 6×8-foot table which stands some four feet above the floor. A sheet of clear glass covers the entire tabletop. Directly under the glass on one side a checked linoleum is laid; but on the other side there is no visual barrier to seeing through the glass. One can look down to the floor, which is covered with the same checked linoleum used in the shallow compartment of the testing table. Between the shallow side and the deep side is a board, an inch or so above the glass, upon which the experimenters poise their subjects. Whichever way the subject moves, he will step down onto the same kind of surface—glass—and if he were to make his decision on the basis of felt firmness of support either side would do. A visual check of his alternatives, however, shows him a close-up checked pattern (on the shallow side) and a far-away checked pattern (on the deep side); the sensation this latter produces is like looking over a cliff. And at a certain stage of development, neither goats nor monkeys nor human babies will willingly move from the center board onto the glass lying over the deep side.

Goats are mobile from birth. If you put week-old kids on the center board, and even though they may peer down at the floor from the safety of the rail while standing on the shallow side of the apparatus, they will not step onto the glass of the deep side. If you force them to, their front legs become rigid and their hind legs push backward.

The developmental timetable for monkeys is a bit slower, but even before they are normally mobile one can see in their behavior the shadow of coming events. Leonard Rosenblum and Henry A. Cross have recently found that at three days of age rhesus monkeys prefer the shallow side of the testing apparatus. Perhaps this precocity is nature's response to the monkeys' normal arboreal environment, from which a fall could be truly disastrous. Walk and Gibson's young monkeys were capable of overcoming this aversion to depth during the first couple of weeks of life; given a lure such as a bottle of milk or a favorite blanket, they managed to get across the glass. By the eighteenth day or thereabouts, when in nature they are fully mobile, neither milk nor blanket would tempt them. And at forty-five days, they showed extreme emotional distress, keeping their heads down, hugging themselves, resisting every effort to get them to move.

Human babies are no different, except that they become mobile at about six months. Walk and Gibson introduced thirty-six of them to the visual cliff just as they began to crawl (and with no history of having fallen from high places). Without exception they refused to tackle the deep side, even when coaxed from its far edge by a mother holding a bright-colored pinwheel that tinkled when it revolved. They *wanted* to crawl across; in fact, some cried in frustration because their innate fear of falling had stalemated another emotion, their desire to respond to their mother's call.

The two psychologists noted, with some amusement, the mothers' reaction to the babies' behavior. The mothers were surprised and upset because even though some babies eased themselves sufficiently off the center board, in their efforts to "come to Mama," to feel the glass under their bodies, their basic behavior didn't change.

"It was as if the infant could not recognize the consequences of his own actions, since he had already been where he now refused to go," Walk and Gibson report. "The predominant attitude of the mothers seemed to be that the child had 'failed' the test because he did not have enough sense to realize that the glass was safe to crawl over."

The reason, of course, was that the innate behavior of the babies had not yet been affected by learning, whereas the mothers had already traveled the full developmental route.

Not that most of us ever wholly conquer our fear of falling, as C. W. Windle demonstrated during the Korean War when he studied the extent to which height fright affected the performance of paratroop trainees. One exercise required them to jump from a tower which permitted an eight-foot free fall before the cable holding them was snubbed. Different groups made the jump from eighteen feet, twenty-six feet, and thirty-four feet. Although the physical fall was the same in each case, the rate of hesitation and poor jumping technique increased with the height at which the jumper launched himself. Perceived visual height made the difference.

At the same time that new research has indicated that babies have more inborn abilities and are "ready to go" sooner than used to be believed, it has been discovered that the rate at which those abilities mature is nowhere near as predetermined as many child development experts have assumed it to be.

Animal experiments, of course, have led the way. I have already mentioned the studies which show that light deprivation causes atrophy or malfunction of the physical structures that enable one to see. The reverse is true too: when an organism develops in an environment which is exceptionally rich in sensory experience, at least some of the physical structures involved in processing that experience grow at an accelerated rate.

Now, there is nothing new about the idea that use of an organ or muscle enlarges it. (For my generation, at least, Charles Atlas demonstrated the possibility beyond doubt.) But there is a difference between the size of one's biceps and the intellectual activity of the brain, and it was this aspect of "exercise" that moved J. C. Spurzheim to say, in 1815:

"Here it may be asked whether the organs [of the brain] increase by exercise? This may certainly happen in the brain as well as in the muscles; nay, it seems more than probable, because the blood is carried in greater abundance to the parts which are excited, and nutrition is performed by the blood. In order, however, to be able to answer this question positively, we ought to observe the same persons when exercised and when not exercised; or at least observe many persons who are, and many others who are not, exercised during all periods of life."

This quotation opens a paper on the chemical and anatomical plasticity of the brain by an interdisciplinary team at the University of California at Berkeley: Edward L. Bennett, a biochemist; Marian C. Diamond, an anatomist: and David Krech and Mark Rosenzweig, psychologists. For a decade now, they have been doing what Spurzheim recommended—observing the brain activity of "many persons who are, and many others who are not, exercised during all periods of life." With this change: they have substituted rats for persons.

Their experiments, which have been exhaustive and exceedingly well controlled, have focused on the chemical and anatomical differences between the brains of rats that have lived in conditions of sensory impoverishment (solitary confinement in dimly lit and bare cages) or in conditions of sensory enrichment (lots of rat and human company, an abundance of "toys," and much opportunity for exploration and learning).

The result? Compared to the impoverished rats, the enriched ones have heightened levels of a chemical activity that is intimately related to the production of acetylcholine (which is a prime conductor of nerve impulses within the brain). They also have thicker and heavier cortexes. This increase in cortical weight and chemical activity is not restricted to young animals; it occurs also in mature rats who are exposed to sensory enrichment. In short, the environmental experience of rats *does* affect brain development or promote physiological changes in it. (And I'll have more to say on the same topic in later chapters.)

And what about humans? Because you can't decapitate human beings and section or centrifuge their brain tissue, nobody knows whether the weight and thickness of our cortexes reflect the amount of sensory experience that has come our way. What *is* known about humans, however, is that the onset of certain physical behaviors can be speeded up or slowed down by environmental conditions.

This has been documented only within the past ten or fifteen years. In the 1930s and 1940s, it was widely believed that certain physical skills of children emerge (like the swimming of Carmichael's tadpoles) according to an innate developmental timetable. The baby books confidently told mothers that babies sit alone at seven months, creep at ten months, walk at fifteen months, etc.; and urged parents not to force the flowering of such skills.

Among the research upon which such advice was based was that of Wayne Dennis, then at the University of Virginia and now at Brooklyn College. He and his wife raised a pair of twin girls from the age of about a month to age fifteen months in an environment in which social interaction was held to a minimum—which also means that it was fairly impoverished from a sensory standpoint, as well. The babies did not see each other, were taken from their cribs as little as possible, were not spoken to by the Dennises, and in every aspect of rearing were treated with as much of a "hands off" policy as the Dennises were capable of. Which turned out not to be a tremendous lot; when the babies were about nine months old, the Dennises' scientific detachment broke down, and from then on the twins' environmental experience began to parallel that of other home-reared babies. Until that point, however, the children had progressed at a normal rate (turning over, finding their hands, smiling, babbling, sitting up, and so on); and Wayne Dennis's conclusion was that if a child's physical well-being is assured his behavioral development is automatic.

Today be believes differently. When he was a visiting professor at the American University in Beirut, Lebanon (in 1958–59), he studied the locomotor behavior of children in Iranian orphanages and observed there a degree of developmental retardation which clearly correlated with environmental conditions.

Whereas most home-reared American babies are sitting up by the age of nine months, fewer than half of the Iranian orphans (in two of the three institutions Dennis visited) could do so even at the age of twenty-one months. Most American children can walk by the age of twenty-four months, but only 8 percent of

Iranian children in one orphanage could walk at thirty-three months and only 15 percent of those in another orphanage were walking at the age of forty-five months.

In these two institutions, babies were removed from their cribs only every other day, to be bathed; otherwise, they lay on their backs until such time as they spontaneously learned to sit up. When they could sit up, they were sometimes put in rows on a bench or plunked down on the floor, but they had no toys and received virtually no individualized attention from hospital attendants.

(These latter, in case good mothers among my readers are feeling critical, were in essentially the same position as if each were the mother of octuplets. There were four attendants assigned to each group of thirty-two infants, and they were responsible for ward housekeeping and food preparation in addition to child care. How much time would *you* have to feed each child individually and run in a game of pattycake if you had eight children of nearly the same age and no household help?)

The third Iranian orphanage that Dennis visited, on the other hand, was a modern showcase institution, where the ratio dropped to three or four children per attendant, where the children were held when fed, had toys, and received more personal attention. There was little developmental retardation among this group.

Dennis's obvious conclusion was that behavioral development does not proceed at a fixed rate independent of circumstances of rearing. In his report on the Iranian children, he notes that the orphans there had suffered far more social and sensory deprivation than the twins that he and his wife had raised in the 1930s, and he also makes some interesting additional comments.

The Iranian babies were slow to sit up, he believes, because they were never propped up in their cribs, and therefore lacked opportunities to practice some of the elements of sitting without danger of toppling over. Nor were they laid prone in their cribs, a posture that fosters creeping. Once they did manage, spontaneously, to learn to sit up, this sitting position became the basis for locomotion. Instead of creeping or walking, the Iranian youngsters whizzed about on the seat of their pants; that is, they were scooters rather than creepers or walkers. Dennis therefore suggests that lack of learning opportunities not only slowed the rate of their physical maturation but in addition *changed the form it took.*

Impressive confirmation for at least the first half of Dennis's conclusion comes from another study involving institutionalized infants—impressive because it is hard to control any experiment involving humans, and from a scientific standpoint this one was impeccable. It was done by Burton L. White of Harvard and Richard Held of the Massachusetts Institute of Technology, using babies born and reared (until at least the age of six months) in a State hospital in Massachusetts.

In overall design, their study had two parts. First, by careful observation, they established norms for the onset of behaviors which characteristically culminate in a child's being able to co-ordinate hands and eyes and grasp an object. Then they exposed babies to three variations of sensory experience, to see whether and by how much their behavioral progress would be affected.

As for the norms:

These infants, as newborns, were visually alert less than 3 percent of the time; at the age of two weeks, about 10 percent of the time. They reached an important visual milestone at about the age of a month and a half, when they discovered their hands; and for the next six weeks or so they spent much of their waking time regarding their fist and finger movements. At around three months they began to "swipe" with closed fists at a toy attached to the side of the crib; at about four months of age they were alternating hand-reach and glance in an effort to calculate exact distance and direct their fingers to the spot; and during the fifth month they finally accomplished the maneuver.

Norms established, the two investigators then modified the environment. First, they instructed the hospital nurses to handle one group of babies for twenty minutes a day, from the sixth through the thirty-sixth day of life. (This, as I said, was a scientifically controlled study with no loose ends; there were no vague orders, like "Handle the babies more than usual.") The outcome: the handled babies (a) became significantly more visually alert than the controls, who received the minimal amount of handling that is the usual lot of institutionalized infants, and (b) discovered their hands about a week *later*, on the average, than the controls. (For the reason, wait a bit.)

Next, another group was exposed to massive sensory enrichment. Not only were the babies handled (same prescription as above) but in addition—this time from the thirty-seventh day of life through the one hundred twenty-fourth day—their environment differed from the controls in three other dimensions. First, they were placed prone for fifteen-minute periods three times a day and the crib liners removed so they could see what was going on in the ward around them. Second, colored or printed crib sheets were substituted for white ones. Third, a huge "stabile" composed of beads, balls, rattles, mirrors, and other brilliantly colored or shiny objects and forms was hung over their cribs. And what happened to *their* visual and reaching behavior?

For one thing, they discovered their hands some twenty days later than babies who had not been exposed to the enriched environment. This finding did not particularly surprise White and Held, and was consistent with the slow-down observed in the group that had merely been handled more than usual. The controls had nothing much to look at *except* their hands (see FIGURE 5), hence they discovered them sooner than the babies in the two experimental groups.

The second finding was a surprise, however. The babies in the enriched group exhibited *less* visual attention during the first five weeks of the experience than the controls, and cried more. Apparently they were so overstimulated, so overwhelmed by sensation, that they tried to shut some of it out.

Peace and progress were restored when the experimenters modified the babies' environment, from the thirty-seventh to the sixty-eighth day, by eliminating prone positioning and the colored crib sheets and replacing the stabile with simpler forms (again, see FIGURE 5) which were attached to the sides of the cribs and therefore didn't loom over the babies, dominating their whole visual field as the stabile had done. On the sixty-ninth day, the massively enriched environment was re-established.

It was the babies in this "modified" group who first achieved two important behavioral goals: on the average they swiped at the cribside toy ten days earlier than the controls and eleven days earlier than the massive enrichment group; and they were able to reach and grasp the toy ten days before the massive enrichment group and *sixty* days before the controls.

Moral for parents of two-month-old infants: take all the dingle-dangles off the crib canopy on the days that both Grandma and the Bridge Group come to visit and the baby is handled or shown off a lot. By the third month he'll be able to take a great deal

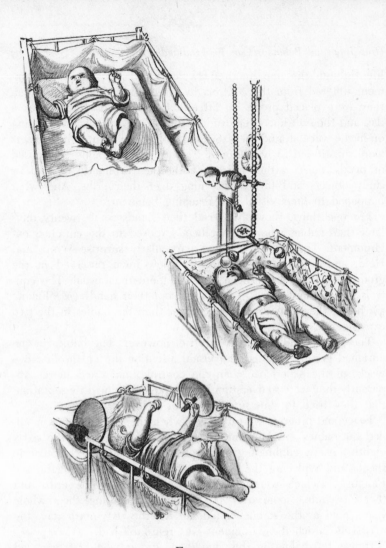

FIGURE 5

In Burton White and Richard Held's study of babies' responses
to differing amounts of sensory stimulation, the controls (top)
had too little; the massive enrichment group (center) had
too much; but for those in the moderately enriched group
(bottom), the amount was just right. (Adapted from photographs
from *The Causes of Behavior: Readings in Child Development*
by Judy F. Rosenblith and Wesley Allinsmith. Copyright ©
1966 by Allyn and Bacon, Inc., Boston. Reproduced by permission of the publisher.)

of sensory stimulation, but until then smallish doses of color, sound, and motion go a long way.

White and Held, cautious investigators, claim only to have demonstrated that these three aspects of early visual-motor development —growth of visual attentiveness, the baby's discovery of his own hands, the onset of visually directed reaching—are "remarkably plastic." To what extent the developmental timetable of other behavior is similarly plastic remains to be seen. But the basic point is indisputable. Although one's physical inheritance determines the sequence in which various abilities emerge, the speed at which they develop, and maybe the form, can be profoundly affected by the learning opportunities present in the environment.

CHAPTER 4

LEARNING TO LOVE OR TO HATE

The great behaviorist John B. Watson believed that all emotions are learned, and did a series of experiments during the 1920s in which he attempted to prove his thesis. Typical was his effort to locate the origin of children's alleged fear of furry things:

First, he presented a variety of animals—cats, rabbits, dogs, rats —to babies four to five months old, all of whom had been reared in an institution and thus had had no previous experience with pets. None of the children showéd fear.

A next step was to condition an eleven-month-old boy named Albert to fear a white rat which he had not feared upon first meeting it. This was done in the standard Pavlovian way by combining a sudden loud sound with the presentation of the rat. Because Albert so disliked the sound, he came in time to fear the rat; and also to transfer the same fear from the rat to other furry things—rabbits, muffs, human hair, and even a Santa Claus mask. (Poor Albert!)

Watson's conclusion: fear of furry things, if a child has it, is learned.

In the end, however, Watson could not so label all emotions. His final list included three innate emotions: fear (of loud noises and of falling); anger (when bodily movements are restrained); and love (upon being petted or stroked). Later psychologists have modified this list. It is now known, for example, that fear can be induced by almost any sudden, intense stimulus, not just a loud sound or threatened loss of support. More importantly, a developmental approach—one which sees specific emotions as evolving from more generalized ones—has acquired wide acceptance in child-study circles.

In the 1930s Katharine Bridges kept careful observations of the development of emotions among a group of sixty-two infants and came to the conclusion that the basic initial emotion is a generalized one of excitement. This early differentiates into distress or delight. By three weeks of age, distress—as a result, say, of waiting to be fed—is clearly distinguishable from general excitation because the baby's cry is louder, more irregular, and higher-pitched; his eyes squeeze shut; his muscle tension is greater. Delight, which is slower to emerge, appears in the second or third month, and its bodily expression is just the reverse of that observed when the baby is distressed. Each of these emotions then undergoes further refinement. By the fifth month, distress splits into anger and disgust; and delight expands into elation (at about the seventh month) or expressed affection (by the eleventh month).

But what controls the rate at which the emotions differentiate? The answer appears to be the same as for perceptual or motor development: sensory stimulation from the environment. Again, deprivation studies with animals throw some light on the process:

McGill University's Ronald Melzack divided four litters of Scottish terriers into experimental and control groups, and for eight months after weaning raised the experimental group in cages from which they could see nothing except the flat surface of the laboratory ceiling. The controls were raised as pets. Three to five weeks after release from restriction and again ten months later, each dog was led into a room in which there were a toy car, a bear skull, an umbrella, a balloon, and similar other innocuous objects—but unfamiliar to the dogs and therefore emotion-provoking.

At the three- to five-weeks test, the dogs that had been raised normally pulled back or watched warily as the balloon was inflated and then moved toward them. Their fear took the form of avoidance. The restricted dogs, on the other hand, whirled about, jumped back and forth, and otherwise exhibited diffuse emotional excitement. At the ten-months test, many of the restricted dogs still behaved the same way but a few showed the avoidance response. The controls, however—the terriers who had grown up in a normal environment—now displayed aggression. They approached the invader balloon with intent to destroy it or drive it away.

There are two explanations for this behavior. One, Melzack's, is that the primitive response of diffuse excitement differentiates into specific emotions only if the animal early acquires a well-organized perceptual acquaintance with its environment. The normal dogs, from puppyhood, had seen and sniffed a great variety of objects, had "placed" themselves and others in familiar space, and in various other ways had developed a concept of what was usual in the laboratory. Thus they could identify the unfamiliar and react to it in a purposeful way. The restricted dogs, who did not acquire such a background at an appropriate time in their development, were helpless.

The other explanation has recently been advanced by John L. Fuller of the Jackson Laboratory in Bar Harbor, Maine. One of the checks and balances built into scientific research is that any investigator's work must be subject to replication by another investigator before its conclusions are accepted. Fuller, too, has isolated dogs and observed the effects of such deprivation. But he has found that *only twenty minutes per week* in the wide world outside their cages is sufficient to make otherwise severely restricted animals behave in an essentially normal fashion.

Inasmuch as this allows them very little time for getting acquainted with the environment, he considered other reasons for the post-isolation behavior of restricted dogs. And he decided that it is not lack of perceptual experience that unhinges such animals but, rather, the stress to which they are subjected upon emerging from isolation. Isolated dogs become habituated to a very low level of sensory stimulation, he says, and respond to moderate stimulation as normally reared animals respond to violent stimulation. This opinion will surely recall to you, as it does to me, the distress apparently felt by White's and Held's babies when exposed to more sensation than they could take.

Whether Melzack is right in his diagnosis of not-enough-sensory-experience-at-the-right-time or Fuller in his diagnosis of too-much-sensation-at-once, the general finding—that emotional as well as physical development can be affected by one's sensory experiences early in life—is still valid.

From an entirely different quarter comes other evidence supporting the belief that one is born with a certain capacity for emotion and that early experience determines its form. But first, here's a historical note and a scientific detective story taken from Daniel Funkenstein's review of medical research into the physiology of fear and anger.

It was the great turn-of-the-century physiologist Walter B. Cannon who first demonstrated the connection between the emotions and physiological changes in the body. When animals (and, presumably, men) perceive a threat, the accompanying emotion of rage or fear automatically stimulates the adrenal glands to produce adrenalin. This hormone then quickens such physical processes as respiration and heartbeat and releases to the blood such organic reserves as the sugar stored in the liver and the corpuscles stored in the spleen. In short, Cannon said, adrenalin marshals all the resources of the body in preparation for fight or flight.

But what determines which response will occur? Why do rabbits characteristically flee and lions characteristically attack? Why do humans also have characteristic reactions to stress, some typically becoming very aggressive (an outward-directed expression of anger) whereas others become depressed (an inward-directed expression of anger) or fearful?

Some clues to the answer have come during the past fifteen or so years, from a variety of sources. Here they are:

1. The biochemists B. F. Tullar and M. L. Tainter discovered that the adrenal glands secrete a second hormone, one that has been named nor-adrenalin. It has a highly specialized effect: it causes the small blood vessels to contract and slows down the flow of blood.

2. The physiologist H. G. Wolff and a group working with him at New York Hospital noted that fear and anger produce different physical effects. An angry man has a bright red stomach lining; its peristaltic movements are accelerated; and the secretion of hydrochloric acid increases. The opposite is true of a depressed or frightened man. And other researchers discovered that there are also fine differences in the behavior of the heart, lungs, and muscles that correlate with anger or fear.

3. Then some investigators at Presbyterian Hospital in New York found that injections of adrenalin and nor-adrenalin, both of which elevate blood pressure, do so for different reasons: nor-

adrenalin by constricting the blood vessels and adrenalin by causing the heart to beat faster.

4. Which caused Funkenstein and colleagues at Harvard's Medical School to wonder about the possible relationship of these hormones to the behavior of psychotic patients. Funkenstein, a sur-
geon-turned-psychiatrist, had been using a certain drug in the
treatment of patients with high blood pressure, and had observed
not only that they reacted physically in one of two distinctly
different ways but also that these reactions correlated with their
chronic emotional states. Those in whom the drug produced a
small drop in blood pressure followed by a quick return to its
former level were also those who were habitually angry at other
people. Those in whom the drug produced a marked drop in
blood pressure followed by a slow return to its former level were
also those who were chronically depressed or fearful.

So he recruited a group of healthy young men and experimentally raised their blood pressure by injections of adrenalin or
nor-adrenalin. Then he injected the drug he had been using on
his psychotics. Sure enough, the drug produced a small drop and
fast recovery in those subjects who had received nor-adrenalin and
a sizable drop and slow recovery in those subjects who had received adrenalin.

The next step was to demonstrate a physiological link between these hormones and the emotions of normal people; maybe
the apparent connection observed in the psychotics was unique
to them. But upon subjecting college students to stress, Funkenstein found that those who reacted to severe frustration with anger
also showed the physiological reactions which accompany injections
of nor-adrenalin, and those who became depressed or anxious
showed the physical changes which accompany injections of adrenalin.

5. But were these changes specific to the *emotion?* That is, would
a given individual show signs of nor-adrenalin secretion when he
was angry and of adrenalin secretion when he was frightened?
Albert F. Ax, also then at the same Massachusetts hospital as
Funkenstein, found the answer to that part of the puzzle. He tested
some forty subjects whom he had managed to first make fearful
and then angry,* and discovered that their physiological reac-

---

* In case you're wondering how a research psychologist sets up a stressful
situation in a seemingly neutral setting, here is how Ax did it.

tions were like those that adrenalin or nor-adrenalin, respectively, produce.

6. Meanwhile, in various labs in various places, biochemists had been analyzing the proportions of the two hormones in the adrenal glands of wild animals shot or trapped in Africa; of domesticated animals; and of human children of differing ages. The results? Lions and other aggressive animals have a high ratio of nor-adrenalin to adrenalin; rabbits and sheep have the reverse; and human infants have higher ratios of nor-adrenalin than older children do.

Which brings us back to the question I posed some paragraphs ago. Why do rabbits flee and lions attack? Why do some humans typically react to a threatening situation by showing fight while

---

He obtained subjects through newspaper ads, offering each person $3 for what sounded like an hour's easy work. He was studying hypertension, he told them, and all they had to do was lie on a couch and listen to music while a battery of electrodes taped to their bodies transmitted a record of their respiration, heartbeat, hand temperature, etc., to a polygraph in the next room.

In due course, each subject began to feel an intermittent shock to his little finger. When he mentioned it, Ax expressed surprise; hastily checked the various wires taped to the subject; unobtrusively pressed a key which created an ominous flash of sparks close to the couch; exclaimed that this was "a dangerous high voltage short circuit"; and for a few minutes created a maximum amount of confusion and alarm. Is it any wonder that people who thought they were wired into a faulty system were frightened? One woman cried out, "Please take the wires off. Oh! Please help me!"

Ax then "found" and "repaired" the "short circuit"; removed the wire leading to the subject's finger; and assured him or her that all danger was past.

Fifteen calm minutes of listening to music and of casual conversation followed. Ax then brought into the talk a mention of the polygraph operator in the next room, saying that he was an incompetent and arrogant fellow who had been fired but had been recalled for this one day because his replacement was ill. At this point the operator entered the room and insisted that Ax swap places with him because he wanted to check for himself that the transmission was properly handled. Ax argued, but eventually gave in.

Then the polygraph operator turned off the music, criticized the nurse (who was there to take blood pressure readings), roughly adjusted the subject's position, upbraided him for moving around too much, called him uncooperative—and, in short, made him good and angry. One man later said to Ax, "Say, what goes on here? I was just about to punch that character on the nose!"

Moral: If you are ever tempted to participate in a research project that requires you only to lie on a couch and listen to music, remember that you may *earn* your $3!

others withdraw? For instance, why does Mark hit Billy when Billy reaches for the fire engine in the nursery school toy box, whereas Billy pulls his hand back and lets Mark have the toy? Why does a grown-up Mark when having a run of bad luck in his business come home and berate his wife for her extravagance while a grown-up Billy, in the same situation, quietly takes to drink?

The likely answer is that potential fight and flight responses are built into the genes; or, if you want to say it physiologically, that the organism naturally responds to stress by producing adrenalin or nor-adrenalin. These responses then develop according to the individual's experience. In the case of animals, little environmental modification of innate action patterns occurs (although it should be mentioned that cowardly lions and belligerent rabbits are not unknown). Human behavior, however, is much more vulnerable to shaping by experience.

Daniel Funkenstein notes that anger directed outward is characteristic of an earlier stage of childhood than is anger directed toward the self or the anxiety generated by inner conflicts over hostile feelings toward other people; and that these last two emotions arise from the child's experiences within his family. If you couple that awareness with the fact that this developmental pattern is normally paralleled by a gradual rise in the growing child's ratio of adrenalin to nor-adrenalin, what emerges is a psychophysiological profile of the "socialization" of a baby. Or, as Funkenstein puts it, "Man is born with the capacity to react with a variety of emotions (has within him the lion and the rabbit), and his early childhood experiences largely determine in which of these ways he will react under stress."

How early in childhood does emotional development begin? At birth, the psychiatrist Bruno Bettelheim believes. A man who kept his own sanity when in concentration camps during World War II by forcing himself to make clinical observations of the inmates' behavior (including his own), Bettelheim is now famed for his treatment of severely emotionally disturbed children at the University of Chicago's Sonia Shankman Orthogenic School.

"We as adults know how helpless the infant is," Bettelheim says, "but the infant does not know it. To him what counts is not the fact of his dependence but the conviction that his efforts are monumental."

A normal baby is eminently active in his own behalf: his cry of distress is one form of action, his vigorously seeking the nipple is another, his squirming during feeding and his rigidity or relaxation upon being diapered are still others—and a good mother is responsive to these cues.

In time, then, the baby "fathoms that he, through his own efforts, has been able to influence the external world—and this is the point at which he begins to become a social being. Conversely, when the infant is kept from being active in the relation, or when his actions evoke no response, he becomes flooded with impotent rage. The experience that his actions make no difference is what stops him from becoming a human being, for it discourages him from interacting with others and hence from forming a personality through which to deal with the environment."

"Personality" is the complex of characteristics that individualizes a person in his relationships with others. One of its keystones is one's concept of self; and "self" is the composite of all *affective* feelings (emotions, attitudes, and values) and all *cognitive* perceptions (awareness of objects and situations and use of this awareness to guide behavior). Although both aspects of the self develop concurrently and with mutual impact, Bruno Bettelheim persuasively advocates the viewpoint which places the affective component slightly ahead of the cognitive.

He cites a study by Peter H. Wolff and Burton L. White in which they tested forty-eight infants, three to four days old, to see whether the babies' emotional state correlated with their attentiveness when visually following a moving disc. It did. Babies who were wide awake and active—waiting for a bottle, say, but not yet distressed by its absence—didn't follow the target as well as babies who were wide awake but quiet because they had been given a pacifier and allowed to suck on it for a few minutes.

Wolff and White explain, "A 'need to suck' acts as an internal excitation and reduces attention. As the intensity of this need is reduced by prolonged sucking, the range of attention increases correspondingly."

To which Bettelheim adds: "An infant is distracted, as we are, when emotionally too preoccupied. How quietly alert he is, and how much chance he has to be active in observing the world, may have far-reaching consequences for his later development.

"But before he can engage in the self-contained activity of ob-

serving, of paying attention, there must *first* have come the emotional experience of having something of a self that can act, and a
sense of its connection to something outside that responds."

I will turn later to the matured concept of self, and discuss how
the older child's behavior is organized around protecting and enhancing that concept. For the moment, the important point to make
is that the establishment of good *affective* relations is of signal importance to good *cognitive* development. Nothing demonstrates this
more dramatically than the studies of what happens to children
when they are deprived in infancy of mother love; not of physical
care, but of maternal responsiveness to them as individuals, in the
mode described just above by Bettelheim. These studies will be the
subject of the next chapter.

CHAPTER 5

BABIES WITHOUT MOTHERS

Everyone "knows" that normal babies love their mothers; it is this love upon which parents capitalize in teaching children how to behave. But what acts or circumstances forge the bonds of infant love? Being fed by the mother? Being held and cuddled? And what effects upon later development does this primary human relationship have?

Some answers to these and related questions have come from a decade of research into the mother-child relationship of rhesus monkeys by the University of Wisconsin's husband and wife team of psychologists, Harry and Margaret Harlow. They have raised several generations of monkeys whose conditions of rearing have included complete deprivation of maternal love, partial deprivation, rearing in isolation, and rearing with other motherless infants. The experiments have varied the timetable for the onset of these abnormal situations, and they have continued long enough to see whether the infant experiences of these monkeys have affected them in adulthood.

One of the first discoveries that the Harlows made was that baby monkeys don't form attachments to a mother because she is the source of food, but because she is soft and pliant and feels good to cling to. Newborn monkeys were put into cages in which they had a choice of two surrogate mothers—angled forms of the right size to be adult monkeys, with immovable and crudely modeled but correctly scaled heads, their "bodies" fitted with nursing bottles in such a way that the nipples protruded from the proper section of the anatomy. One of these mother surrogates, however, was made of bare wire mesh and the other was sheathed in terry cloth. (See FIGURE 6.)

The babies nursed from either mother—to eat, after all, is an imperative of life—but spent no more time with the wire mother than was required for feeding. Unanimously they climbed, cuddled, and clung to the cloth mother. Furthermore, when something frightened them—a mechanical teddy bear, for example—they ran for comfort to the cloth mother. Snuggling there for a few moments invariably reduced their fear sufficiently so that curiosity could take over and they'd either look with interest at the strange object in their environment or go over and investigate the teddy bear at close quarters.

In dozens of similar tests, the babies used the cloth mother as a psychological home base, coming briefly back to "her" for reassurance after an exploratory foray into the far corners of the cage or a tentative examination of a new toy. If the cloth mother was removed and only the wire mother was available, the infant monkeys ran across the test room, threw themselves face down on the floor, clutched their heads and bodies, and screamed in distress. Clearly, the wire mother was the same as no mother; the babies' "emotionality scores" nearly tripled.

Harry Harlow says, "No quantitative measurement can convey the contrast between the positive, outgoing activities in the presence of the cloth mother and the withdrawn and disturbed behavior in the motherless situation."

It is therefore the Harlows' opinion that bodily contact is the single most important requirement for the formation of an infant's attachment to its mother. (A monkey infant, anyway.) Also important, but less so, is rhythmic motion. Baby monkeys like to be rocked as much as human infants do, and if given a choice between a stationary cloth mother and a cloth mother that rocks, they opt for the latter. Furthermore, little monkeys "discover" the heads, faces, and eyes of their surrogate mothers at precisely the same stage of development that human babies do, and attempt the same kind of exploratory touch and manipulation with which human mothers are familiar. The Harlows therefore believe that visual and

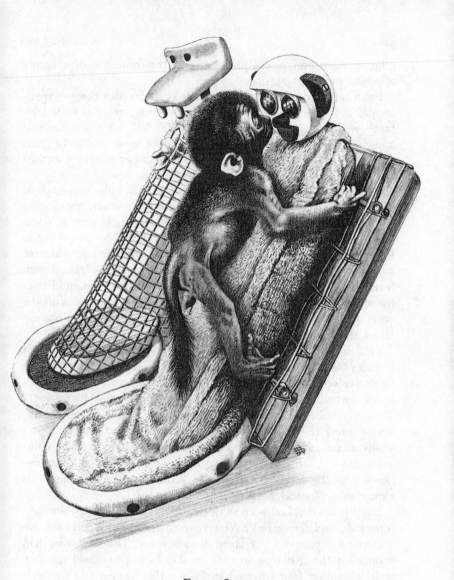

FIGURE 6

Harry Harlow has raised several generations of rhesus monkeys who have been "mothered" by wire or cloth-covered dummies like these. Because the infants will feed from the wire mother but always go to the cloth-covered mother for comfort, Harlow concludes that bodily contact is of prime importance in establishing a baby's attachment to its mother.

other sensory stimuli also play a role in the formation of a baby's affective tie to its mother.

From another branch of the animal kingdom also comes experimental evidence that the mother's presence is essential to the infant's well-being. Cornell's Howard S. Liddell, who is a violinist and a Civil War buff on his days off, has done some studies of goats that show how the mother's presence buffers her offspring against stress—and what the long-range effects are.

In one set of experiments, Liddell has put twin kids, at the age of three weeks, into adjacent rooms—one with the mother, one alone—and harnessed them so that instruments monitoring heartbeat, respiration, and other body processes can be affixed to proper sites. (These harnesses, however, allow the kid complete freedom of movement.) The kids are then conditioned to react to darkness with fear. The room lights are turned off just before they get a mild electric shock in one leg; a shock which they shortly associate with the onset of darkness, after which they respond with fear to the turning off of the lights.

Liddell has found that the kid which is housed with its mother bounces back very nicely from this traumatic experience. When the lights are on, it roams freely around the room and otherwise behaves normally. The solitary kid, however, becomes increasingly disturbed. It begins to avoid the center of the room and moves cautiously along the walls; then it restricts itself to just one wall; and finally it cowers in a corner—as unhinged as any baby monkey without a real or cloth mother to cling to. Liddell says, "These tensions impose on the isolated animal a psychic strait jacket almost as strong as a physical harness."

Eight goats that had been subjected to this experiment when they were kids, and seemed to have recovered from the experience, underwent a reprise after a lapse of two years. The four who had endured it the first time in their mothers' company held up very well. The other four reverted to their earlier neurotic behavior.

When the Harlows raised their first generation of motherless monkeys, they concluded that "the cloth-covered mother surrogate is eminently satisfactory. She is available twenty-four hours a day to satisfy her infant's overwhelming compulsion to seek bodily contact; she possesses infinite patience, never scolding her baby nor biting it in anger. In these respects we regard her as superior to a living monkey mother."

Nothing, it turns out, could have been further from the truth, and the Harlows have retracted their earlier opinion. At maturity, the monkeys raised on cloth mothers, both male and female, were totally incompetent sexually. The several females who did become pregnant, thanks to the persistence of normal males in the Harlows' breeding colony, turned out to be "hopeless, helpless, heartless" mothers. They either ignored their babies or brutally abused them. The Harlows now say, "It is perfectly obvious that monkeys which have known no affection can never develop either normal sexual behavior or normal maternal behavior and are bound to live out their lives as social failures."

Using human babies for similar controlled experiments is, of course, out of the question.* So the evidence for the relationship of maternal care to children's mental health comes primarily from what are called retrospective studies; the kind in which you match a group of children who have been reared normally with a group who have been deprived of maternal care, and see whether and how they differ.

One of the best and most convincing of such studies was done some years ago by William Goldfarb, who is now the director of the Henry Ittleson Center for Child Research in New York. His subjects were thirty adolescents aged ten to fourteen, matched as to age and sex, all of whom had long lived in foster homes. The foster homes were essentially the same, as was the overall adjustment to those homes of all the children. The thing that differentiated them was that fifteen of them had been put into hospitals or orphanages at about four months of age and had remained in these institutions for about three years before going to foster homes; whereas the other fifteen children had gone, while under two years of age, directly from their natural homes to their foster homes.

By the age when Goldfarb studied them, there were great differences in intelligence between the two groups. Despite many

---

* In a thirteenth-century chronicle by Salimbene von Parma, it is related that Emperor Frederick II, something of a scholar, was curious as to what language chilen would speak if they had no model to copy. Hebrew, the oldest language? Greek, Latin, Arabic? Or the tongue spoken by their parents?

So he assembled an experimental group of boy babies and told their wet nurses to care for them physically but otherwise to pay no attention to them and not to speak to them. The Emperor's curiosity as to their innate language was never satisfied because all the children died. The reason, von Parma said, was that they "could not live without petting and joyful faces and loving words."

years of family living, the early-institutionalized children were retarded in language and speech development, were less thoughtful
in problem solving, and less capable of sustained effort. The average
IQ of the group was 72.4 as against 95.4 for the children who had
not been institutionalized. They tended to be apathetic, unambi-
tious, less responsive to approval, lacking in a clear sense of personal identity, and were unable to form satisfying relationships with
other people.

A more recent foster home study, by Jessie M. Williams of Guys
Hospital, London, concentrated on children aged five to eleven who
had had to be removed from foster homes because of unsatisfactory
relations between the children and their foster parents, not because
the home itself was of poor quality. These children were compared
to a control group of family-reared children who, for one reason or
another, were newcomers to foster homes. Of the children who had
to be removed from their foster homes, 80 percent had been first
separated from their mothers before the age of two. They were
significantly below the control group in verbal ability, were lonely
and confused, and "grossly lacked self-regard."

These are only two of many studies which have come to the same
conclusion: infants deprived of maternal care may be damaged in
rather special ways. Their physical development is little affected,
but their intellectual development may be retarded, especially verbal ability, and neither the sense of self nor the ability to form close
relationships with other people may develop to the extent that it
should. It is largely because of such studies that the orphanage is
now a vanishing institution in the United States and Europe, and
social service agencies are concentrating on finding foster or adoptive homes that will welcome unwanted children as soon after birth
as possible.

Now, what of the child who never leaves his natural home, but
finds an abnormal lack of responsiveness to his needs in his own
mother?

It is exceedingly difficult to do objective studies of intrafamily
behavior, and hardly conceivable that a controlled experiment could
be set up to see what would happen to home-reared children if
their mothers were abnormally cold and inattentive. Therefore, such
evidence as exists of bad mothering in a child's own home is in the
form of clinical observations by people who deal with emotionally
disturbed children.

Among these are a group of case histories by Joyce Robertson, of the Hampstead Child Guidance Clinic in London. This institution maintains both a well-baby clinic and a nursery school, and children who have been patients at the former often attend the latter. In 1960, Robertson reports, she was struck by differences in muscular tone among the nursery school children—"the strong sturdiness of some as contrasted to the flabby limpness of others, the directed and skilful movements of some and the clumsy incoordination of others." Having seen many of these toddlers at younger ages in the well-baby clinic, she went back to their records, and discovered that "the clumsy ones were those whose mothering during the first year had been regarded as unsatisfactory." Then she undertook a systematic comparison of infant records with nursery school behavior, eventually going beyond her initial interest in motor coordination to a consideration of total personality.

Among the mother-child pairs whose records were checked was a handsome cherub named Peter. When his mother brought him to the well-baby clinic, she did not talk to him or play with him. "In the waiting room they sat silent and still like two wooden figures. If he cried, she did not comfort him. He gradually learned to control his tears; by the time he was a year old, nothing made him cry. It had become clear that subdued unresponsiveness was what his mother wanted of him." At age three, there was no animation or pleasure in his bodily movements; he was a passive watcher, not a doer; and his response to excitement was to stand rigid and tremble.

Beatrice was also a child whose mother looked after her physical welfare but otherwise lacked empathy for her baby. "When Beatrice was three months old, it was noted that she and her mother looked at each other silently, with expressionless faces. By six months of age, the child's looking had a staring, intense, and apprehensive quality. When the child cried after an injection, the mother would look away from her and continue talking. When Beatrice wanted attention—to be lifted from the floor, for instance—she would again look away. It was painful to witness a baby trying to get protection and response from a mother who defended herself by being blind to these demands."

Maurice and Gordon were brothers, Gordon being the younger by twenty-one months. Maurice was a crying baby; in fact, he screamed at everything and everybody, practically from birth. The clinic staff "tended to think that his mother's imperturbable calm was rather wonderful" until Gordon came along. *He* was an abnormally quiet, unresponsive baby "over whose whole being there was an air of diffuse anxiety." The mother was never seen to fondle or kiss either child, and avoided bodily contact with them insofar as possible.

Incidentally, it was not lack of intelligence or absence of counseling that caused these mothers to persist in their patterns of child-rearing. When the clinic staff suggested changes, the mothers found ingenious ways—born of their own emotional problems—to follow the suggestion without honoring its spirit. One mother, for instance, reacted to the suggestion that her baby needed more human company by moving his pram from the side yard to the front garden and propping him up so that he could see pedestrians and traffic on the street.

Joyce Robertson concluded her report by saying, "A baby mothered without warmth will develop broadly on the same lines as other babies. He will focus his eyes, smile, babble, find his limbs; but he will do it largely alone. There will be no fusion between the baby's achievements and the mother's pleasure and support; and for lack of his mother as an intermediary there will be less reaching out to the environment. The balance between adequate stimulation from his surroundings and potentially overwhelming new experiences will not be maintained, and the baby may try to take over part of his own protection.

"As early as eight to ten weeks of age, the consequences are low quality and quantity of body movement, slow responses, serious facial expression, and eyes that are incongruously alert and watchful. The mother will say, 'But he is so contented,' meaning that he is undemanding; or, 'He is happiest when alone,' unaware that he may be withdrawing. With the passage of time these deficiencies become more gross. The uncomforted baby who swallows his tears at seven months may not cry at twelve months.

"A baby will adjust to almost any condition and survive—but at a cost."

That the cost can be enormous was first fully documented by John Bowlby, a psychiatrist who heads the Child Guidance Department of the Tavistock Clinic in London. In a 1951 report that had great impact on the child study and child care fraternity, he said: "When deprived of maternal care, the child's development is almost always retarded—physically, intellectually, and socially—and symptoms of physical and mental illness may appear. Such evidence is disquieting, but skeptics may question whether the retardation is permanent and whether the symptoms of illness may not easily be overcome. Other studies make it clear that such optimism is not always justified and that some children are gravely damaged for life. This is a sombre conclusion which must now be regarded as established."

The report was controversial. Many people in the child-study field took exception to certain of its conclusions, their objections falling generally into one of three categories:

1. Does deprivation of maternal care *permanently* damage the child?

The British psychologists A. D. B. and Ann Clarke, now at the University of Hull in Yorkshire, are among those who doubt the inevitability of this outcome. They believe instead that "exceptionally adverse experiences in childhood prolong the immaturity of the organism" rather than irretrievably retard development. The Clarkes are among those who have found that the IQ can move upward during the years of later childhood, despite severe maternal deprivation in infancy.

2. Are all children equally vulnerable to the distorting effects of maternal deprivation?

The answer to this, of course, is "no"; Bowlby himself said only that *some* children are gravely damaged for life. If one can extrapolate from animal studies, in which breed makes an enormous difference in reaction to isolation or stress, there are innate differences of responsiveness to environment among children too. Furthermore, the degree and duration of maternal deprivation experienced by any individual child is likely to be different.

3. Just exactly what is meant by "maternal deprivation"?

It is too loose a term to cover a number of variables in childhood experience, some say. The absence, from birth, of a single mother-figure? The somewhat later separation of a baby from a person with whom he has established a close affective tie? These are very different situations: in the first case, the infant never *had* anyone; in the second, as many an observer has noted, his reaction to separation is akin to the grief felt when a loved one dies. Still another, and perhaps more commonplace, situation involves the temporary separation of a baby from its mother (because of his or her illness, say) with a later reunion.

Kellmer Pringle and V. Bossio, of Birmingham University in England, are typical of the researchers who have refined the meaning

of "maternal deprivation." They studied a group of children between the ages of eight and fourteen, all of average intelligence, all
of whom had lived apart from their parents for more than half their
lives and were at the time of study in an institution. The children
were chosen because they were rated "notably stable" or "severely
maladjusted" (on standard personality tests and by clinical observation); then their histories were compared.

Of the maladjusted children, nine out of eleven had been separated from their mothers during the first year of life; of the stable
children, only one child had been institutionalized so early. Most of
the children in the maladjusted group were illegitimate, hence it is
not surprising that neither their mothers nor any blood relative
wanted to be reminded of the indiscretion—but the effect on the
children was to deny them any parent-figure or link with the world
outside the hospital or orphanage. In contrast, the children in the
stable group had been deprived of mothers by chance, and other
members of the family never wholly abandoned them.

Pringle and Bossio say, "Our maladjusted group may be described as being psychologically deprived while the stable group
was deprived of family life but nevertheless loved and cherished by
adults who were important to them." Therefore, these psychologists
say, "Physical separation and prolonged institutionalization themselves do not necessarily lead to emotional difficulties or character
defects. Susceptibility to maladjustment and resilience to the shock
of separation and deprivation appear to be determined by the
quality of human relationships available to the child during critical
periods of growth."

Bowlby's landmark report was updated in 1962 by the Canadian-
born psychologist Mary Ainsworth, who worked for a time at the
Tavistock Clinic and is now at Johns Hopkins. She says that minor
amendments should be made but that Bowlby's basic conclusion
still stands. If an unmothered baby gets a mother—anyone to whom
he can form a stable and loving relationship—within the first two
years of life, progressive retardation of *general* development may be
arrested or reversed. This would include the general level of intelligence—which is what the IQ tests measure. But the bulk of
the evidence still suggests, Ainsworth says, that it is not possible to
reverse impairment to certain intellectual and emotional processes
which seem to be *specifically* vulnerable to disturbance during
early development. These include language and abstraction, the

ability to establish deep and meaningful interpersonal relations, and the ability to control impulse in the interest of long-range goals.

It is hard to think of qualities more important for success in our kind of society than these very ones. I will consider the development of language and abstraction in more detail later, but suffice it to say now that the employment of abstract concepts is the cornerstone of our ability to communicate with other human beings or to order our own mental processes into the activity known as thinking. Look at the following words: "space," "time," "cause," "effect," "color," "roundness," "excellence," "friendship," "morality." None describes an object, something with material substance; all are abstract concepts which describe relationships among material things. To develop an understanding of them is a long, slow business that normally occupies some fifteen to twenty years of our lives.

As for the emotional processes whose growth is thwarted by absence of maternal care in infancy, think of the central importance to marriage and parenthood of the ability to establish and maintain meaningful interpersonal relations. Both of these human institutions are in deep trouble if the individuals concerned have only superficial and impersonal involvement in each other's lives. And few human enterprises of any sort are realized quickly or without effort; one usually has to work toward a specific goal in a consistent manner, an activity in which denial of some competing demand or desire is implicit.

There aren't many studies of human beings that show the effect of extra-attentive mothering. One, however, was made by Marcelle Geber, who tested over three hundred East African babies (from Uganda) during their first year of life, to see how their motor coordination compared to that of children of the same age in our culture. The tests used were those standardized by Arnold Gesell of the Yale Clinic of Child Development. The findings—in a report which predates by two years Wayne Dennis's observations of the children in Iranian orphanages—are almost too perfectly opposite.

The African babies came from lower class families where ancient tribal customs are still practiced. Babies remain with their mothers day and night. They are talked to, cuddled, and stroked; they are fed whenever they wish to eat; and they are watched for cues as to what they want to do—sit up, for instance—and are then helped to do it. The Uganda mother is wholly child-centered.

And the child she produces is noticeably superior to Western European or American children. At seven weeks, for example, he can sit up unaided and watch himself in a mirror; at seven months, for another example, he can walk to a box and look inside it for toys. These accomplishments occur in our children at about twenty-four weeks and fifteen months, respectively.

This superior coordination could be explained by earlier physiological maturation; on the whole, African peoples *do* mature earlier than Europeans. But that isn't the complete explanation, because the Uganda babies were also ahead of their Western-culture counterparts in adaptivity to novel situations, social relationships, and language skills.

Lest Western-culture readers still resist the implication of these findings and defend our ways as "best," here is one more item from Geber's report. A few babies in the study came from the upper classes, which means that their families were somewhat Westernized and therefore raised their children more as we do—less bodily contact with the mother, more emphasis on scheduled feedings, more attention to "training." These particular African babies, Geber found, were much less precocious than the babies reared in the tribal environment.

CHAPTER 6

CRITICAL PERIODS

The thalidomide disaster of a few years ago demonstrated beyond doubt that there are times in the development of a young organism when it is maximally sensitive to chemical interference with the normal processes of growth. Pregnant women who took the drug during the first seven weeks of gestation were most likely to bear babies with stunted or missing limbs. Likewise, expectant mothers who happen to contract German measles—such a mild disease in itself!—during these same weeks of rapid fetal growth are likely to have deaf, blind, or mentally retarded babies.

After birth, too, there are critical periods in physical, emotional, and intellectual development. Some of these can be pinpointed in time quite specifically; others, especially those pertaining to emotional and intellectual development, can as yet be bounded only generally. But even if one can't say that Johnny's speech will be forever abnormal if he doesn't make certain sounds by the tenth week after birth, one *can* say that Johnny will be severely handicapped in his use of language if he doesn't progress from random vocalizing of vowel sounds to consonants to syllables to simple words within the first two years of life.

At the 1952 Oxford Conference of Mental Health, John Bowlby presented a paper which so neatly summarized findings and tentative theories from a number of scientific sources that a longish excerpt seems indicated. He said:

"The organization of perceptual and behavior patterns appears to pass through critical phases during which these patterns are highly plastic and after which they become comparatively rigid. If, for example, the perceptual organizations of the first two or three years of life are consolidated by experience in the third and fourth years, they are maintained thoughout life—even if deafness or blindness supervene. But if deafness or blindness supervene earlier, say before the second birthday, the organization fails to consolidate; and if hearing or vision are restored, all has to be learned afresh—and learned with infinitely greater difficulty because the plastic phase of development is over and different organizations for communication and perception of form have become organized and consolidated.

"There is good reason to think that something similar occurs in regard to social perceptions and social responses. Children of between six months and three years who are separated from their mothers often undergo intense emotional experiences of rage and despair and then proceed to organize their social relations on a new pattern; often one in which no particular human being is sought after and loved. It would appear that if this new and psychopathic organization is permitted to consolidate at around the age of three or four years, it tends to become permanent.

"Clearly this 'setting' of the perceptual and behavioral patterns in the third and fourth years of life must have as its base important maturational changes in the physiology and anatomy of the brain . . . My own guess would be that the cerebral centers concerned complete their basic patterns of growth at this time and thenceforward do not change greatly in their general organization.

"The social responses of sophisticated adult human beings are enormously complex . . . and thus depend on the highest cerebral centers. But there are very good grounds for believing that if we strip away the sophistications, the simplest and most highly motivated responses and those most charged with feeling are not only learned in childhood but depend on centers in the older* parts of the brain, parts not very different from those with which the other mammals are provided."

So let us consider some evidence from animal studies.

One of the liveliest centers for behavioral research is McGill

* Author's note: "Older," as Bowlby uses it here, means the parts of the brain that evolved first.

University in Montreal. Ronald Melzack, whose work on the development of emotion in dogs was mentioned in Chapter 4, is one of the McGill group. Two of his colleagues, William R. Thompson and Woodburn Heron, have reported a comparable experiment testing the problem-solving capacity of dogs after prolonged isolation. They raised Scottish terriers for eight months in solitary cages from which they could see nothing and in which they had an absolute minimum of contact with the outside world; then compared the dogs' adult ability to solve problems with that of littermates who had been raised normally. A year after their removal from isolation—that is, after twelve months of freedom to explore the environment—they remained far less attentive and observant than the normally reared dogs.

For instance, if all the dogs were trained to run from one corner of a test room to a food dish in another corner, and the food dish was then placed in a different corner, dogs who had been restricted continued to run to the original corner first—even though they had watched the feeder place the dish in the new spot, had heard him thump it down to emphasize its new location, and could see it sitting there. When shown a morsel of meat which was behind a wire fence and obtainable only if they ran around the open end of the fence, the restricted dogs took more than twice as long as the controls to solve the problem. It is clear, therefore, that sometime during the first eight months of life there is a critical period during which Scottish terriers must have certain kinds of perceptual experience or be permanently handicapped in their ability to solve problems.

And then there's the evidence from many studies of imprinting in fowl. This process, which creates in certain animals a social attachment to their parents, was first described in detail by the zoologist and ethologist Konrad Lorenz. He divided a clutch of eggs laid by a graylag goose into two groups, one of which was hatched normally and the other in an incubator. The goslings hatched by the goose subsequently followed their mother, but those hatched in the incubator—who did not see their mother—following the first moving thing they *did* see: Lorenz.

Imprinting has since been studied experimentally by many investigators. Foremost among them is Eckhard Hess at the University of Chicago, who has concentrated on the behavior of mallard ducklings.* To eliminate even the earliest visual experience, the incubator in which his birds are hatched is kept dark. From it, the ducklings are exposed, at different periods after hatching, to a decoy duck (male) mounted in the center of a circular runway. (See FIGURE 7.) In some experiments, the moving decoy has been the sole feature; in others, a recording of the human voice making a "gock, gock, gock" sound has accompanied the movement of the decoy. Ducklings are adaptable: they will accept as their mother the moving decoy, the moving-and-gocking decoy, or even the sound alone.

To test them for depth of imprinting, ducklings are later released between two decoys—the male model with which they had been imprinted, and a female model. If the gock-gock sound had originally been paired with the male decoy, a recording of the sound that mallards make when calling their young is paired with the female decoy. Each duckling is placed four times in a test situation and is scored according to the number of times it goes to the male model. This record is correlated with the age period after hatching when the duckling was first exposed to the decoy.

Thus, Hess has shown that imprinting is deepest and firmest if it occurs between thirteen and sixteen hours after hatching. Delayed beyond twenty-four hours, it collides with the onset of an equally important and innate behavior pattern—fear of moving objects—which develops by thirty-two hours after hatching. It is

* The history of scientific research abounds in "accidental" discoveries, which some people equate with pure luck. This is not true in many cases, for the operating factor is the alertness of the scientist in question—his quickness to recognize the significance of a spontaneously occurring event and his subsequent ability to reproduce it under controlled experimental conditions. That is the background of Lorenz's discovery of the imprinting phenomenon, a discovery upon which Hess built an investigative laboratory technique.

Hess, too, has an "accidental" discovery to his credit. One night, when his wife was reading in bed—a book with text on left-hand pages and pictures of animals on right-hand pages—he noticed that the pupils of her eyes dilated when she looked at the right-hand pages. But pupils expand or contract only for a *physical* reason, to adapt to light intensity, don't they? No; as subsequent investigation showed. When women look at pictures of babies and when men look at pictures of pretty girls, regardless of their ability to maintain an overall deadpan expression, their eyes give them away. This knowledge could be a secret weapon for schoolteachers who suspect that Johnny's absorbed interest in a textbook might in fact be absorbed interest in a comic book tucked into the textbook's pages.

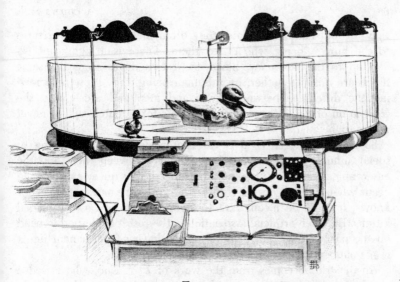

FIGURE 7

In nature, many species of young fowl are "imprinted"—that is, form an attachment to a member of their own species—by following their mothers. In Eckhard Hess's laboratory, however, this duckling is being imprinted to a decoy of a male mallard. (From *Scientific American*, March, 1958. Reproduced by permission of Dr. Eckhard H. Hess and *Scientific American*.)

obvious that a duckling in the wild hasn't much chance for survival if something goes wrong with this timetable of development.

Imprinting also occurs in insects, fishes, and many kinds of birds.* Erich Klinghammer has studied the early experiences of doves and similar birds which are dependent on their parents for the several months it takes them to develop sufficiently to fly and to leave the nest. Such birds, if hand-raised in a laboratory, will behave very differently if they are removed from the nest before or after the eighth day of life. Klinghammer reports that they all tame quite easily, but only those removed from the nest before the eighth day remain tame throughout adulthood; in fact, when

---

* A student of Hess once imprinted a duckling to herself and a quail to the duckling. The three of them made a charming parade when they went for a morning stroll on the university campus.

they are old enough to mate, they often make courting overtures to the human being who raised them. There is a significant exception to this tendency, however: if two doves from the same hatch are raised together, by a human being, they grow up knowing the difference between doves and men and are spared the frustration of gathering nesting materials for a match that is never going to be made.

So necessary to survival is the requirement that the young of social animals have an adult intermediary between them and the environment, so insistent is the inborn need, that queer pairings can occur when nature's design is thwarted. As every newspaper reader knows, it is by no means rare for female dogs to raise orphaned kittens. But such artificial association is the result of desperate need on the part of the young, and seems to have no permanent effect if a member of the same species is handy.

An illustration comes from the work of Z. Y. Kuo, who raised a number of kittens in cages with rats—one kitten paired with one rat—and discovered that the kittens had no innate hostility toward rats. At the age of six months, furthermore, when normal cats have become enthusiastic rat-killers, *these* cats refused to kill the species of rat they'd been raised with. However, when Kuo raised several kittens and several rats in the same cages, he found that no social bond had been forged: the grown-up cats killed any rat they could catch. A rat will do as a parent-figure if it is the only living creature available—but given a choice between an adult rat and another kitten, kittens "imprint" to their own kind. (Not that such behavior would do them any good in nature. Kitten-to-kitten, like kitten-to-rat, is a combination that can survive only in the laboratory.)

Now, what about the primates—chimpanzees, monkeys, and men? The Harlows have discovered that being motherless is not the worst thing that can happen to young monkeys; what finishes them off as social beings is isolation. Those that are raised in cages with other infant monkeys turn out pretty well. This does not prove that baby monkeys imprint each other, but it does indicate that monkeys share with doves and cats a basic need for close association with others of one's own species during some critical period of early life.

Most psychologists shy away from use of the term "imprinting" as applied to human beings, but recognize that human infants must form an attachment to a particular adult during their earliest months if they are to develop properly. Philip H. Gray, who is now at Montana State, is one of the few who believe that babies form the bond just as ducklings do. Further, he has suggested that the human infant's first social smile (at four to six weeks) is the equivalent of the "following response" which occurs in ducklings a few hours after hatching. Gray says that both are biologically programmed for a very special survival purpose: to bind the young to the parent and thus give it a proper model to learn from.

John A. Ambrose, a colleague of Bowlby at the Tavistock Clinic in London, disagrees with many of the specific assumptions which led Gray to his conclusion but nevertheless agrees that smiling serves the same social purpose as imprinting, and that its onset signals a critical period of development. He points out that the stimuli which trigger the following response in young fowl and of smiling in babies are similar: for birds, sound or motion; for babies, sound or one particular part of the human face, the eyes. Ambrose equates a human mother's eyes with "the first moving object seen" by a duckling, pointing out that tiny babies can't fixate *their* eyes on very large objects, and that of all features of a mother's face the most mobile are her eyes. Not only do they move in their sockets, but they have a light-reflective quality and often a sparkle which is akin to movement.

Unlike ducklings, human infants are physically incapable of following a parent. Neither can they cling, as monkey infants can. Yet a baby has the same need as other young for close contact with a mother. His cry of distress will fetch her from a distance, and normally results in the satisfaction of his basic physical needs. But man does not live by bread alone; and it is a rare mother who fails to respond to a baby's smile by cooing to him or picking him up for a cuddle. (*Her* response is also built in by the genes, Ambrose says.) Thus, greater contact between the two is encouraged, and the normally reared baby therefore has abundant opportunity during his early months to piece together a picture of what a human being is like.

He learns from this first member of the species with whom he interacts that human beings have a characteristic form, sound, smell, touch—and behavior. Ambrose says, "Depending on what his mother is like, his picture of a human being may turn out to be anything between two extremes. At one extreme it may be a loving, need-satisfying, anxiety-reducing, benign person, whom he can depend on. At the other extreme it may be a hating, rejecting, poor need-satisfier who frequently elicits anxiety, lets him in for long periods of frustration, and cannot be depended on. Every infant must in fact have some degree of each sort of perception of his mother. Where infants vary will be in the balance between the amount of good and bad aspects built up."

At about the twentieth week of life a baby starts smiling selectively, his signal that he has learned to differentiate familiar individuals from strangers. But Ambrose believes that the infant transfers to strangers whatever emotional attitudes he has developed toward his mother during the period when he was "learning the species" by contact primarily with her. If she has engendered a high amount of anxiety in him, his tendency to withdraw from other people will exceed his tendency to approach; this withdrawal will prevent his learning that other people are in fact different from his mother; and his capacity to establish and maintain human relationships in general will be attenuated.

Children raised in institutions where close contact with a single mother-figure is denied them are thus seen as coming to the six-month mark without a clear sense of their human identity. In addition, the high level of frustration which they experience (hospitalized adults who have to wait for attention undergo it too!) enormously reduces their ability to attend to what's going on around them. (Remember what Wolff and White had to say, in Chapter 4, about the relation of the emotions to attentiveness.)

Not all child development experts would accept the foregoing explanation, but all would agree that something very important happens in a child's life between the second and sixth months. The evidence has been piling up ever since René Spitz—who, incidentally, has *three* M.D. degrees—published a classic 1945 paper on "hospitalism." In that report, he told how he had followed a group of infants in a foundling home from the first to the twelfth month, and had noticed a "precipitous drop" in developmental quotient (the child's maturational age divided by his chronological age) between the third and sixth month. This was followed by a more gradual drop during subsequent months.

Somewhat later, Liselotte Fischer—who is now chief psychiatrist at the Child Guidance Clinic run by the Childrens Hospital in Buffalo, New York—found that the IQ's of institutionalized children rose on the average about ten points between the ages of six and ten months but that certain personality traits stabilized by the sixth month. That's when the children she was watching either became exceedingly passive, apathetic, and uninterested in adults except as a source of food; or became aggressive, hyperactive, and frantically anxious for adult attention.

From this point onward, toys had little or no meaning to these children. The passive ones sucked their thumbs and the active ones shook the bars of their cribs or screamed for attention. And this at a developmental stage when normal children are notable for their strong urge to manipulate things, in the course of which they familiarize themselves with size, shape, weight, and texture!

Finally, there's the testimony of Bruno Bettelheim, who has treated a number of autistic children at the University of Chicago's Sonia Shankman Orthogenic School. Autism, according to Bettelheim, is an emotional disorder in which a child sees the world as potentially so destructive to himself that he wholly withdraws from it. Take "Marcia" as an example:

Bettelheim says that this child had been aware from infancy that "her father wanted her out of the way so that he could have more of the mother, and the mother wanted her out of the way so that she could be free of them both." Marcia obliged her parents by creating for herself a life of nonexistence. She came to the Orthogenic School at age ten, a nontalking child who either sat motionless in a yoga-like position or rocked wildly back and forth in a frenzy of holding herself together. She left the school at age sixteen, able to lead a sheltered life outside of an institution, but unable to function well in the adult world because her intellectual abilities never caught up to her emotional development. She never learned to read, for example, beyond the fifth-grade level.

Bettelheim, thinking over the school's experiences with Marcia and other autistic children, says, "Generalizing from both our failures and our successes, we are impressed that for all our children the so-difficult establishment of affective relations was achieved far more readily than [intellectual] functions.

"Marcia's case may illustrate here, since she gained the whole range of affect—first to significant persons and then to the world. But while her ability to reason, to read with comprehension, and to master nonaffective aspects of reality showed marked development, they never reached normal levels.

"These findings suggest again that in infantile autism we are dealing with an inborn time schedule that cannot be delayed too long. There seems to be no biological time clock that governs development of our emotions, but there is one for the intellectual development based on those emotions . . ."

There are many theories as to why early learning has such a powerful effect and is so difficult to alter later. As indicated in this chapter, the imprinting studies suggest that learning is most firmly fixed during a particularly sensitive period which is biologically determined. Some psychologists theorize that the things we learn before we can talk are buried in the unconscious and therefore cannot later be tested for validity against the perceptions we store in conscious memory. Others ascribe the persistence of early learning to its constant repetition over a long period of time. If, in countless ways and every day from birth onward, a child is not responded to, he will come to school age with over two thousand days of that kind of learning behind him and no one should be very surprised if a teacher's effort to "give individual attention to each child" isn't a huge success with that particular one.

And then there's the "resolution of crisis" theory proposed by Erik Erikson of Harvard. He says that each stage of psychological growth is characterized by a particular conflict which must be resolved in a positive way if future conflicts are also to be resolved. We are never wholly successful in this task, he says, and carry with us through life some residue—small or large—of failure at each developmental stage. If the residue is large, it limits our ability to cope successfully with the next conflict, just as a shallow foundation limits the height of a building.

The first of these crises of development, according to Erikson, is the infant's need to develop a basic sense of trust in himself and in his environment. If he finds that he will be fed when hungry and held when frightened, he learns to trust his mother; and through her, others. As his sensory and motor skills improve, he learns to trust his own body. From these experiences he learns that the world is fundamentally predictable and consistent, and that to be alive in it makes sense.

Babies should have acquired this basic faith in existence by their first birthdays, because the next developmental stage is by that time at hand. It does not wait upon the child's readiness for it; his own physical maturation and the expectations of his culture thrust him into a period of about two years during which he must learn to walk and talk, establish himself as an individual distinct from other individuals, learn self-control, and develop self-esteem.

Quite a large order, that, for any unfortunate toddler who hasn't learned during the preceding period that it is an orderly, predictable, and basically satisfying world—and therefore one in which purposeful action is possible.

CHAPTER 7

THE ANATOMY OF THE BRAIN

Man's great biological specialty is his ability to learn; he does this better than any other animal. For the purpose, he possesses an ovoid mass of tissue which in the adult weighs about three pounds and, if removed from its protective skull and viewed from above, looks like a shelled walnut. Nothing about its appearance indicates that the brain is the remarkable organ it is. Yet this is the source of man's uniqueness among living species.

Nature appropriately starts him out by allocating proportionately more space to his brain than to the rest of him. (The rest of him increases twentyfold before reaching maturity; the brain enlarges only fourfold.) His brain matures faster than much of the rest of him. (By age seven, overall brain growth is largely complete; the skeletal framework of the body isn't done until age twenty.) Finally, the human child remains dependent on adults for a longer percentage of his life span than any other species, so that his brain may acquire and organize the vast amounts of information which must be put into it if he is to become an adult fitted to live in human society.

The exterior of the brain is pinkish gray, but the interior is white. The whiteness comes from a material called myelin, which surrounds each of the brain's many millions of nerve fibers, just as insulating material sheaths the electrical cords on your toaster, telephone, or television set. The analogy is deliberate: the brain, too, is powered by electricity. The great neurologist Sir Charles Sherrington once described the brain as "an enchanted loom where millions of flashing shuttles weave a dissolving pattern, always a meaningful pattern but never an abiding one." The "flashing shuttles" are fast indeed: tens of millions of electrical impulses per second reach the brain, reporting on both internal conditions of the body and on its external environment; and within the same second more tens of millions of electrical impulses course outward from the brain, regulating internal health and external activity by controlling the glands and muscles of the body.

The human brain is often compared to a computer. Mechanically, this is a good comparison, for both are switching networks with multiple interconnections; both are capable of scrutinizing and evaluating incoming data, determining what is relevant to a given situation and what is not; and both store and retrieve information and dispatch messages that will determine action elsewhere. But the brain outperforms the computer to an astonishing degree, both in the quantity of information it can store and in the quality of discriminative acts of which it is capable. The research engineer Dean Wooldridge has said, "The memory capacity of one cubic inch of the neuronal material of the brain exceeds that of a roomful of electronic components."

To which W. Ross Ashby adds: "Cybernetic studies are showing that [the brain] works not so much mechanistically as statistically, developing its adaptations by processes of selective feedback working on a basis that is, to a certain degree, random. This might seem to invite disorder, but in fact can be shown to give the mechanism potentialities available in no other way. It is the fact that the brain works statistically, unlike any man-made machine, that gives it powers so obviously beyond those possessed by any machine yet made . . . The brain makes the biggest computer look like an abacus."

The circuitry of the nervous system begins with single thin nerve-cell fibers on the periphery of the body and leads inward toward the backbone. Eventually bundled into cables within the spinal cord, these massed fibers become the body's trunk lines to the brain. Some electrical impulses are sidetracked during their passage up the spinal cord or when they reach the lower parts of the brain; others go all the way to the top.

As the spinal cord enters the brain, it angles forward and elabo-

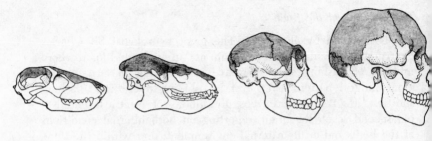

FIGURE 8

Greater mental powers accompany the enlarged cerebrum. Among living creatures, it is most highly developed in man.

rates into a structure called the brainstem. This is all the brain that many animals possess; in man it is called "the old brain" because in appearance and function it links us to our evolutionary past. It directs such unconscious or reflex action as the contraction of the eyes when coming from a dark room into a light one, or the expansion of the chest muscles which cause the lungs to breathe in air. It also contains a concentration of nerves called "the reticular activating system" which serve as an alarm clock for the higher regions of the brain. This is the site of consciousness; it wakes us up in the literal as well as the metaphorical sense, and keeps the mind alert to incoming sensation.

What are little more than protuberances on the brainstems of lower animals have evolved in higher animals into two major structures. One is the cerebellum, a lump about the size of a baseball, which is behind the brainstem at the base of the skull and just above the nape of the neck. The other is the cerebrum, the part that lies just under the top of the skull and behind the forehead. This is the part which increases in size and forward thrust as one follows the evolutionary development of ever-higher species. (See FIGURE 8.)

The cerebrum is composed of two anatomically identical hemispheres, each covered by cortex, which means "bark." The word for this one-sixth-inch layer strikes me as not too well chosen because one tends to think of bark as flat on the underside—and the cerebral cortex squeezes down into the hemispheres so that the internal outline of this gray matter looks in cross section like the coast of Maine. (See FIGURE 9.) Again quoting Wooldridge, the convolutions of the cerebral cortex "give the impression that Nature has gone to considerable pains to pack into the limited space available as much yardage of this sheet material as possible."

Not surprisingly, the cerebrum and its cortex are the site of those intellectual processes that have earned man the label of *Homo sapiens.* This organ has taken over many activities that at some point in our evolutionary past were handled by the old brain. It also refines activities that are still initiated by the brainstem or the cerebellum. If the cortex is damaged at a point somewhat behind the crown of the head, for example, one loses the ability to localize pressure on the skin or is unable to distinguish between rough and smooth textures. A person so afflicted is aware of pressure *somewhere,* and may find a certain object pleasant or unpleasant to the touch; that's because these gross sensations are controlled by the thalamus, a body lying between the brainstem and the cerebellum. Muscular movement, similarly, has its beginnings in the cerebellum but depends upon the cortex for such finishing touches as smoothness and coordination.

Neurologists and others concerned with the physiology of the brain have identified a number of specific areas in the cortex whose activity correlates with particular functions—either by observing what behavior is impaired when the brain is damaged or by implanting electrodes into animal brains and artificially "firing" the

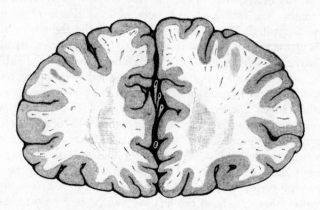

FIGURE 9

Cross section of the human brain shows how convoluted the cerebral cortex is. This is the site of the intellectual abilities that distinguish human beings from other animals.

animal's own nerve circuitry. This latter technique (which is not painful) has been especially useful in locating the apparent center of the emotions: a cluster of cells near the thalamus which is called the limbic system.

But as you can see in FIGURE 10, there are great unmapped areas in the brain. Somewhere within this unknown territory—or perhaps all through it—we do such complicated tasks as substituting symbols for absent objects and events (the ability that underlies language and thought). Here too we make important associations—correlating the sound of a spoken word with the shape of a printed one, for example, or the size of an object with its texture. Stanley Cobb gives these large unspecialized areas of the brain the credit for the development of human intelligence. Short circuits are capable only of direct specific responses to signals, he says, and if we didn't have the elaborate long circuitry that he believes is characteristic of these association areas we wouldn't be able to reflect upon the significance of incoming stimuli before we respond to them.

The cerebrum's division into two hemispheres gives us a generous margin of safety (as does the doubling of lungs, kidneys, and limbs). Take the optic nerves: one of the two from each eye runs to the hemisphere on the opposite side of the head, crossing at a point in the base of the brain; but one nerve fiber from each eye runs to the hemisphere on the same side of the head in which the eye is located. (See FIGURE 11.) Thus, if the right hemisphere, say, is damaged at the point where the optic nerves terminate, the individual will still be able to see half the visual field from each eye—because the optic nerves to the left hemisphere remain.

There is much transfer of information from one hemisphere to the other. Roger Sperry, California Insitute of Technology psychobiologist, has learned a great deal about how this occurs by doing "split-brain" experiments on cats. First, he cuts the optic nerve going from the left side of the right eye and the nerve going from the right side of the left eye at the point where they cross en route to the cortex. (This point is marked with an A in FIGURE 11.) Thereafter, messages from the left eye can be sent *only* to the left hemisphere and messages from the right eye *only* to the right hemisphere. Then, with the right eye blindfolded, a cat is taught to discriminate a square from a triangle. Finally, the left eye is blindfolded and the cat is given the same problem. It performs

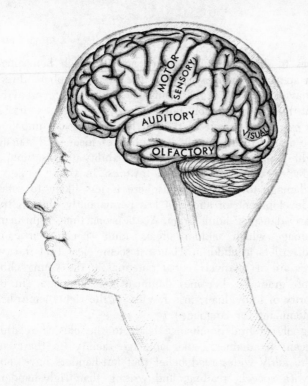

FIGURE 10

In this diagrammatic sketch of the brain, the visual, motor, auditory, and other centers are indicated—but of equal importance are the unmapped "associative" areas in between, where information is correlated and stored.

equally well—which can only mean that learning which occurs in one hemisphere has been transmitted to the other hemisphere.

The pathway for this transferral is a bundle of fibers (B, in FIGURE 11) which spans the two hemispheres a little forward of the crown. When Sperry has cut this bundle, his cats have been limited to behavior learned by one or the other hemisphere of the brain. (Such a complete split has been useful to researchers, incidentally, because the net effect of such surgery has been to create two living brains in one animal. Scientists can train one hemisphere and use the other as a control, or the separated halves can learn opposite behavior without causing any psychic discomfort to the animal.)

Although, as I have just indicated, it is normal for the two hemispheres to duplicate each other's activity, each hemisphere also has a specialty. In most people, the left hemisphere directs verbal behavior and the right hemisphere directs nonverbal behavior—but this specialization builds slowly over the years. In adults, for example, damage to the left hemisphere can impair or destroy the ability to use words as symbols of ideas, and damage to the right hemisphere can affect one's ability to discriminate between shapes, colors, sounds, and textures. In young children, however, damage to the left hemisphere is less likely to retard language development, or affects it less permanently, than is true of a similarly damaged adult brain. At the same time, right-hemisphere damage—which seldom affects adult speech—*can* cause language disorders in children. Hence it seems clear that the two hemispheres are of relatively equal potential in the young child, and the left gradually becomes dominant for language (in the great majority of individuals; in a few cases, the right hemisphere becomes dominant for language).

Speaking of cerebral dominance leads to the elusive relationship between "handedness" and language facility. Is there any truth to the fairly widespread belief that left-handers have more difficulty with speech, reading, and writing than right-handers?

First, let's consider the development of handedness. On the basis of the design of primitive tools, it appears that Stone Age men (20,000 to 10,000 B.C.) had no preferred hand.* In this they were like modern primitive peoples: handedness is less strongly developed among societies that do not use many implements. Bronze Age men (3000 to 2000 B.C.) were strongly right-handed, however, and to this day the great majority of human beings are right-handed.

As observed by Arnold Gesell and Louise B. Ames of the Yale Child Guidance Clinic, children use either hand or favor the left hand until they are about a year old; shift to the right hand but swing back to mixed handedness from time to time until they are about seven years old; then settle down—95 percent of them—to uncompromising right-handedness. Is this the result of a *cultural*

---

* The professionals' term for this is "mixed laterality," and it is not synonymous with ambidexterity. The latter connotes equal competence in the use of the hands, whereas mixed laterality means that an individual may do some things with one hand, other things with the other hand, and do them well; or he may use his hands indiscriminately and be clumsy with both.

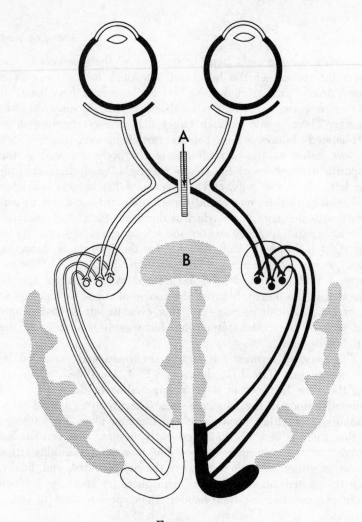

FIGURE 11

In this diagram, the optic nerves that run from each eye to the hemispheres of the brain are drawn light and dark to enable one to trace those that lead to the same-side hemisphere and those that cross to the opposite-side hemisphere.

In his "split-brain" experiments, Roger Sperry cuts these cross-over nerves at point A and thus limits the left hemisphere to the visual sensation provided by the left eye and the right hemisphere to sensation provided by the right eye. Both hemispheres soon have the same information, however, unless the bundle of nerves labeled B is also cut.

preference for the right hand, a training by their parents to use the right instead of the left hand? Or does it have a genetic base? Animal studies show that cats and monkeys have hand or paw preferences too; preferences that are virtually impossible to change. There is also a much larger than chance distribution of left-handed children whose parents are left-handed too.

Now, motor control of each side of the body is vested in the opposite hemisphere of the brain: the right hemisphere controls the left side of the body, and vice versa. If handedness *is* related to language facility, one would expect preferred hand use to correlate with the hemisphere which is dominant for verbal behavior. Therefore, the language center for left-handers ought to be in the right hemisphere. Unfortunately for the hypothesis, however, the majority of left-handers are *not* right-brained. The neurosurgeon Wilder Penfield—who has located many areas of specific function in the human brain in the course of repairing damage to it from accident or disease—says that even in left-handed people the area of the cortex responsible for speech is usually in the left hemisphere.

This personal testimony is largely confirmed and expanded by the neurologists Harold Goodglass and F. A. Quadfasel, who studied the case histories of over a hundred individuals who had suffered lesions in the language area. They report (among other findings) that either hemisphere can function alone for language if the other is severely damaged early in life; that left-handed people are possibly more susceptible to verbal disability from lesions of either hemisphere than are the right-handed; and, finally, that the specialization of the left hemisphere for language is much more extreme in most right-handers than specialization of either hemisphere in left-handers.

Relevant too is a study done by the British neurologist T. T. S. Ingram. His subjects were healthy six- to nine-year-olds, all of average intelligence, yet all plagued with reading and writing problems. Left-handedness was not typical of the group, but neither was right-handedness: 69 percent of these children had mixed handedness. All had been unusually slow in the development of speech—58 percent having said their first words after the age of eighteen months, another 35 percent after age two, and 8 percent after age three. Furthermore, family histories indicated that their parents, when children, had had similar problems.

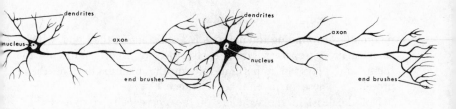

FIGURE 12

Human nerve cells are extremely varied in size and shape; they may be as small as 1/5000th of an inch or as "large" as 1/250th of an inch, and from 1/5000th of an inch to two feet long. But all have the basic parts shown in the diagram above.

What appears to need further study, then, is not the relationship of left-handedness to language difficulties but the relationship of weak cerebral dominance to handedness, to language difficulties —and maybe to some other attributes as well. In short, current evidence points toward a developmental slow-down in the normal process by which one cerebral hemisphere becomes dominant. But no one, so far, has pinpointed the cause.

What all these parts of the brain, and the nervous system that carries electrical impulses to it, have in common is the individual conductor of those impulses—the nerve cell, or neuron.

Newborn babies have all the neurons they will ever have, but many of those in the cerebral cortex are incapable of function because they do not acquire their sheaths of myelin for some months after birth. This immaturity of the basic unit which is involved in sensation and response is believed to explain the very young infant's limitation to reflex actions and gross movements of the type that are controlled by the old brain. Not all neurons become myelinated, and they vary considerably in size and shape according to function and location. They are as small as 1/5000th of an inch in diameter and about the same length, or as large as 1/250th of an inch and two feet long.

But all have three basic parts: a central section with a nucleus (in which respect they are like all other cells in the body); a fringe of thin tendrils called dendrites, which act as receptors; and a "sending" part, which is called an axon and terminates in fibers called end brushes or end plates. (See FIGURE 12.) Immediately surrounding the neurons is a substance called glia, which keeps neurons separated from each other, transports nutrients to them, and plays an important role in the manufacture of their proteins. (Those in myelin, for instance.)

Not the least of the wonders of the nerve cell's design is that no neuron is physically attached to any other. The electrical impulses which are initiated by a stimulus must jump a tiny gap (called a synapse) from one neuron's axon to an adjacent cell's dendrites. And since there are always many dendrites to choose from, impulses can jump in various directions. From neuron A, say, an impulse might jump to neuron B and then to G and then to P; or the course might be from A to C and then to H and Q and T; or from A to D and L and S and Y: with ten *billion* nerve cells in the brain alone, each of which receives impulses from hundreds of other nerve cells, the human brain is capable of almost infinite modification in its responses to the electrical messages that are fed into it from elsewhere in the nervous system.

But isn't "modification of response" the same thing as "learning"? Certainly; only now it is not the behavior of the whole organism that concerns us but the development *at the cellular level* of routes or methods for responding to stimuli. I said, a couple of sentences back, that the electrical impulses carried by the neurons can jump in various directions because there are many dendrites, many adjacent neurons, to choose from. How is the choice made? Is it accidental, or is there some element of selectivity involved? And what causes the final establishment of a given neural network— the use of the route from A to P, for instance, rather than the route from A to T or from A to Y?

The posing of these questions brings us to a controversy—one that seems to me, an outsider, to have generated more bitterness among psychologists than any other issue. I'll describe the two (at least two!) opposing viewpoints in the next chapter.

CHAPTER 8

THE BIOLOGY OF LEARNING

Learning is the process by which the brain's neural networks are developed—those that haven't been built in by heredity—and it is common to all animals and men. But there is a great deal of disagreement among the .experts about the way it operates or the mechanisms underlying that operation.

One school believes that neurons respond automatically to incoming stimuli and send on the resultant electrical impulses by various and accidentally chosen pathways. If one of these pathways happily leads to the satisfaction of some need—for food, say—it is thereafter preferentially used and progressively strengthened.

In its purest form, this theory of learning links a specific stimulus to a specific response via the reinforcement provided by a reward. It is a mechanistic viewpoint; one with an inherent neatness because it enables one to reduce fairly complicated acts to a series of simple and logically related steps.

Those who subscribe to it are called "associationists" or "S-R psychologists" (the S-R standing for "stimulus-response"). The early twentieth-century psychologist Edward L. Thorndike—who once said, "Learning is connecting"—was of this school. So were Clark L. Hull, Kenneth Spence, and Edwin Guthrie. All profoundly influenced psychological thought from the 1920s onward.

The "behaviorists" also operate from this theoretical base, although I dare say some will take exception to my saying so—for a reason I shall explain shortly. The dominant historical figure in behaviorism was, of course, John B. Watson, a contemporary of Thorndike. It was Watson who said:

"Give me a dozen healthy infants, well-formed, and my own specified world to bring them up in and I'll guarantee to take any one at random and train him to become any type of specialist I might select—doctor, lawyer, artist, merchant-chief, and, yes, even beggarman and thief, regardless of his talents, penchants, tendencies, abilities, vocations, and race of his ancestors."

Some say that Watson was deliberately overstating his case in an effort to counteract the weight then given to heredity as a determinant of behavior. Regardless of his intent, however, a couple of generations of Americans took him so seriously that the basic idea in his statement still echoes in our mythology: that the environment of rearing controls development.

(Watson, incidentally, left academic life in the mid-twenties and wound up in the advertising business.)

Now, some S-R psychologists consider themselves to be behaviorists *too* and some behaviorists do not consider themselves to be S-R psychologists *at all*. These subtle gradations of ideology seem to swing around the degree to which the man in question is interested in the internal activity of the brain. Simon-pure behaviorists are interested only in what the organism *does*. Probably the best-known contemporary member of this group is Harvard's B. F. Skinner.* Since we can't observe what goes on inside the brain, he says, why not stop worrying about how information is transmitted and concentrate instead on creating the behavior which indicates that one possesses that information? Break down behavior into small

---

* I should probably not classify Skinner as a member of *any* group; he seems to be a whole movement in himself. Part psychologist, part engineer, part evangelist, he left college in 1926 with the intention of becoming a writer. Shortly, he says, "I discovered the unhappy fact that I had nothing to say, and went on to graduate study in psychology hoping to remedy that shortcoming." He has. He has written quantities of scholarly articles and six books, among them *Walden Two* (a novel about a Utopian society in which human development is guided by a "technology of behavior").

He is famous among psychologists for (among other reasons) his invention of the Skinner box, in which untold thousands of rats and mice have learned to operate levers to get food. Laymen of my generation identify him with the Air-Crib that he invented in the 1940s—a controlled-environment glass compartment in which he and his wife raised their daughter Debbie until she

enough pieces, reinforce it systematically, and in due course you will shape behavior in a way that adds up to learning.

The psychologists who oppose this view are not so easy to classify because they disagree with each other as well as with the S-R psychologists. The one thing they have in common is doubt that all learning can be explained in terms of a simple cause-and-effect relationship between a single stimulus and a single response.

The early dissenters were called "field theorists" because they held that almost any event is altered by its field—that is, by setting and circumstances—and that the interrelationships between the reacting organism and its environment can cause highly variable responses. The whole of an experience, in short, is more than the sum of its parts. Because the German word that connotes "whole" is "Gestalt," field theorists were also called "Gestalt psychologists." One early member of this school was Wolfgang Köhler, whose observations on ape behavior were mentioned in Chapter 2.

A later and most influential field theorist was Edward C. Tolman of the University of California at Berkeley. Tolman did not .deny that stimuli ultimately lead to responses, but suggested that "the intervening brain processes are more complicated, more patterned, and often more autonomous" than S-R psychologists believed. In a famous 1948 monograph he summarized the field theorists' position as follows:

"We believe the nervous system to be surprisingly selective as to which stimuli it will let in at a given time. We assert that the central office"—the brain—"is far more like a map control room than it is like an old-fashioned telephone exchange. The stimuli are not connected by simple one-to-one switches to the outgoing responses."

His own theory was that stimuli are evaluated in terms of how they fit into a "tentative cognitive map" of the environment. "It is this tentative map, indicating routes and paths and environmental relationships, which determines what responses, if any, the animal will finally release," he said. Further, he believed that these cognitive maps could be narrow strip maps, or broad and comprehen-

---

was two years old, and in which their granddaughter Lisa has since been raised too.

Skinner is also strongly identified in the public mind with teaching machines, and has just invented a new method of teaching writing. Called "Write and See," it uses a special workbook and ink that becomes visible only if the child makes a letter or word properly.

sive ones. If narrow, the organism would be able to use its internal map successfully only if the problems to be dealt with were susceptible to similar solutions. Broader and more comprehensive maps, on the other hand, would permit variations in behavior and thus make possible greater flexibility in dealing with new situations.

Field theory is a little-used term today; the newer version is "cognitive theory." It should be mentioned that some contemporary psychologists who are *not* S-R psychologists do not consider themselves to be cognitive theorists, either. These are the two broad orientations of twentieth-century psychological thought, however; and at this point I will not attempt to describe the numerous theories that have shot off from bases in one or the other of the two major philosophies.

However, neither S-R nor cognitive theory explains what happens to the physical structure of neurons or to nervous networks while a stimulus is eliciting a response or is being fitted into a cognitive map. Somehow or other the passage of electrical impulses is recorded and remembered, and thereafter can be retrieved. In what form is it stored?

There are those who say that the electrical activity engendered by a stimulus and its response is fed into "reverberating circuits"—closed systems of neuronal loops in which the electrical impulses go round and round for indefinite periods of time. This theory is currently believed to be a possible explanation for short-term memory (the kind that operates while one is learning a task) but it has been discarded insofar as long-term memory (the later recall of that learning) is concerned. Anesthesia, coma, or electroconvulsive shock are now known to cause massive disruption or temporary cessation of the brain's electrical activity, but do not interfere with long-term memory. So what some investigators call "engrams" and others call "memory traces" must be converted for storage purposes to something less perishable than electrical circuits.

A popular theory leans heavily on the idea of changed functional patterns at the neurons' synapses. An increased amount of synaptic chemical activity could spread through a whole group of cells, linking them into assemblies that are unique for each bit of learning. Such assemblies are not thought of as permanently fused agglomerations of cells, merely as groupings whose linkage is capable of re-establishment. Some think that such assemblies may be labeled with chemical markers, like blazed trees on a forest trail—markers which are followed by the electrical or chemical agent of recall in order to reactivate the particular assembly of cells that equates with a given memory.

It is also generally believed that one's genes are involved in the process; if not in learning itself at least in the consolidation of that learning into memory. The reason is a common sense one. Here is how it is stated by the neurologist Robert Galambos:

"A baby sleeps, cries, suckles, salivates, swallows, makes a fist, kicks its legs, and performs every other response it is born with because human genes can be counted on to generate an object that not only looks human but acts human as well.

". . . If despite lack of exact knowledge of the details we can agree that genetic mechanisms read into the brain memories characteristic of the species, what about the probability that they also contribute to memories arising out of experience? To me it seems very high.

"Once cells discover how to organize themselves in a baby's brain so that hunger leads to crying, it is unlikely they would devise some other mechanism, based on entirely different principles, to enable the baby to learn that crying commands attention. The original solution is so elegant, simple, and exact; why should nature (or physiologists) abandon it in favor of some other?"

Great efforts are being made, therefore, to find out how—or if— the "genetic mechanisms" whose operation is "so elegant, simple, and exact" contribute to learning and memory. Because the biochemists seem to be in the lead, I'm going to concentrate in the following pages on the scientific activities of a representative sample of them.

First, however, a short excursion into molecular biology is necessary.

The basic unit of any organism is the cell. Our cellular organization is our first, and our fundamental, "inherited characteristic." Externally obvious traits like eye color (the average person's example of an inherited characteristic) are really of second-order importance, for they are the product of a hierarchy of metabolic processes in many cells.

Among the constituents of cells, two are of overriding importance: the genes, which are segments of the deoxyribonucleic acid (DNA) that fills the chromosomes in our cell nuclei; and cell proteins. These are of two basic kinds. They may be structural, in the

sense that bricks are part of the structure of a wall; a protein
sheath is part of the structure of the chromosomes, for example.
Or they may be those activist proteins called enzymes, which control the rate of cells' chemical reactions. To a biochemist, therefore, the significant aspect of an organism's inheritance is the link
between these proteins and its DNA.

DNA carries, and preserves from generation to generation, the
manufacturing directions for the proteins required by any given
kind of cell. These directions are "written" in the form of sub-units
called nucleotides, hundreds of which are chained together in every
DNA molecule. The sequence in which nucleotides are arranged
can be almost infinitely varied and therefore so can the proteins
they specify. DNA, in short, is a molecular code, the master code
of life; and like any master code, it deserves to be safeguarded.
Therefore nature uses it only as a template from which a transcribing molecule takes off a copy.

That transcribing molecule is ribonucleic acid—RNA; and because
of its function it is called "messenger" RNA. Its nucleotides differ
from those of DNA, just as the dots and dashes of Morse Code
differ from the letters of the English alphabet. But just as messages
in Morse and in English can carry identical information, so does
messenger RNA duplicate in its structure the arrangement of
nucleotides characteristic of the DNA upon which it is modeled.

RNA is made in the nucleus of the cell, by DNA. Then it moves
into the cell's cytoplasm, which is a storehouse of the amino acids
that are the building blocks of protein. Already there are molecules
of another kind of RNA, which cruise through the cytoplasm like
submicroscopic barges until they find amino acids that fit their own
molecular configuration. These "transfer" RNA molecules tow their
amino acid freight to "docks" provided by messenger RNA. Here
the amino acids are linked into a sequence that corresponds to
the nucleotide arrangement of messenger RNA; which, of course,
corresponds to the sequence in the DNA template. Then the transfer
RNA molecules disengage themselves from the amino acids they
have ferried into position and go off on a hunt for more.

I left out some steps, but this is essentially the process that creates
whatever proteins a given cell requires for its growth, maintenance,
or function. Now, at which point in this chain of events are "memories arising out of experience" read into the brain? And into which
of its structures?

Let's take the last point first. Many scientists believe that one's experience alters the structure of molecules within one's neurons; that the physiological base of learning is *intra*neuronal. They cite the fact that whereas most cells of the body degenerate and are replaced many times, our lifetime supply of neurons is present at birth and does not diminish until old age, if then. This circumstance supports a theory that sees neurons as permanent repositories of cumulative records. (If information were kept in cells that are continually being replaced, how would early-stored memories be transferred to the new cells?)

This intraneuronal theory is not the only one around, but let's accept it for the moment; and consider how any of the macro-molecules within the neurons—that is, the DNA, the RNA, or the constituents of proteins—might be altered during learning.

Is the DNA code changed, as when a mutation occurs? Nobody seems to think so. The reason is partly emotional, scientists having grown fond of the concept of DNA as an extremely stable molecule. Besides, such a change in the code would eliminate whatever directions were previously carried by that particular segment of DNA, and it is difficult to envision a process selective enough to make only "good" changes. Mutations, after all, are random changes which are mostly harmful; and it's obvious that learning doesn't disrupt the fundamental operation of brain cells. What it seems to do is to *add* something.

This has led some people to speculate that a portion of the DNA in various body cells is more or less permanently deactivated after the cells specialize. Although brain cells and liver cells have the same complement of chromosomes, neither kind of cell makes the proteins programmed in their DNA for the other kind of cell. So perhaps the deactivated DNA is available for the impression of new coded information based on one's experiences after birth?

Yet another theory is based on knowledge of the body's immune system. Those who hold it say that the specifications for making whatever proteins may be involved in memory are coded from conception in one's DNA—which has a practically limitless coding capacity—and that one's learning experiences simply trigger their manufacture.

This is what happens when the body is invaded by disease-producing viruses or bacteria, or by vaccines derived from them. The invading agent produces a protein substance called an antigen, and to combat it the infected organism produces another protein substance called an antibody: and up until four or five years ago the antigen was given all the credit for the formation of its organic opponent. The theory was that the antibody is formed on a molecular pattern that complements that of the antigen—the principle that governs the fit of a key into a lock—and that the antibody then fits itself so snugly to the antigen that the antigen can't function. This latter part of the theory is still accepted, but recent research indicates that antibodies do not use antigens as their model. Rather, the antigen is a stimulator of a gene or genes that are already present in the cell's DNA, but remain passive until there is need for them to go to work.

But what is the analogy with learning? The immune system develops during the lifetime of the individual and is a response to his unique experiences—as is learning. The formation of each antibody permanently changes the immune system, just as learning brings about permanent changes in the central nervous system. Finally, because more and better antibodies are produced if "their" antigens enter the body on several occasions, the immune system—again like the central nervous system—"appears to have a memory that enables it to benefit from previous experience."

The quotation is from the immunologist N. K. Jerne of Germany's University of Frankfurt. He points out that some amino acid sequences in antibodies are identical for all members of a species and other sequences in the same antibodies differ within individual members of that species. This suggests, he says, that the DNA directing their manufacture is in part constant and in part variable; from which it theoretically follows that "learning from experience could be based on a diversity in certain parts of the DNA, or to plasticity of its translation into protein." Jerne even has a name for the neuronal proteins that would thus be created: "synaptobodies." He sees their role as one of enhancing or depressing the activity of certain synapses, of opening or closing particular gates of recall.

Only the future will reveal how much of the foregoing speculation was truly prophetic. That DNA is involved seems clear, but how it does whatever it does is still shrouded in mystery.

For hard experimental evidence as to what happens to the biochemistry of the brain during learning, therefore, one has to shift the focus from DNA to later steps in the manufacture of the brain's proteins—and even that evidence is inconclusive.

There are three main investigative approaches:

▶ To transfer brain extracts from animals that have learned something to animals that have not learned the same thing, then determine whether the recipients' learning is speeded up;

▶ To compare biochemical changes in the brains of animals that have learned a new behavior with those that have not;

▶ To interfere with the formation of brain proteins, then determine whether learning and memory are affected.

The most controversial of these are the transfer-of-learning experiments. They are also the ones that have been most sensationalized by the popular press, which views them with mingled horror and fascination—understandably enough, for they stir atavistic memories of the belief that certain attributes reside in certain organs. Courage was once thought to be lodged in the heart, for instance; and primitive peoples believed that you could acquire a foe's courage if you ate his heart.

The laboratory variant involves the use of planarians, a kind of flatworm, which investigators such as the University of Michigan's J. V. McConnell and UCLA's Allen L. Jacobson have trained to avoid electrical shock by moving into one chamber of an apparatus rather than another one. Then the trained worms are chopped up and fed to untrained planarians. (The species has no taboo against cannibalism.) In many such experiments, it has been reported that the worms which ingested their trained counterparts had a head start in learning the same behavior.*

* When such experiments first began to be publicized, interest among scientists, especially the younger ones, was intense, and a great many of them jumped on the bandwagon. But they found it difficult to keep up with what others were doing, partly because there is normally quite a lag between the submission of a scientific paper for publication and its appearance in print, partly because competition for space in scientific journals reduces the number of papers that can be published about a given specialty, and partly because the skepticism of journal editors reduced the space given to reports of experiments with planarians.

Michigan's McConnell therefore undertook to bridge the gap. He started *The Worm Runners' Digest,* a journal which keeps its readers on the intellectual *qui vive* because he regularly includes, along with the serious papers, some articles that are outright spoofs.

D. J. Albert of the University of British Columbia has taken a different tack. He chemically "depresses" one hemisphere of a rat's brain—a procedure that makes that hemisphere temporarily non-functional—and then teaches the animal a discrimination task; to go to the white end of its box, say. Presumably, this learning is stored in the functioning hemisphere of the brain. When the inhibitory chemical has worn off and the other hemisphere is again normal, he removes the relevant part of the cortex of the hemisphere that learned the discrimination task; makes an extract of it; and injects it into the same rat. He reports that such animals relearn the task faster than untrained controls.

Other investigators have transferred brain extracts from one animal of a species to another, and between animals of different species. Some have claimed that it is brain RNA which has been transferred; others, more cautiously, say only that "macromolecules" are the carriers of learning—which, as I said earlier, could mean proteins as well as RNA.

Their reported results have been criticized by other scientists on a variety of grounds: the use of questionable techniques in preparing, purifying, and injecting the brain extracts, for instance, or allegedly insufficient control of a host of variables in the behavioral situation. Furthermore, these experiments have proved so difficult to replicate that more conservative scientists tend to write them off.

Not so the psychiatrist Gardner C. Quarton, who heads the Neurosciences Research Program in Brookline, Massachusetts.° In recently reviewing the transfer-of-learning studies, he described the original

° The Neurosciences Research Program is an international, interuniversity organization which was formed in 1962 under the sponsorship of the Massachusetts Institute of Technology and has been funded by Federal grants. Its members include mathematicians, physicists, biochemists, psychologists, neurologists, and others whose object in membership is to bring the specialized knowledge of each discipline to bear on the organ of their common concern, the brain.

In 1967 the Program published an enormous book (972 pages) entitled *The Neurosciences,* in which all current theories about the physiology of learning and memory are described and analyzed. Most of it is exceedingly difficult reading for a nonscientist, but if you really want further details about some of the work discussed in this chapter you might want to dip into it. I know of no other modern work which includes a like amount of differently oriented but related studies within the same covers.

You will find it listed among the References that conclude this book, after the name of Gardner C. Quarton.

experiments as "wild gambles" and agreed that failure to replicate has cast doubt upon their validity, but at the same time warned that these negative findings should not be used as an argument to kill further research on the problem. He said, "In many areas of research that began with similar vague exploratory experiments, original efforts to repeat the early positive studies were unsuccessful and it was only after the phenomenon had been considerably clarified that the reasons for the failure to replicate became clear."

In a second kind of approach to the biochemistry of learning, investigators train animals to do specific tasks, then kill them and compare certain constituents of their brain tissue—the amount of RNA present, for instance—with that of animals which were untrained on that particular task but whose life experience was otherwise the same as the experimental animals'. (Rodents and fish are the commonly used subjects in such experiments.) It has been found that increased sensory experience not only induces the synthesis of neuronal RNA but in addition increases the amount by 10 to 100 percent. This could indicate that "experience stimulates gene areas first to synthesize primary products"—RNA—"and, eventually, protein end products."

The quote is from the Swedish neurobiologist Holger Hydén, of the University of Göteborg, who has focused his research on the brain's production of RNA. His findings have led him to take a step beyond the intraneuronal theory of brain protein synthesis. In the preceding chapter, you may remember, the glial cells were mentioned; they fill the spaces between neurons and play an important role in providing the nerve cells with nutrients. Given this close structural association, it was no surprise to Hydén to find evidence of chemical collaboration between the two kinds of cells— transfer of RNA from one to the other, for example. He theorizes, for this and other reasons, that a partnership of neurons and glia is responsible for making the proteins that attend learning or consolidate memory.

But you may be thinking, the intraneuronal theory was so *logical*; the neurons' existence for the lifetime of the individual makes them ideal sites for the cumulative storage of records. But the case for inter- or extraneuronal participation is logical too. Glial cells, for example, increase after birth: could this not reflect a response to sensory stimulation from the environment? Some glial cells are involved in the myelination of neurons, and myelination proceeds roughly from a child's motor and sensory projection areas in the brain to the unspecialized association areas. This, again roughly, is the sequence that the human infant follows in learning. (He sees, and he moves his arms, before he can recognize objects and pick them up.)

Distinct from the glial cells but growing among them are some tiny, short-axon cells called "microneurons." They are structured so that they could make highly specific two-way linkages; but nobody knows for sure what they link. Microneurons also develop after birth and increase in relative number as one goes up the scale from lower animals to man—facts that are consistent with a theory of their genesis in response to sensory stimulation from the environment and man's superiority to animals in learning ability. The microneurons of rats and cats are known to multiply in the cerebellum concurrently with the young animal's improving motor ability, a growth pattern that ceases when the animal has learned to walk, jump, or climb. The same may be true of man.

There are other theories of learning or remembering which involve more than the neurons, but I find them too recondite—especially those placing heavy stress on the electrical side of the brain's activity—to discuss here. Again, for those readers who don't like other peoples' abridgements, I suggest *The Neurosciences*.

In summary so far, then, there is a lot of lively inquiry as to how, and where, DNA and RNA direct the synthesis of brain proteins; but no sure knowledge of all the details—yet. Now let us consider the end product, protein. Underlying most of this chapter is the assumption that information storage in the brain depends upon protein synthesis. But *does* it?

Among the many who believe that it does is the University of Michigan's Bernard Agranoff. His research tool is the common goldfish. He trains his subjects in plastic tanks with two compartments, in both of which there are lights and grids by means of which the fish can be given a mild electrical shock through the water. The task that Agranoff sets them is to learn (a) that a turned-on light signals an imminent electrical shock, and (b) to avoid the shock by swimming to the unlighted compartment. Goldfish readily learn this task, and remember it (without intervening reminder) a month later.

Having established the existence in his subjects of long-term memory, Agranoff then interferes with it by injecting the antibiotic puromycin into their skulls. (*Over* the brain, not *into* it: it must take a very steady hand and superb knowledge of fish anatomy to successfully give a goldfish such an injection.) When the drug is injected immediately after the goldfish have first learned to swim from one compartment to the other as the light goes on, memory is obliterated: the fish have to relearn the task the next time the problem is presented. If, however, Agranoff waits for an hour after the fish have learned the task, the puromycin injection has no effect upon memory. If he injects the fish at the half-hour mark the effect is intermediate. The unarguable conclusion is that it takes learning (goldfish learning, that is) about an hour to consolidate into memory; and that puromycin interferes with this consolidation. Why?

You will remember from a few pages back that a specialized form of RNA—transfer RNA—builds a molecule of protein by hooking onto amino acids that are floating about in the cell cytoplasm, then towing them to the staging area provided by messenger RNA, where it links them into a chain. This is a mechanical process, one in which the molecules involved "recognize" each other by the chemical bonds which form between them when the configurational fit is right. There is no way for a growing chain of protein to discriminate between real and fake amino acids, and if a correctly configured but spurious one happens to come along—which, in essence, is what puromycin is—the protein chain will incorporate it. The puromycin molecule sufficiently resembles one end of an RNA-plus-amino-acid assemblage so that it is accepted, and then the trouble begins. The other end of the puromycin molecule is the wrong shape to fit the amino acid that is supposed to come next in the sequence, and therefore protein manufacture is blocked at that point.

But because puromycin interferes with protein synthesis *and* with consolidation of learning does not prove that memory depends upon protein synthesis. Especially when other scientists, using different metabolic monkey wrenches, find that blockage of brain protein synthesis does *not* affect memory.

Among such scientists are a lively group of researchers at the University of Pennsylvania, headed by the husband-and-wife team of L. B. and J. B. Flexner; in fact, their use of puromycin in mice encouraged Agranoff to try it on goldfish. Both the University of Michigan and the University of Pennsylvania groups have also employed another drug, one with the jawbreaking name of acetoxycy-cloheximide, which doesn't prevent the brain's manufacture of protein but merely slows down production. Agranoff finds that it prevents the consolidation of memory in goldfish whereas the Flexners find that it does not similarly affect mice. And because it is an article of faith among biologists that fundamental processes are the same for all living things, the idea that the chemistry of goldfish memory is basically different from the chemistry of mouse (or human) memory is unacceptable.

Until clearer cause-and-effect relationships can be demonstrated between biochemical processes and mental behavior, therefore, all that can be claimed is that protein synthesis is involved somehow in learning and remembering. Which means also that RNA and DNA are involved somehow in learning and remembering.

I know that this has not been an easy chapter to read. It is also a frustrating one for readers who have made the effort, because they have not been rewarded with answers to any of the questions posed. Think, however, of how much more frustrating these problems are for those doing the research. They are engaged in assembling a jigsaw puzzle as confusing in detail as one of those made from a reproduction of a Jackson Pollock painting. The borders have now been pieced together, but the majority of the pieces are still on the sidelines. The scientists are trying first this one and then that one, seeking a match with the few pieces already in place—realizing all the while that new pieces will surely be added and that some of those now on the table may not belong in the picture at all. Nevertheless, since so much more is known about the brain than was the case even five years ago, there is a persistent and tantalizing feeling in the air that any moment now . . .

It also occurs to me that science-oriented young people might find this chapter encouraging rather than frustrating. There has never been better proof that a host of exciting new discoveries await a new generation of investigators.

CHAPTER 9

MOTIVATION

A sentence so often heard at parent-teacher conferences that it has become a joke (although a wry one) is this: "Johnny's intelligent enough; it's just that he lacks motivation." In other words, he is capable of mastering his schoolwork; what's absent is an energizing force that encourages or impels him to do it.

One is motivated to do many more things, of course, than to acquire the information offered in schoolrooms. One can be motivated by hunger to seek food, or by pain to escape the pain-producing situation: these are basic biological drives. But one can also be motivated by curiosity to explore a novel situation, and at least some of a champion athlete's effort is motivated by his need for the approval of others. These are psychological and social drives. Psychologists argue a great deal as to whether and which drives—especially those in the second category—are innate or learned; by what processes they develop; and how they become motivators of action.

During the first forty years of this century, the prevailing theory of motivation was that it seeks to relieve "deficit tensional states." These could be biochemical: tissue deficits, for example, of the sort that occur when the blood sugar level is rising, the water level is falling, or the body's heat loss is beginning to exceed heat production. They could be physiological, as when an empty stomach contracts or when overworked muscles become painful. Or they could be psychological, as when a baby indicates by crying that he is afraid of strangers.

In each such case, the theory went, the individual is impelled to reduce the resulting inner tension. A "motivated act" was therefore defined (and still is, in some textbooks) as "one that is complete when a goal is reached—the goal being some substance, object, or situation capable of reducing or temporarily eliminating the complex of internal conditions which initiated action." An influential advocate of this view was Clark L. Hull, whose phrase for it was "drive reduction."

Hull was an S-R psychologist, and like others of the same persuasion believed that the building blocks of behavior are a series of single events—the single event being a specific response by the organism to a specific stimulus. Chains of such single events, linked to each other via the mechanism of the conditioned response, explain the motivation for, say, one's efforts to gain the approval of others. The baby, stimulated by a basic biological drive such as hunger, responds by crying. This action fetches his mother, whose ministry reduces his hunger. In time, therefore, the baby connects his mother's presence with relief of tension. If, as she normally does, the mother speaks gently and lovingly to the infant while she is caring for him, the baby then connects her tone of voice with relief of tension; and as he grows older is motivated to seek her verbal approval with as much ardor as he expended in seeking the food or comfort she initially provided for him.

In recent years, however, experimental psychology has produced a good many facts that are hard to reconcile with the drive reduction theory. Take the hunger drive, for example. It became increasingly difficult to explain hunger solely in terms of tissue deficits or contractions of the stomach. Experiments showed that eating allays hunger long before any food is actually absorbed by the intestines (hence no tissue deficit could have been relieved); that rats whose stomachs have been removed (and therefore can't contract) exhibit the same hunger symptoms shown by rats with intact digestive systems; and that electrical stimulation of a certain region of the brain will cause a well-fed animal to eat as if it were starving. What, then, is "hunger"? What impels a living creature to seek food?

The process of amending the drive reduction theory began in the late 1930s, with Karl S. Lashley, who is sometimes described as "the American Pavlov." He argued that motivated behavior varies greatly on different occasions and among different individuals; that conditions within the organism alter the responses that a given stimulus will elicit; and that even when a single stimulus triggers a response, a complex pattern of other stimuli are usually involved too. To Lashley, the concept of a chain of stimulus-response patterns seemed much too simple and too rigid. Motivation must be controlled, he said, by the central nervous system.

Lashley was then the director of the Yerkes Laboratory of Primate Biology, and assembled there during the 1940s a brilliant group of psychologists with special interest in brain structure and function. They sat, not over coffee cups in a faculty lounge, but over bag lunches in the warm Florida sunshine, and argued about the hows and whys of learning. Among those who took away from such sessions a host of stimulating ideas to ponder in private was Donald O. Hebb, who subsequently returned to his native Canada and to a professorship at McGill University. In 1949 he published *The Organization of Behavior,* one of those rare books that revitalize an entire academic discipline. In it, he said:

"The tradition in psychology has long been a search for the property of the stimulus which by itself determines the ensuing response, at any given stage of learning. This is no longer satisfactory as a theory. Almost without exception psychologists have recognized the existence of the selective central factor that reinforces one response, now another . . . Responses are determined by something else besides the immediately preceding sensory stimulation. To say this does not deny the importance of the immediate stimulus; it does deny that sensory stimulation is everything in behavior."

Hebb said that to be active is the essence of being alive, and that the concept of motive is necessary only to explain the *directedness* of activity. As the source of that directedness, he interposed, between sensations at the periphery of the body and the organism's final response to them, assemblies of brain cells which order and analyze those sensations and eventually direct the organism to behave in a certain way.

"Consider the salted nut phenomenon," he said. "Ordinarily, one can take salted nuts or let them alone—until one has eaten a mouthful, when it becomes much harder to let them alone.

Hunger has increased: but how? A lack of food cannot be increased by eating something, and stomach contractions are stopped
by chewing and swallowing. If, however, we consider hunger to be
neither a particular condition of the body, nor a set of sensations
from the stomach, but an organized neural activity that can be
aroused in several ways, the puzzle disappears."[*]

One of the central tenets of the drive reduction theory of motivation was that a *deficit* tensional state was being relieved; that the
goal of motivated action, at base, was to avoid or reduce some
unpleasant or stressful situation. But what deficit tensional state is
present, what drive is being reduced, some psychologists of the
1950s asked, when one is motivated to explore one's surroundings—
as so many creatures are?

Robert A. Butler trained rhesus monkeys to solve problems for
which the only reward was•the opening of a window which permitted them to see what was going on elsewhere in the lab. A. K.
Myers and N. E. Miller found that rats would learn to press a bar
for the sake of poking their heads into an adjacent compartment
and being allowed to sniff around. Harry Harlow and G. E.
McClearn reported that monkeys learned a number of problems
involving pairs of screw eyes for no apparent reason other than
the fun of manipulating them. (See FIGURE 13.) None of these
activities served to reduce a biological drive such as hunger or thirst;
in none of the animals was there evidence of anxiety or any other
state of discomfort.

In fact, animals and children often behave as if they want to
prolong rather than reduce "the complex of internal conditions
which initiated action." Harlow says, in describing the behavior
of the young rhesus monkey, "It can see and it must see; it can
manipulate and it cannot help itself from manipulating. This is a
strong, powerful, compulsive motive. If the best plaything available
is only a piece of chain hanging down into the cage, the infant

[*] Harry Harlow is famed not only for the breadth and quality of his research
but also for his wit and caustic tongue. Agreeing with Hebb and others about
the role of a central control system in the development of learned behavior,
he snapped, "Learning efficiency is far better related to tensions in the brain
than in the belly."
If you would enjoy more than this glimpse of the battles which psychologists of different schools fight in the pages of their professional journals—words
being the weapons—you might read Harlow's "Mice, Monkeys, Men, and Motives" in *Psychological Review* (1953), Vol. 60, pp. 23–32.

FIGURE 13

To get food or to escape pain have been standard motivating
forces in laboratory experiments involving animals. But many
animals, it is now known, will work just as hard on learning
a problem if the reward is a chance to explore their surroundings or to manipulate something interesting—as this monkey
is doing.

will bat it back and forth or pull it or climb it or swing from it dozens or hundreds of times a day." Any mother who has run herself ragged replacing the contents of drawers and cupboards emptied by her toddler will agree that his exploratory and manipulatory drives, too, are "powerful and compulsive."

The Harvard psychologist Robert W. White, considering behavior of this sort, has suggested that there is a kind of motivation which is less intense and less urgent than that which occurs in order to relieve "a deficit tensional state." Although the biological drives are primary, he says, no organism lives in a constant state of crisis. There is plenty of time, especially in the life led by man, for him to experience the more moderate motivation provided by his innate desire to make something happen in his environment—to be the cause of a consequence. White calls this "effectance motivation."

Life itself depends upon accommodation to one's environment, and the more information we have about it the better off we are. White notes that strong drives cause us to learn lessons well° but hamper breadth of learning. This contention is borne out by such experiments as one by Edward E. Johnson, now at Southern University in Baton Rouge, who tested the ability of well-fed but thirsty rats to learn where food might be found in the same maze they were running in search of water.

One group of rats was deprived of water for twelve hours, another for six hours, and a third group ran the maze neither hungry nor thirsty. Later, when all were hungry rather than thirsty, their ability to find food in the same maze depended upon how thirsty they had been during the first test. Those rats that were least thirsty on the first round noticed and remembered the location of food, whereas those that were most thirsty were so intent on finding water that they had no attention to spare for something they didn't, at that moment, need.

"The narrower but efficient learnings that go with the reduction of strong drives are an important element in our capacity to deal with the environment," White says (and indeed it *was* important for those thirsty rats to find water), "but this capacity needs also to be fed from the learnings that take place in quieter times.

"It is then that the infant can explore the properties of things he does not fear and does not need to eat, learning to gauge the force

° Up to a point, as will be documented shortly.

of his string-pulling when the only penalty for failure is silence on the part of the attached rattles, and generally accumulating for himself a broad knowledge and a broad skill in dealing with his surroundings.

"The effectance urge represents what the neuromuscular system wants to do when it is otherwise unoccupied or is gently stimulated by the environment."

There are two ideas implicit in that final sentence that deserve elaboration. One is that learning can be associated with differing motivational intensities. The other is that the problem to be solved or the external circumstance in which the learner finds himself— that is, the objective characteristics of the situation—are not the sole determinants of his behavior; there is a subjective element involved, too. Let's take them in turn.

A famous experiment, and a long-ago one, was done in 1908 by Robert M. Yerkes and John D. Dodson, using mice. The apparatus consisted of a white box and a black box, each of which was illuminated in such a way that the contrast between them could be very great or very little. As the degree of brightness diminished, of course, the job of visual discrimination became progressively harder. The white box was the "correct" choice, and whenever the mice tried to enter the black box they got an electrical shock. The motivation for learning to choose the white box, then, was to escape pain.

Yerkes and Dodson discovered, not surprisingly, that the mice learned faster when the job was easy; that is, when there was strong contrast between the whiteness and the blackness of the two boxes. Further, the rate of learning correlated with the strength of the stimulus: the more intense the electric shock, the quicker the mice learned to avoid it by choosing the white box. But this was not the case when the learning job was difficult. When the two boxes were so nearly of the same degree of brightness that it was hard for the mice to tell which one was light and which one was dark, too painful a dose of electricity actually retarded learning. The experimenters found that their mice learned best when intensity of stimulus was midway between the weakest and strongest shocks given during the set of tests.

"This leads us to infer," the two psychologists said, "that an easily acquired habit—that is, one which does not demand difficult sensory discrimination or complex associations—may readily be formed under strong stimulation, whereas a difficult habit may be acquired only under relatively weak stimulation."

Some thirty-five years later, the New York psychiatrist Herbert G. Birch made the same point. His research subjects were young chimpanzees; their motivating drive was hunger; and their problem —after having been deprived of food for two hours, six hours, twelve hours, twenty-four hours, thirty-six hours, or forty-eight hours —was to learn to use sticks to obtain food that was beyond arm's reach.

The chimps with low motivation (those who had fasted only two to six hours) ignored the problem. They played with the sticks, but did not direct themselves in any purposeful way toward getting the food. The chimps with high motivation (those who hadn't eaten for twelve or more hours) did a bad job of problem solving too. The hungrier they were, in fact, the poorer their performance. They persisted in repeating wrong solutions; one ravenous animal made twenty-six ineffective sweeps with his stick, then had a temper tantrum. The chimps who did well were those in the groups that had gone without food for six to twelve hours. Birch's conclusion: an intermediate degree of motivational intensity is more conducive to rapid mastery of a problem than either extreme.

There is a lesson here for parents who are so upset because their children haven't learned skills that other children of the same age *have* learned that they lean too hard on the youngster in question. If he doesn't make it to the toilet in time, he is spanked. If he fumbles with his shoelaces for eons of time, the job is snatched away from him and performed by a parent who makes no secret of his or her exasperation. If Sonny still has that baby lisp when his same-age cousins have lost theirs, his speech is disparaged by parental mockery.

Since children are strongly motivated to gain their parents' approval, might it just not be that overanxious parents subject such children to motivational intensities that actually *retard* learning? This is not to say that one should take a casual attitude toward a child who lacks bladder control or has a speech impediment at age ten—but it might be a good idea for parents to keep Yerkes' rats and Birch's chimps in mind whenever they begin to tense up because the Joneses' Caroline has passed some developmental milestone several months before their Susan even approaches it. Such parents might even ask themselves, when they find themselves pressing the child, "What's *our* motivation, anyway?"

Now, let's turn to the subjective element in motivated behavior. White said that the effectance urge represents what the neuromuscular system "wants to do" when it is otherwise unoccupied. This suggests that organisms not only react to the stimulation that circumstance presents but also actively seek stimulation. In fact, Donald Hebb once made the point that we drive cars at high speed, look at horror movies, and in other ways seem bent on increasing the impact of the environment—even in the direction of creating mild degrees of frustration and fear.

Experimental evidence for such self-motivated behavior came, in 1954, from work in Hebb's own laboratory at McGill. In fact, it resulted from another of those happy accidents which an alert investigator can sometimes convert into a significant discovery. The story goes this way:

For an experiment using mild electric shock to interfere with brain wave patterns, James Olds (now at Caltech) had implanted electrodes in certain areas of rats' brains, a procedure that inhibits the animals' mobility about as much as putting a dog on a long leash. In the course of the experiment, Olds noticed that his essentially unrestrained rats kept coming back to the corner of the table where he had held them when he had administered the shock. One would almost think that they had *enjoyed* it . . .

So he and Peter Milner set up a new experiment, one in which caged rats could give themselves electric shocks by pressing a bar that functioned like the switch on a lamp. The rats not only learned to do this, but behaved as if it were a thoroughly addictive experience: one rat pressed the bar every two seconds and another racked up seventy-five hundred bar presses in a twelve-hour period. When the circuit was broken, so that no current flowed to the brain, the rats stopped pressing the bar—but just as soon as the circuit was re-established, the rats resumed their self-stimulation.

Olds and Milner subsequently reported, "Our subjects from the first day after the [implantation of electrodes] are quiet, non-aggressive; they eat regularly, sleep regularly, gain weight. There is no evidence in their behavior to support the postulation of chronic pain." Nor were the rats hungry or thirsty. So what drive could they have been seeking to reduce? Instead, the experimenters said, the rats' behavior represented "strong pursuit of a positive stimulus rather than escape from some negative stimulus."

Since then, other "reward areas" have been located in the brain. Therefore, learning theorists now consider the willful seeking of

pleasure to be as important a motivator as the compulsive avoidance
of pain. One such theorist is Harvard's David C. McClelland. He
says that our brains maintain a record of whether we feel pain or
pleasure during a certain experience, along with a set of cues
which—if subsequently triggered—will recall that emotion. Those
cues may be internal (such as a tissue deficit), external (such as
the sight or smell of food), or both. When the cues are triggered,
we are motivated to take action that will either recapture the
original emotional state (if it gave us pleasure) or prevent its
recurrence (if it gave us pain). McClelland calls this "the affective
arousal" theory of motivation—"affect," you will remember, being
the totality of emotions, attitudes, and values surrounding a given
experience—and illustrates its workings by following a rat's efforts
to learn a maze and then a child's efforts to manipulate a toy.

He begins by asserting that certain expectations attend every
experience and so do discrepancies from those expectations, and
then says: "Suppose that a rat runs down an alley, turns left,
proceeds three or four steps further, finds and eats a food pellet
of certain size and consistency. If this series of events occurs with
sufficient frequency, we argue that the rat has built up a chain of
associations of high probability or certain 'expectations' as to what
will happen. But these expectations may fail to be exactly confirmed in a variety of ways. An obstacle may delay him so that it
takes him longer to get to the food; the food may differ, mash for a
pellet; he may eat it where it is or pick it up and carry it somewhere else to eat . . .

"So long as the animal is uncertain in his expectations (i.e., is
still learning the habit), there will be a tendency to limit the
variability of responses so as to increase the probability of expectations. But once the habit is overlearned, the animal will tend to
introduce variations—now to increase *uncertainty* to a 'pleasurable'
level. In short, exactly confirming expectations produces boredom
and a tendency to discontinue the act unless enough minor variations are permitted to produce positive affect."

And now the child:

It is Christmas morning, and Johnny has just unwrapped a new
toy car. McClelland says, "Unless he has had other toy cars, his
expectations as to what it will do are nonexistent, and he can
derive little or no positive or negative affect from manipulating
it until such expectations are developed. Gradually, if he plays

with it, he will develop certain expectations which will be confirmed or not confirmed. Unless the nonconfirmations are too many (which may happen if the toy is too complex), he should be able to build up reasonably certain expectations as to what it will do *and confirm them*. In short, he gets pleasure from playing with the car.

"But what happens then? Why doesn't he continue playing with it the rest of his life? The fact is, of course, that his expectations become certainties, confirmation becomes 100 percent, and we say that he loses interest or gets bored with the car. According to the theory, the discrepancies from certainty are no longer sufficient to yield pleasure. However, pleasure can be re-introduced into the situation, as any parent knows, by buying a somewhat more complex car, by making the old car do somewhat different things, or perhaps by letting the old car alone for six months until the expectations about it have decreased in probability or otherwise changed."

At this point, I can hear some parents saying, "That's all right in a play situation. But in other areas of life? After all, there are *some* things that have to be learned whether a child finds them pleasant or not."

If this is your reaction, ask yourself first what you mean by "pleasant." Frivolous? Amusing? Easy? McClelland uses "pleasure" in the sense of "satisfying" or "gratifying"—and situations yielding this kind of pleasure are often far from amusing or easy. A baby who is learning to walk is not engaging in frivolity. A six-year-old who is learning to read may be working harder than he ever will again. But both can—and should—get pleasure out of the effort.

Wise parents or teachers will structure each learning situation so that the challenge of novelty is coupled with the promise of achievement. If there are no unknowns, no mystery, the learner will ignore the task. If the situation is so unfamiliar that it is incomprehensible, and therefore frightening, the learner will do everything possible to avoid the task. Given a pleasurable level of uncertainty, the child will continue to approach the task; and will probably accomplish it. Which ought to give *you* pleasure too!

Robert B. Livingston of the University of California at La Jolla has a nice last word on motivation. He says, "Feelings provide the 'go/no go' switch for all behavior."

CHAPTER 10

FREUD'S IMAGE OF MAN

This is the century of science, of controlled experiment and objective research. As men of their times, therefore, most psychologists—wherever they may be located on the spectrum that stretches from "pure" S-R behaviorists at one end to "pure" cognitive theorists at the other end—have attempted to conduct their studies within a scientific framework. They have in consequence had to rely heavily on the use of animals and have been limited to studying those facets of human behavior that are relatively simple to test or are naturally available for observation.

One can't, for example, set up an experiment in which a hundred identical twins are separated at birth and subjected to radically different but carefully controlled environments for five years. One can only find as many twins as possible who have experienced separation and compare their characters and abilities after a certain amount of time has elapsed—making allowances for the inevitably differing ages and circumstances of separation and the inevitably differing characteristics of their subsequent environments. Such comparisons often provide valuable insights into developmental processes, but the findings are not the result of "scientific experiment."

In addition, much human behavior is too complex for easy breakdown into separate pieces which can be objectively studied—at least by the techniques currently available to experimental psychologists. You witnessed, in the preceding chapter, the difficulties one gets into when trying to explain all human motivation as a series of separate responses linked by specific stimuli to basic biological drives. That's because much human motivation is a stable and enduring force in the life of each individual; it's a trend of behavior rather than a specific action aimed at reaching a concrete goal.

The fruits of the scientific approach in psychology have been considerable. The functioning of the mind has been illuminated, many developmental patterns have been traced, and many theories have been devised against which further research could be tested. But the emphasis has fallen on particulars—for example, upon the nature of motivation or the mechanics of learning or the relationship between physiological and psychological processes. The end product of development, the psychic entity into which all experience is synthesized, is the human personality; and psychologists have been unable so far to construct a comprehensive general theory as to its structure.

Credit for that achievement goes to the great psychoanalyst Sigmund Freud, whose thinking has provided the most widely accepted "model" of personality in which a framework is systematically related to a structural whole. There is no scientific proof for Freudian theory, inasmuch as it is based on Freud's clinical observations of specific individuals who were mentally ill—and according to Jerome Bruner, it is not even a theory in the conventional sense, "it is a metaphor, an analogy, a way of conceiving man, a drama."

Bruner, co-director of Harvard's Center for Cognitive Studies, is not a psychiatrist but a psychologist whose special interest is in perception (perhaps because he was born blind and acquired vision only at the age of two). Now in his mid-fifties, he has behind him a period of wartime Intelligence service here and in Europe as well as much participation in the affairs of professional societies and government committees. Harvard legend has it that Bruner was once a consultant for sixty research projects all at the same time. That allegation couldn't possibly be true, even for a man of his energy, but it nicely captures his driving, action-oriented personality. His essay on Freud, from which the preceding quotation and some following ones were taken, is thus a surprise because of its reflective and literary quality. Later in this book, you will meet Bruner again—as a scientist; but listen to him now as an intellectual historian and philosopher:

"Two figures stand out massively as the architects of our present-day conception of man: Darwin and Freud. Freud's was the more daring, the more revolutionary, and in a deep sense, the more poetic insight. But Freud is inconceivable without Darwin.

". . . What Darwin had done was to propose a set of principles unified around the conception that all species had their origins and took their form from a common set of circumstances—the requirements for biological survival. All living creatures were on a common footing . . .

"When the post-Darwin era of exaggeration had passed . . . what remained was a broad, orderly, and unitary conception of organic nature, a vast continuity from the monocellular protozoans to man. Biology had found its unifying principle in the doctrine of evolution . . .

"As the summit of an evolutionary process, man could still view himself with smug satisfaction, indeed proclaim that God or Nature had shown a persistent wisdom in its effort to produce a final, perfect product.

"It remained for Freud to present the image of man as the unfinished product of nature: struggling against unreason, impelled by driving inner vicissitudes and urges that had to be contained if man were to live in society, host alike to seeds of madness and majesty, never fully free from an infancy anything but innocent. What Freud was proposing was that man at best and man at worst is subject to a common set of explanations: good and evil grow from a common process."

Freud, a Viennese, was trained as a neurologist. Because one of his teachers used hypnosis to alleviate hysterical symptoms in patients, Freud became interested in hysteria and from there progressed to other psychic disorders. He was a brilliant and creative thinker and left a rich heritage, both to clinicians involved in treatment of the mentally ill and to theoreticians interested in the workings of the healthy mind.

His great contribution, Bruner says, lies in the continuities of which he made us aware: that in the human mind, the primitive, infantile, and archaic exist side by side with the civilized and evolved; that the rational purposefulness of waking life is connected to the seemingly irrational purposelessness of fantasy and dream; that there is no all-or-none distinction between mental health and mental illness, but that the one can shade into the other, or replace the other, given the right set of circumstances.

Among Freud's many provocative ideas, the three that are most pertinent to the content of this book are his division of the mature personality into the id, the ego, and the super-ego; his insistence that the unconscious mind exerts tremendous influence on behavior; and the importance he attached to the influence of childhood experiences upon adult life. In treatment of patients, he was struck by the frequency of unresolved conflicts that originated in the very early years, hence he came to stress this period in life as the foundation—shaky or strong—upon which all later development of personality depends.

The id, Freud said, is the site of our primitive instincts and urges—of which one, the libido, is transcendant. "Libido" is popularly translated to mean sexuality, but in Freud's usage it meant all physically pleasurable, self-gratifying activities. The id is wholly in the unconscious mind.

In the mature person, the hedonistic demands of the id are opposed by the super-ego—the conscience. This is the part of the psychic structure that judges the rightness or wrongness of any thought or contemplated action. The super-ego is partly in the unconscious.

The middleman, the third part of the personality, is the ego. It collects information about the external world and the subjective reactions of the individual, takes note of competing necessities or desires, then works out a realistic plan of action. The ego, which is sometimes called "the executive of the personality," is wholly in the conscious mind.

Both the ego and the super-ego develop over a period of time, in response to the experiences of the growing child, and via a series of steps correlated with physical maturation. Take, for example, the relationship of adequate mothering in infancy to the development of both the child's intellectual processes and his social relationships. In psychoanalytical terms, and in John Bowlby's words, this is what happens:

"The functions of the ego include appraisal of our long- and short-term needs, their arrangement in an order of priority, the inhibition of some and the acceptance of others, so that action may be purposeful and integrated instead of haphazard and self-frustrating. Because one of our foremost long-term needs is to remain on friendly and cooperative terms with others, we must keep their requirements firmly in the front of our minds; and so important is this for us that we [have] machinery especially designed for the purpose—our conscience, or super-ego.

". . . It is not surprising that during infancy and early childhood these functions are either not operating at all or are doing so most imperfectly. During this phase of life, the child is therefore dependent on his mother performing them for him. She orients him in space and time, provides his environment, permits the satisfaction of some impulses, restricts others. She is his ego and super-ego. Gradually he learns these arts himself and, as he does so, the skilled parent transfers the roles to him. This is a slow, subtle, and continuous process . . .

"Ego and super-ego development are thus inextricably bound up with the child's primary human relationships."

Freud's word "ego" corresponds to the psychologists' word "cognition"—the term that sums up the intellectual processes of perception, language, and logical thought. Freud's "id" and "super-ego" roughly equate with "affection"—the psychologists' word for the totality of an individual's emotions, attitudes, and values. The struggle of the ego and super-ego to hold the id in check is consistent with the psychological theory of motivation as drive reduction; in fact, all of Freudian thought places great stress on biological drives as central forces in behavior.

When one is mentally healthy, Freud said, the ego successfully mediates the conflicting demands of the id and the super-ego. Hostility toward others, for example, can be "sublimated" into the socially acceptable activity of engaging in competitive sports; and failure to excel at sports can be "compensated" by learning to play the hottest trumpet in the school band. If the ego is unable to engineer compromises such as these, the affected individual will develop a neurosis; that is, he will still be able to function in society, although others may find some aspects of his behavior rather odd. If the ego loses the battle altogether, and is overridden by either the id or the super-ego, the individual will become fully psychotic; that is, he will be too sick to function in society.

And here's Bruner again, himself as much of a poet as he considers Freud to be at base:

"It is Freud's imagery, I think, that provides the clue to his ideological power. The characters are from life: the blind, energic, pleasure-seeking id; the priggish and punitive super-ego; the ego, battling for its being by diverting the energy of others to its own use. The drama has an economy and a terseness. The ego develops canny mechanisms for dealing with the threat of id impulses: denial, projection, and the rest. Balances are struck between the actors, and in the balance is character and neurosis. The imagery of the theory . . . has an immediate resonance with the dialectic of experience. True, it is not the stuff of superficial conscious experience. But it fits the human plight, its conflictedness, its private torment, its impulsiveness, its secret and frightening urges, its tragic quality."

Nothing could seem more remote from the provenance of a Viennese psychoanalyst with a nineteenth-century Victorian background than a modern community of twenty-six hundred American Indians in Fort Hall, Idaho; but a description of the breakdown pattern common to this group will indicate how universal is the application of Freud's image of man. The compassionate chronicler of Fort Hall's Indians is Larry H. Dizmang of the National Institute of Mental Health; and suicide among these Indians is the particular problem that he has been studying for the past seven years.

In Fort Hall, the suicide rate is ten times the national average. In addition, the majority of those who take their own lives are young: half of them (during the period 1960–67) were twenty years old, or younger. The reverse is true of the general American population, where suicide is the old man's way out.

What circumstances have caused this high incidence of self-destruction?

It has been only a little over a hundred years since our Indians were conquered, confined to reservations, and forbidden the nomadic life that had been their way for centuries. The Shoshone-Bannock Indians did not by tradition function in large, stable communities, and the problem of these particular ones was further complicated by the Federal government's forcing various unrelated bands to live together at Fort Hall.

"In the time scale of cultural evolution the containment was abrupt, intrusive, and severely damaging to an otherwise healthy social group," Dizmang says. The conflict, disruption, and disorganization that followed this change hampered group adaptation to a new pattern of existence. The Fort Hall Indians could not find the key to a way of life that would make them self-sufficient, and the outcome was complete dependency on the government. Thus, whatever self-esteem this vanquished people had managed to hold onto was further diminished.

Mothers who do not themselves find the world a pretty decent place cannot build trust into a child's developing consciousness, nor can they play their traditional role in helping a child's ego develop. Thus, Dizmang says, many young Indians in Fort Hall are psychically defective in their ability to moderate between internal needs and external reality. And, in addition: "A beaten, depressed, dejected father who has to depend on welfare to support his family, who can no longer hunt and fish his well-known territory, and who quickly discovers that alcohol will temporarily dissolve his depression, soon ceases to be a useful model after whom his son can develop healthy patterns. Depression and low self-esteem breed more of the same and become self-perpetuating . . ."

Young Indians are like all other young humans: in adolescence, they experience a tremendous internal drive toward independence. The best way to achieve it is to adopt the white man's culture, yet few Fort Hall teenagers have the emotional strength to withstand the rejection by their friends and relatives that follows any tendency to "go white." Distrust and alienation from the whites (bred in part by a long history of inconsistency and abrupt changes in the government's Indian policies) has by now reached the point, Dizmang says, "where 'to become like a white man' will raise more group disapproval than almost any other behavior."

So there they are—stuck in a social milieu characterized by hopelessness and helplessness. For anyone, this is a state of intense anguish; among the few alternatives for its relief are alcoholism, severe depression, or suicide. Too many of Fort Hall's young Indians experience all three.

Dizmang is specific as to the reason. "Suicide is always the result of a defective or temporarily malfunctioning ego," he says. "It is the breakdown or absence of psychic defense mechanisms under the pressure of stress that fail to protect the individual from his own inner violence."

CHAPTER 11

ACQUIRING A SEX IDENTITY

Freud did not cut his pie of personality into three equal slices. He considered the ego less important than the id and the super-ego. This downgrading of the intellect explains in part the early opposition to Freudian theory. If there's one thing that men like to believe about themselves it is that they are wholly rational beings; and here was Sigmund Freud telling them that the pull of the emotions within the unconscious mind motivated their behavior far more than intelligence.

The other shocker was Freud's insistence upon infantile sexuality, the most famous example of which is the conflict he called "the Oedipus complex" (after the Theban hero of ancient Greek legend who killed his father and married his mother). Freud asserted that little boys, somewhere around three years of age, feel hostility toward their fathers because they see them as rivals for their mother's love. Fearing retaliation by the father—Freud says that the basic fear is of castration—the child then tries to achieve, for his own protection, the qualities of strength and power that he senses in his father. By thus identifying with the dominant male in his life, he acquires the model upon which his own behavior as an adult male is based. In the case of girls, the process is a bit more complicated, but ends the same way: hostility toward the mother is transmuted into identification with her. Furthermore, Freud said, it is the resolution of this conflict that brings the super-ego into being.

Certainly it is true that children have only the most minimal sense of right and wrong—that is, the conscience is undeveloped—in the preschool years. But whether the super-ego develops out of the Oedipal conflict is a moot point. Later psychoanalysts°—including Freud's daughter Anna, a distinguished member of the profession whose special interest is in children—have tended to believe that Freud ascribed too large a role in adult behavior to juvenile conflicts over sex.

Both the psychoanalysts and the psychologists agree, however, that children *do* have sex-linked emotions and behaviors at very young ages. What Freud called "the primacy of the genital zone" comes with puberty; but long before a youngster goes to school he is aware that he is sexed, and behaves in ways that are unique to that sex. By age three or four, in fact, children have acquired that exceedingly important component of their mature personality, their sense of sex identity.

This awareness of being masculine or feminine is not a simple outgrowth of being physiologically male or female—as the Harlows discovered when rearing their unmothered monkeys. Psychologically, a developing human must *perceive* himself or herself as male or female in order to act toward members of the same sex and members of the opposite sex in accordance with the expectations of society. And perception (as I shall explain in more detail in a following chapter) is a mental process which is much affected by learning; by experience.

How much the perception of one's sex identity is affected by learning is disputed; so I'll give you a choice of four opinions.

Freud said, and many still agree, that young humans are innately bisexual (psychologically speaking), and develop their sex identities out of the trauma of the Oedipal conflict.

Not so, say John Money, Joan Hampson, and John Hampson: children are sexually neutral at birth and acquire their psychological sexuality entirely as a result of learning. Money and the Hampsons

---

° Among them: Alfred Adler, who believed that the dominant influence on personality was an urge for self-realization, for superiority (and thus gave a generation of parents one of its most overworked phrases, "inferiority complex"); Carl Jung, who not only gave us "introverts" and "extroverts" but also added to the unconscious mind of each individual a "collective unconscious" which preserves memory traces from all of mankind's past experience; and neo-Freudians like Erich Fromm and Karen Horney, who assign more weight in personality development to the social environment than Freud did.

are leaders in the Johns Hopkins group whose work on endocrine disorders has been mentioned in other chapters, and their opinion on the genesis of sex identity is based on studies of the hermaphrodites who have come to the Hopkins clinic for treatment. (A hermaphrodite is a person who has both male and female physiological characteristics, as did the mythical son of Hermes and Aphrodite, whose body was joined to that of a nymph.)

Such individuals may be born with a mixture of male and female sex organs, or as a result of endocrine imbalances may later develop characteristics of the opposite sex. Their true—or, at least, their *dominant*—sex can be determined by internal examination (to see what gonadal structures are present) and by cell studies (since males have XY chromosomes and females have XX chromosomes).* Once it is ascertained which sex predominates, it is often possible to use surgical or chemical therapy to alter those structures which are discordant. But diagnosis and treatment do not necessarily occur in babyhood, and therefore Money and the Hampsons have interviewed and tested a good many adult hermaphrodites.

They have found that an overwhelming majority have accepted "the sex of rearing"—even those with external genitalia that belie the sex classification given them by their parents. In other words, if parents—unwittingly, or for neurotic reasons—have dressed a girl in trousers, favored a crew-cut hair style, used the pronoun "him," encouraged baseball rather than doll play, and praised aggressive and "manly" behavior, the child develops a masculine sex identity in which she feels thoroughly comfortable. Sex orientation, in short, is wholly learned.

Of two children with female hyperadrenocorticism, a disorder which causes the genitals to look male, Money and the Hampsons

---

* Successful laboratory techniques for determining a given individual's chromosomal constitution are fairly new, but have already been used for other than medical reasons to help settle a difficult question: At the Olympic Games, are all athletes entering the women's events *women?*

In the period just before World War II, a prize-winning high jumper called Dora and a track star called Clare turned out to be men, and in the 1950s a number of "female" entrants were found to have an abnormal condition in which chromosomes and gonads are male but external virilization is incomplete.

At the 1964 Tokyo Olympics, therefore, physical examinations of all women athletes were instituted, and in 1968 at Mexico City the cellular studies of chromosomes were added. Knowing that the tests would be given was, apparently, a sufficient deterrent; and only women competed in the women's events.

say, "It is indeed startling to see two such children in the
company of each other in a hospital playroom, one of them entirely
feminine in behavior and conduct, and the other entirely masculine.
One gets no suspicion that the two children are chromosomally
and gonadally female."

The same investigators tested a group of fourteen adult hermaphrodites who had been switched from the sex of rearing to the
opposite sex, to see how normal their sexual psychology was. Of the
nine who made the shift *before* the age of two years and three
months, six showed no signs of emotional disturbance. Of the five
who changed sex *after* the age of two years and three months,
"only one person could possibly be rated as psychologically healthy."
Therefore Money and his colleagues suggest that there may be a
critical period somewhere during the second year of life when children are in effect imprinted with their sex identity.

You will remember (Chapter 6) that Erich Klinghammer's doves
fixed on their adult love-objects when they were nestlings. Those
that had human company rather than that of doves during the first
eight days of life subsequently courted humans rather than doves.
Perhaps the sex identity of the young human similarly stabilizes
during a certain period, making it as impossible for a child who
considers himself male to become female as it is for doves who are
prepared to "love" humans to settle for doves?

This suggestion is appealing to ethologists and biologically
oriented psychologists who believe that the human infant, like the
young of other species, is genetically sensitized to specific aspects
of the environment. But that's about all of an innate nature that
John Money and his colleagues permit in their theory of how sex
identity develops.

And that's short-changing heredity, says the University of Louis-
ville's Milton Diamond. He speaks for those who believe that babies
have an inborn sexuality, a built-in "bias" which affects the way
they interact with their environment.

Diamond objects to Money's assumption that the behavior of
hermaphrodites can be extrapolated to normal individuals. All that
the John Hopkins team has shown, he says, is that human beings
can adjust to an erroneously imposed gender role. It is Diamond's
belief, furthermore, that individuals who successfully make such
adjustment are prenatally and biologically predisposed to do so.

Animal studies show, he says, that gene-dispatched hormones

differentiate the developing sex organs of the fetus into male or female; these organs then secrete substances which differentiate the hypothalamus (an important structure of the brain) into a male or female type; and the hypothalamus, in its turn, is involved in adult endocrine activity and the physical expression of emotional states. If one part of the nervous system is "potentiated" along sex lines before birth, Diamond says, it is reasonable to believe that other neural structures are too.

Animal studies have also shown that removal of a certain part of the brain affects the sex behavior of males and females differently; in rats, cats, rabbits, and guinea pigs, loss of the cortex abolishes the male mating pattern but does not similarly affect the female.

As for humans, it is well established that the sexes normally differ in sensory and perceptual behavior. Diamond points out that girl babies as young as three days of age show a lower threshold to electric shock stimulation than do boy babies; at around age two, girls show more interest in size and color than boys, and build basically different kinds of structures with blocks; and as adults women have a keener sense of smell than men.

To which one might add the interesting finding by H. Lansdell of the National Institute of Neurological Diseases in Bethesda, that there are sex-linked changes in perceptual abilities following surgery in that hemisphere of the brain which is concerned with non-verbal behavior (usually the right hemisphere).

Before and after such operations, twenty-two patients were given a test of artistic judgment, in which they were asked to look at a series of abstract designs in which "the inartistic ones contravene principles of esthetic order and are often symmetrical or nearly so." After surgery, the men picked the simpler, more symmetrical, less artistic designs more frequently than they had before the operation —but this was not true of the women.

Lansdell, after noting that a similar disparity in verbal ability has been found by another investigator upon testing the effect of surgery in the hemisphere dominant for speech, then says:

"The effects of the operations suggest that some physiological mechanisms underlying artistic judgment and verbal ability may overlap in the female brain but are in opposite hemispheres for the male. Some [other data from school-administered tests] could be interpreted in the same way: girls show positive correlation between their level of artistic interest and their competence on tests of verbal reasoning and language usage, whereas boys do not."

It is Diamond's belief, therefore, that babies' nervous systems are predisposed toward behavior typical of one sex, and that Money's hermaphrodites lacked the crucial (and probably hormone-induced) "potentiation" during fetal or immediately postnatal life which causes normal individuals of different sexes to react differently toward the environment.

I should add that Diamond does not argue against the importance of learning in the development of a child's sex identity, only against a theory that a child's environmental experience is all that matters. "In analyzing human behavior," he says, "trying to separate genetics and experience may be like trying to separate hydrogen and oxygen in their importance with respect to the properties of water . . . In the development of any behavior pattern we must consider not only the stimuli serving to mold the pattern but the nature of the receptive medium which is to be molded."

And then there's a fourth hypothesis pertaining to the genesis of sex identity. This, the view of some cognitive theorists, is that a child's perception of himself as male or of herself as female is primarily an intellectual achievement—like learning to count.

When a four-year-old boy asserts, for example, that he intends to be a mother when he grows up, Freudians claim that the child's wishes and fears motivate the fantasy. The position of the cognitive theorists is that four-year-olds simply don't know yet that gender is constant. Not until children are six or seven do they perceive that material things have *invariable* qualities (weight, mass, length, etc.). A four-year-old's unrealistic assumption that his sex can change, therefore, is only part of his overall confusion about which things in this world are alterable and which things are not. That is, his deepest emotions are not involved—only his cognitive immaturity.

Psychoanalysis is speculative rather than scientific; psychology is a less exact science than biology or biochemistry; and even in the biological sciences there have until very recently been taboos which inhibited truly scientific research on sex.* So none of the

* Three scientists at a West Coast university, whose interest is in the relationship between hormones and sexual behavior, ruefully reported in a 1965 paper that there has been little research in their field because of "the stigma any

above theories can be considered "proved," and you will have to decide for yourself which one you favor (if any). The final one, however—that of the cognitive theorists—brings us logically to the great Swiss psychologist Jean Piaget.

Piaget's published work on child development dates from the 1920s, when it was criticized more than it was praised, and he is still relatively unknown to the public. In recent years a dramatic reversal has occurred. A steadily growing number of behavioral scientists have "discovered" Piaget; have set up experiments to test his theories; and have found that he knows what he is talking about. He is even being described as "the Freud of cognition"— meaning that he has constructed for the intellect a theory of development which is as complete and as persuasive as was Freud's theory of how personality develops. Piaget's studies of cognition, therefore, will be the subject of the next chapter.

---

activity associated with sexual behavior has long borne. In our experience, restraint has been requested in the use of the word 'sex' in institutional records and in the title of research proposals . . . and the propriety of presenting certain data at scientific meetings and seminars [has been] questioned . . ."

Chapter 12

THE DEVELOPMENT OF CONCEPTS

Facing a tumbled pile of household laundry that she has just spilled out of a hamper onto the basement floor, how does a housewife bring order out of chaos? She sorts the pile. First she classifies the laundry by properties of fabrics: their response to bleach, to heat, to abrasion, to kind of soap, or to water itself. After the various items have been washed and dried, she separates those that should be ironed from those that should not be. A third sorting regroups them according to site of use, after which the housewife carries them upstairs for storage in kitchen drawers, linen cabinet, or bedroom.

These three principles of classification are only the gross categories that guide her actions; at each stage of the washday job, the housewife makes dozens of subclassifications too. But for the purposes of this analogy, the important point is not how many times she sorts the laundry, nor her principles of classification. The important point is that she continually reclassifies the *same* items.

In every aspect of daily life, and many times each minute, we all do similar sorting jobs. Sometimes they are of the kind just described, in which mental classifications are expressed in overt physical activity. But more often and more fundamentally, without external expression, we "sort" the objects, people, and events which impinge on our consciousness. Only by screening, evaluating, and somehow relating to each other the diverse sounds, sights, tastes, odors, and textures that bombard our senses can we move about in the environment with safety, precision, or confidence.

The intellectual process which enables us to do this—to group diverse things according to certain common properties, then speedily to dissolve that grouping and relate the same items to each other in different ways or to different objects on the basis of other common properties—is called conceptualization. The general ideas that result from this practice are called concepts.

Concepts may deal with concrete things, but are themselves abstractions. For example: golf balls, mothballs, oranges, marbles, peas, and pearls are round. Round objects can be touched, tasted, smelled, heard, or seen—but the concept of roundness exists only in the mind. Our brain cells create it, nobody knows precisely how, out of our numerous experiences with round objects. There simply comes a time in the development of the mind when we recognize ball-shaped things as members of a class of objects which have in common the quality of "roundness."

A concept like roundness speeds thought and therefore action because it substitutes a single idea—the commonality of shape—for separate awareness of that quality in each golf ball, mothball, orange, marble, etc., that we come across. So, too, for everything else in our environment. We organize all experience into abstractions—clumsily at first, then with more and more skill. Roundness is easy compared to "weather," and weather is easy compared to "morality." It takes us, in fact, fifteen or more years to acquire the full complement of concepts and the techniques of using them that underlie the rational thought of adults. And some of us, alas, never fully accomplish the job.

How do concepts develop? According to that meticulous observer and persuasive theorist, Jean Piaget, our cognitive development occurs via a series of stages which are invariant, interdependent, and subject to the same rules that govern any other process of physical growth. Note that I said "any *other* process of physical growth"—so biological at base is Piaget's philosophy of learning.

This is not surprising in view of Piaget's early experience. A precocious child, he published his first scientific paper in 1906, when he was ten years old—a short note on a partly albino sparrow he had observed in a public park. A bit later he worked as a volunteer assistant to the director of the natural history museum in his home city of Neuchâtel. Before he was twenty-one, he had published some twenty papers on mollusks, and on the basis of the scholarship evidenced in this work was offered a position as curator of mollusks in a Geneva museum before he had left secondary school. At the university, his specialty was zoology.

But his interest in the natural sciences waned somewhat after he got his Ph.D. He drifted a bit, looking for the right job. What opened the door to his permanent vocation was a project in which he was supposed to adapt, for French-speaking children, some reasoning tests that had been developed in the United States. As he tested elementary school children, he became increasingly fascinated by the mental processes they used to arrive at their answers —especially their *incorrect* answers. It is still central to Piaget's view of intellectual development that the nature of a child's misunderstandings and inconsistencies as he gropes for new levels of comprehension are the most revealing source of information as to his cognitive structure.

But Piaget was still a biologist. This was clearly apparent when he began to publish his unconventional theories, in the 1920s. In order to survive, he reminded his readers, all living things must adapt to their environment; in fact, living systems are organized to this end. Basically, they use twin processes of function—which Piaget illustrated by using the example of food intake, and so will I.

To live, one eats. In order for food to nourish the system, however, it must change its form. First, we chew it into pulp; then, via digestion, we finish the job of destroying its original identity. Only then can it be incorporated into the structure of the body. This process, by which various elements in the environment (not just food) are changed and absorbed by the organism, is called *assimilation*. But at the same time, the mouth must open, the teeth must chew, the throat must swallow, peristaltic action must occur, digestive juices proper to the chemical properties of that particular food must be secreted, etc. In short, the organism must *accommodate* itself to the individual attributes of the particular food which it is trying to assimilate.

All living things adapt to their environments by use of these complementary processes. Why, asks Piaget, should the functioning of the mind be governed by different principles? In cognitive development, however, it is not foodstuffs that are being assimilated; it is the reality of the world. What this reality must be assimilated to is the body of knowledge that the child currently possesses about the world. What does the assimilating are the structures of the brain. In the course of the effort, the structures of the brain accommodate themselves to the individual peculiarities of whatever it is that they are trying to assimilate—an object or an event— and in consequence of this accommodation, they change. These processes, furthermore, take place within an organized entity and operate in accordance with laws which systematize all actions of that entity. For living things in general, that entity is the entire organism; in Piaget's analogy, it is the intellectual framework of the mind.

For example, let's suppose a child has learned that cats and dogs belong to a category of things called "animals," and that the child's classifying principle is the fact that cats and dogs have four legs of about the same size. He can therefore fairly easily assimilate horses and cows to the same concept. In doing so, however, his mind has to accommodate to such individual peculiarities of horses and cows as horns, hoofs, and greater size relative to cats and dogs. The result is a slightly broader concept of what constitutes an "animal"; a slight bending of cognitive structure to fit the reality of the world. The same process will be repeated as, over the years, the child becomes aware of rabbits and ducks and reindeer, as well as giraffes and kangaroos and monkeys and ostriches at the zoo. To assimilate these to his concept of "animal" requires a series of accommodations over a period of time, in the course of which the classifying principle will be forced to shift by degrees and through various possibilities to, perhaps, the common possession of a backbone by all these creatures.

But I am anticipating; this mature concept of "animal" doesn't develop until the school years. What must happen first are much more fundamental discoveries about the universe: that objects exist, that they differ from one another, that they have permanence. Also: that one thing happens because of something else (cause and effect); that things happen *somewhere* and that objects are positioned (concept of space); and that activities occur at measured intervals (concept of time). To start acquiring these concepts is the task of the newborn baby.

Nobody knows what kind of cognitive structure he starts out with. Piaget says that incoming stimulation from the environment may at first do no more than "feed" those reflex actions which are built in by heredity. But the baby's first random rooting around when he feels pressure on the cheek quickly becomes a purposeful search for a nipple. His blank newborn gaze soon becomes a focused scrutiny of his mother's face. Piaget says that every act of intelligence, however rudimentary, presupposes an interpretation of something in external reality—an assimilation of that something *to* some kind of meaning system in the brain and an alteration *of* the structure of that meaning system as it accommodates to the shapes and sounds and textures that reality presents to it.

This, as you can see, is a very dynamic theory of intellectual development. It proposes that our cognitive structures—neural networks, presumably—are formed by the functioning of the brain, and only by such functioning. The baby is not seen as an empty vessel into which learning is poured, nor as a lump of clay which is molded by external forces. Instead, he is an active participant in his own intellectual development. He constructs his own world. The *process* (assimilation and accommodation) is constant throughout development, but the *product* is an ever-changing body of knowledge which step by step comes into balance with the realities of the environment.

To illustrate these steps, let's take the concept of permanence.

If you put something of interest to a five-month-old baby—a ticking watch, say—within reach, he will try to pick it up. But if you cover the watch with a handkerchief as he reaches, the baby will withdraw his hand. Why? Lacking a concept of permanence, he thinks that the watch has vanished.

Seven months later, however, you can't fool him *that* way. By this stage, one of his favorite games is to hunt for concealed objects. He will watch you hide a ball or block under a cloth, then crow with glee and retrieve it. Has he now acquired the concept of permanence? Not quite—for if you take the same ball or block and, in full view of the baby, place it under another cloth, he will look for it under the cloth where you first hid it—even if its outline bulges up under the fabric which now covers it. (See FIGURE 14.)

Piaget says that the concept of permanence is tied to the concept of space, which is slow-coming. At birth, the only space of which a baby is aware is the area he occupies or acts upon. It takes many months for him to realize that he is one object among many and that he shares space with others. Even at a year of age, his sense of locality is still subjective, tied to himself and his actions; not

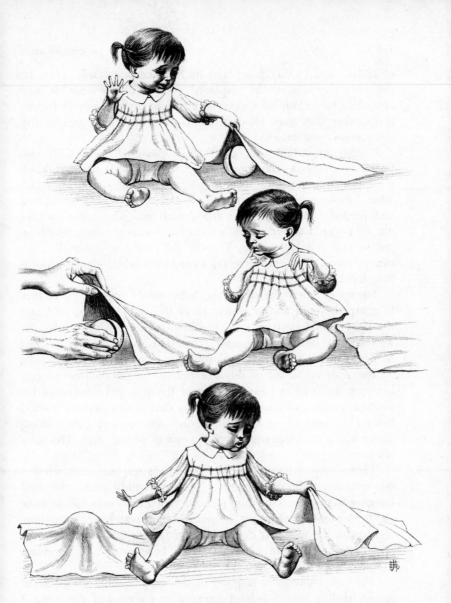

FIGURE 14

This year-old baby has not yet learned that solid objects exist independently of her actions upon them. That's why she is looking for the ball under the cloth where it was first hidden. According to Jean Piaget, children do not develop the concept of permanence until the second year of life.

objective, tied to the object and its displacement. Only when he discovers that objects are displaced *relative to one another,* and according to certain laws, does he attribute permanence to them— a discovery that most children don't make until sometime during the second year of life.

Another important concept, that of cause and effect, is also linked by Piaget to the concept of space. His own three children were probably the most closely observed infants in history, and what follows will give you an example of how Piaget watched and recorded their progress. When each was about five months old, he covered the crib with a transparent canopy upon which he put several celluloid rattles. Then he gathered the material of the canopy into a knot and attached a cord to it which dangled down into the crib.

"Sooner or later," he says, "the baby would happen by chance to grasp the cord and of course make the rattles bounce. At first the baby would be frightened by these unforeseen noises, but he would soon become enchanted and pull the cord harder and harder, watching the dance of the toys above him.

"But does an infant of this age perceive a physical connection between the cord and the covering of the crib and comprehend a physical cause and effect? In order to decide this matter, I stand behind the crib where the baby cannot see me and gently swing above him a toy suspended from the end of a long stick. The baby watches it, smiles, coos, and so on.

"Then I stop swinging the toy. The baby's response now answers our question with utter clarity. He immediately seizes the cord hanging from the canopy and pulls it! When his yanks fail to make the toy resume its swinging, he pulls harder, watching the motionless toy all the while. It does not occur to him to follow down the stick with his eyes to see what might have caused the previous motion.

"The baby may even respond in the same manner to a distant sound. Hiding myself behind a screen in a corner of the room, I whistle at regular intervals until the baby has acquired a sufficiently lively interest to stretch his head and look in the direction of my corner. Then I stop whistling. The baby's eyes explore the corner for a moment; then he pulls the cord hanging in his crib, looking back to the corner from which the whistles came.

"In short, the action of pulling the cord has been generalized to represent a means of prolonging interesting experiences, without any thought being paid to distances or points of contact. This is perfectly consistent with what we have learned of the infant's initial inability to organize space and his consequent lack of the concept of permanent objects."

Seven months later, however, the child may behave quite differently.

"Toward the end of the first year, we seat him before a blanket with an object placed on the other end. He tries at first to seize the object directly. Failing to reach it, he may immediately comprehend that pulling on the blanket will bring the object closer. If not, he may discover this accidentally, by random jerking of the blanket. In the latter case we can make a test which shows how much he comprehends of the significance of his discovery.

"We put the object not on top of the blanket but on the floor just off the end or the side. If the child still has only a generalized concept of causality, he will pull the blanket, watching the object as if he expects it to move toward him. But if the child has reached the stage where his sense of causality has become spatialized and objectivized, he will pull the blanket only if the object is lying on top of it."

Piaget's scholarly output is so great that it would be impossible to discuss a tenth of it in a book of this kind.° I have quoted from his studies of the first stage of cognitive development because this is the period he has studied in greatest detail and partly to give the reader the flavor of his language and a glimpse of his ingenuity in setting up observational situations. From now on, however, his stage-dependent theory overall will be described in rather bare-bones fashion.

Thought, says Piaget, is internalized action. We begin, as babies, by having basically slow-paced physical interactions with concrete objects; progress, as children, to a state in which we replicate such action sequences mentally; and finally, as adults, transmute these actions into symbols and systems which flash through our brains too fast for conscious comprehension. In the course of the years it

° To read Piaget in the original leads one to a very large number of books and journals, some of which have not yet been translated into English. For laymen who wish to delve more deeply into Piagetian theory, therefore, I suggest John H. Flavell's *Developmental Psychology of Jean Piaget*, which is generally agreed to be a masterly review of Piaget's work. You will find it listed among the References at the back of this book.

takes us to do this, we pass through a series of clearly marked developmental stages. Each stage is characterized by a distinctive mode of thought which determines our *general* approach to organizing experience as well as our specific responses to specific events. We can't skip any stage or experience it out of order. It would be unrealistic of a parent who knows his Piaget to expect a child to use the mental *modus operandi* of a later stage when his cognitive structure is that of an earlier stage. (Keep this point in mind: I will be coming back to it at the end of the chapter.)

The first period, which lasts for about two years, is called by Piaget "the sensory-motor period" because the infant's knowledge of the world derives entirely from his bodily interaction with concrete objects. Piaget stresses the necessity of this interaction being one in which the child is personally active; he says, for example, that actual handling of things is an essential preamble to the formation of such concepts as permanence and causality.

During the early part of this period, the child's big problem is to separate himself from other objects. Characteristically, Piaget says, he views objects or sensations as extensions of himself until he is six or seven months old. This may explain the peculiar significance of the sixth or seventh month in institutionalized infants' behavior (which was mentioned in Chapter 6). At any rate, this is the belief of H. R. Schaffer of the Royal Hospital for Sick Children in Glasgow, after studying the posthospitalization behavior of children who were three weeks to a year old when admitted for treatment and stayed for four days to a month and a half.

Those who were *under* seven months at admission were so preoccupied with the environment upon their return home that they virtually ignored everything else. "For hours on end sometimes the infant would crane his neck, scanning his surroundings without apparently focusing on any particular feature and letting his eyes sweep over all objects without attending to any particular one," Schaffer reports. Neither toys nor maternal attention diverted them. This behavior continued for a matter of hours, or as long as four weeks.

Babies who were *over* seven months when hospitalized, however, became excessively dependent on their mothers upon returning home, clinging and crying when left alone, and exhibiting acute fear of strangers. This behavior lasted as long as thirteen weeks.

Schaffer explains these reactions in light of Piagetian theory. If there is no distinction between the self and the environment for the first six months of life, and "objects do not exist in their own right but only as functional elements serving the infant's own activities," a baby would not recognize his mother as a person clearly distinguishable from himself—and miss her—until he had passed the seventh month. Since Schaffer's study showed that children of seven or eight months were just as upset by separation from their mothers as children of eighteen months to three years of age are also known to be, he concluded that a child's attachment to his mother (as a particular and identifiable individual) does not build gradually over the first year or so, but hits all at once, in full intensity, at the seven months mark of cognitive development.

And why do children *under* seven months of age develop their distinctive posthospitalization preoccupation with the environment? Babies as young as this are unable to stand, are often confined in solid-sided cribs, are rarely picked up—hence their hospital environment is perceptually dull, even static. If a child sees himself and the environment as one, a change from the monotonous setting of the hospital to which he has adapted himself would be, Schaffer believes, an exceedingly stressful experience. The rich variety of sounds and sights in the home setting would be a veritable assault; and not just on his senses, on *himself*. Hence, his posthospitalization posture of intense watchfulness. (I am reminded here of Joyce Robertson's case histories of babies whose mothers did not mediate sufficiently between them and their environments.)

Back to Piaget now.

For children in the sensory-motor period of development, the time dimension is *now;* the space dimension is *here;* and the orientation is *me*. Mental functioning is dependent upon the perception of events that the child has seen occur or has made occur; in fact, one of the signs that he is approaching the next period of development is his ability to anticipate the trajectory of a thrown ball which lands out of his sight, or conceive of something happening where he can't see it at the same time that something is happening where he *can* see it. Piaget believes that children under two live in a world of essentially disconnected episodes; of static frames projected upon their minds like slides upon a screen.

They move into the "period of preoperational thought"—age two to age seven—as they become capable of letting one thing stand for another. When a toddler uses the word "mama" to signify his mother's possessions as well as her self, he is beginning to think symbolically. Likewise, his imitative play demonstrates the same capacity: when he "drives the car," using a pot lid for a steering wheel while sitting in a big carton from the grocery store, he is symbolizing his past experience and relating it to the present. He is a very long way from grasping a sweep of events in one encompassing intellectual act of recall-recognition-and-anticipation— as adults do—but he is making a start.

At the younger end of this developmental period, children often attribute cause-and-effect relationships where none intrinsically exists. For instance, if the phone rings just as a toddler falls down and hurts himself, he may think that the phone hurt him. He tends, in fact, to take everything at face value—a trait that is charmingly illustrated by a study conducted at the University of Chicago by Rheta DeVries. She used some sixty little boys aged three to six and a "reluctantly obliging" black cat named Maynard. With judiciously dispensed bits of liver, she persuaded Maynard to accept and wear either of two helmet-like masks. One, covered with white fur, was modeled to look like a rabbit's head; the other covered with black fur, looked like the head of a schipperke, a small Belgian dog which is about the size of a cat and has similar bodily conformation.

First, the children were invited to see and pet Maynard, in his own identity. (See FIGURE 15.) Then, out of the child's sight, one of the other of the masks would be slipped over the cat's head, and Maynard would be returned to the child's company. "What is this animal now?" the experimenter would ask. After the child responded, the mask would be removed (while the child watched), and he would be asked questions designed to reveal his beliefs about the possibility of identity change. Here are two sets of responses typical of the two age-groups represented:

Christopher, about four, said, "Hi, rabbit!" when Maynard appeared with the rabbit mask in place.

"Is he a real rabbit?" the experimenter asked.

"Yes," Christopher answered.

"What happened to the cat?"

"He ran away . . . Bring the cat back. I want him to be a cat."

The experimenter removed the mask while Christopher watched. The child identified Maynard as a cat. Then the mask was replaced, this time in front of the child. Christopher identified Maynard as a rabbit.

FIGURE 15

Can a cat be a dog? Yes, when a child is four years old;
no, when a child is six. This was Rheta DeVries' finding when
she persuaded a cat named Maynard to appear first as himself (top) and then with a mask (bottom) which made the
younger children in the study believe that the cat had turned
into a dog.

"But don't you think this might still be a cat?" the experimenter asked.

"No, it *isn't* a cat," Christopher said. He was annoyed. "It's a rabbit. I *told* you that *before!*"

Finally: "Did I do magic?" the experimenter asked.

"Yes," Christopher replied, and ran back to his classroom to tell his nursery school teacher that Maynard was a cat *and* a rabbit.

On the other hand, Paul, aged six and a half, knew exactly what was going on when Maynard appeared wearing the dog mask.

"You put that on him," Paul said.

Later, after Paul had watched the mask being removed and then replaced, he was asked, "Is there any way a real cat could become a real dog?"

"No."

"Why not?"

"'Cause he's *not* a dog."

"Could magic change a real cat to a real dog?"

"No. There's no such thing as magic."

All through this period of cognitive development, children tend to particularize. If two things are alike in one respect, they must be alike in all respects: if one toy fire engine makes a siren sound, all toy fire engines should do so. Youngsters two to six tend to "center" on just one characteristic of an object: if you pour water from a tall narrow vase into a wide low bowl, they believe that the amount of water has decreased. That's because they can't attribute both height and width to the same object.

Although by five or six a child has become aware of classification —of the concept of classes and the usefulness of classifying—he still hasn't mastered what the psychologists call subordinate and superordinate classes. If you show him a box which contains wooden beads, twenty brown and two white, and ask whether there would be any left if you were to string all the brown beads into a necklace, he will promptly answer that the white ones will be left over.

"And if I string all the wooden beads into a necklace?" you ask next. "Would there be any left?"

The child will tell you that none would be left.

"Then which would be longer, a necklace made with all the wooden beads, or a necklace made with all the brown beads?"

The child almost invariably says that a necklace made with all the brown beads would be longer, and when you ask him to explain

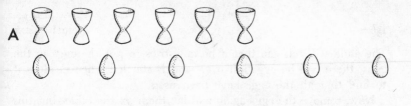

FIGURE 16

Whether one uses eggs, beads, or blocks in the experiment dia-
grammed above, the typical five-year-old cannot accurately relate the units in one group to those in another, even if he
"knows" that they are equal in number. He believes that
there are more eggs than cups when the eggs are spaced
farther apart than the cups (top), and he believes that there
won't be enough eggs to fill the cups when the cups are more
widely spaced than the eggs (bottom).

his answer, he says something to the effect that "there are more
brown beads than white ones."

In other words, children at this stage of cognitive development
can compare brown and white beads (members of the same subordinate class); or they can think of brown and white beads as
being wooden (recognition of a superordinate class); but they
cannot compare brown or white beads with wooden beads (cannot
establish the subordinate-superordinate relationship). This is one of
Piaget's classic experiments; it has been varied in a multitude of
ways, by a multitude of other investigators, and children's responses are the same.

The biggest achievement of the child approaching the end of the
period of preoperational thought is his ability to count; and after
this to acquire the concept of "number." The two are not the same
—as this experiment makes clear:

Put out six egg cups and a carton of eggs, and ask a five-year-old
(one who can count to six or beyond) to take out just enough eggs
so that there will be one in each cup. After he has placed them in
the cups, remove the eggs and place them on the table parallel to
the egg cups but spaced farther apart than the cups. (FIGURE 16A.)

The child will tell you that if he now tries to put the eggs in the cups, there will be eggs left over—and is startled when he does it to find that all the eggs have been used.

Now, remove the eggs again and lay them on the table—but this time space them closer together than the egg cups are spaced. (FIGURE 16B.) The child will insist that there will be cups left over, and is sometimes upset enough to cry when he replaces the eggs in the cups and finds, again, that numbers correspond.

In other words, the ability to enumerate collections of things— six eggs, for example—is a long way from understanding "number." At five or six, a child's thinking is still dominated by the appearances of things—and "number" requires him to treat objects as alike even though they are diverse, and to ignore what they look like or what they are used for. If conceptualization has previously been based on the principle of similarity, it takes a mental leap to see a *numerical* relationship between two blocks or five fingers; another leap to see "three-ness" as the relationship between a spoon, a crayon, and a shoe; and still another leap to give three or any other number an abstract life of its own.

A related problem is that of seriation: of learning to arrange things in order. First one must acquire a mental basis for placing this one first and that one second, an awareness of what the logicians call "asymmetrical relationships." Children are six—and a bright six at that—before they can tell you that if the red stick is longer than the yellow stick, and the yellow stick is longer than the blue one, then the red stick is longer than the blue one.

Then there's the concept of reversibility. Because the young child is very much tied to what he sees and experiences, and because actions in the real world are not reversible (e.g., spilled milk cannot swoosh back into the cup), he is slow to grasp the idea that mental operations *are* reversible. He will be eight or nine years old before he knows that three times four is twelve and that twelve divided by four is three. And that's not all he needs the concept of reversibility for: it is essential in many activities to know that one can return to an original state of affairs or, in reasoning, to know that one has the option of returning to an original premise.

Mastery of this concept is, in fact, one of the measures of a child's achievement of Piaget's third developmental stage, which spans the ages seven to eleven. He calls it the "period of concrete operations" in order to distinguish it from the final stage, between ages eleven to fifteen, called the "period of formal operations." Emphasis in those two phrases should fall on the word "operations," which Piaget defines to mean an organized network of related mental acts that are carried on simultaneously and with regard for the changes wrought by each of the others. The main difference between the mental functioning of a nine-year-old and fourteen-year-old is that the younger child bases most of his operations on concrete objects or specific situations and cannot transfer what he has learned in one physical context to another.

As an illustration, let's take the ability to "conserve" quantity, weight, and volume. The concept of conservation requires one to know that certain properties of objects are invariant. By age eight, most children can conserve quantity; they know, for example, if you pour water from one container into another of different shape, and none spills over and none is left, the amount of water has not changed. But they cannot extrapolate from that point to an awareness that the volume of the two containers is the same. Only at ten or twelve can a child identify the high narrow vase and the broad low vase as alike in capacity. The ability to conserve weight falls somewhere in between. One of Piaget's classic experiments was to use one ball of modeling clay as standard; squeeze an identical one into a radically different shape; and then ask children of varying ages to estimate whether the altered ball weighed less than, more than, or the same as the standard. Children do not realize that the two balls of clay weigh the same until they are about nine years old.

With the period of formal operations, children are finally divorced from thinking in terms of concrete things. The red, yellow, and blue sticks of early childhood turned, in middle childhood, into an awareness that "if A is longer than B and B is longer than C, then A must be longer than C." Now, however, the adolescent can integrate this knowledge into the proposition that "any item to the left is longer than any item to the right of it." He can take account at last of all the multiple dimensions of a thing or situation—swiftly and automatically, in a radar-like sweep of his mind—and in so doing he can perceive the possible variables that would affect the outcome of an action. Thus he can anticipate what each of these possibilities would mean if it were to occur, and eliminate the unimportant or unworkable ones—before he lifts a finger. In short, he has become capable of hypothetical deductive reasoning, and is cognitively mature.

You didn't realize how much you've been through to get where you are, did you?

Some investigators, in duplicating Piaget's experiments, have found that his age norms are too high for children of superior intelligence. W. H. Kooistra, for example, found that children whose IQ's averaged 135 could conserve quantity, weight, and volume when they were two years younger than the ages assigned to these abilities by Piaget. (Piaget himself, incidentally, has always said that his age divisions were intended as general guidelines rather than as fixed boundaries.) And Columbia's Millie Almy, in testing children of different socioeconomic background, found that middle class children were about a year ahead of lower class children in their ability to accomplish Piaget's conservation tasks.

But so far no one has faulted Piaget's assertion that children achieve these and other cognitive abilities in a sequential fashion which cannot be altered.[*] In fact, various efforts seeking to teach conservation to children who are not, according to Piagetian theory, ready for it, have at best had only limited success—and then only when the children have been very close to the period when they would achieve this ability anyway. (You can demonstrate endlessly to a five-year-old that six eggs are always going to fill six egg cups, regardless of how they are spaced on a table, and he won't believe you—until he has reached the point in cognitive development when he would normally acquire the concept of number.)

In addition, there is evidence that Piaget's age periods are universal. Children in primitive societies seem to go through the same stages of cognitive growth, and in the same sequence, as civilized children. Here are two examples of such studies:

D. G. Price-Williams of the London School of Economics tested a group of illiterate children, aged five to eight, who belonged to the Tiv, a Central Nigerian tribe. He put the same amount of fine earth into two identical containers; poured the contents of one of them into smaller containers of equal dimensions; then asked the children whether the amount of earth in the smaller containers

[*] Unless you count a report from Red China quoted by Millie Almy. Its authors, Tsu-hsin Cheng and Mei-ke Lee, say that their study of six- and seven-year-old children runs contrary to the contention of "the bourgeois scholar Piaget that children's conception of number is completely determined by age."

was *hemba* (more than), *dhar* (less than), or *kwagh mom* (the same as the amount of earth in the remaining large container). None of the five- or six-year-olds, half of the seven-year-olds, and all of the eight-year-olds answered, *"Ka kwagh mom."* This is approximately the age at which civilized children can conserve quantity.

To compare children's reactions to dreams was the object of another cross-cultural study made by Harvard's Lawrence Kohlberg. (It is difficult for a young child to differentiate between subjective and objective components of his experience. He confuses thoughts with things, and symbols with the reality they stand for; for instance, he may half-expect a picture of a snake to bite him. Hence his progress toward reality is easily measured by the way he reports his dreams.) The typical American four-year-old believes that the bad man he dreamed about was really, physically, in his bedroom. Not until five does he recognize that the dream originated inside his own head. At six, he is aware that his dream had no material substance but was a *thought*. And at eight he realizes that he himself had caused that thought.

And so it is also with the Atayal, a group of aborigines who live in Taiwan. Kohlberg interviewed four- to eight-year-olds in that culture; discovered that they were a bit older than the American children when they hit a given stage; but otherwise their reactions to their dreams followed the same age-related sequence.

To sum up: Piaget believes that a child's mind is a psychic entity which consistently evaluates by one general mode of thought all the various stimuli which impinge on his consciousness—but that this entity, this structured whole, is continually being *re*-structured by its own interaction with the environment. This means that the thought of infants and children is not a miniature version of adult thought. It is *qualitatively* different. It changes its form as it "grows up."

This also means that a wise parent, although seeking always to clarify reality for a child, will not expect him to see that reality as the parent does. You will be cautious, for example, about citing the Golden Rule in arbitrating quarrels between preschoolers—waiting until you are sure they have sufficiently separated themselves cognitively from other objects so that they can *really* put themselves into someone else's shoes. You will not scorn as sissified a four-year-old's request for a night light in his bedroom because "it will scare away the bears." And you will refrain from calling your seven-year-old stupid because he insists that an airplane flying away from the viewer actually shrinks in size.

Support for this radical notion that each stage of mental development has its own logic comes from an odd quarter. Psychologists have long noted that there is virtually no correspondence between intelligence tests given at early ages with those given at later ages. You simply cannot predict from a child's test results at age two what his abilities will be at age ten. Dozens of researchers have puzzled over this problem; a summary listing of their papers, recently made by Michael A. Wallach, takes two pages of a good-sized book. Then he cites a study made by Peter R. Hoefstaetter, whose use of a complex statistical procedure called factor analysis suggests that the composition of "intelligence" changes with age.

The reason for the quotation marks around "intelligence" is that it is not a unitary attribute. No one is equally good at all intellectual tasks. It has been proved and proved again that some of us do better, on tests and in life, when we are dealing with concrete materials, and others when dealing with symbolic materials like words and numbers. In fact, over sixty separate and specialized intellectual abilities, or *factors,* have now been identified as components of that thing called "intelligence." And although most intelligence tests still end up with a single score—such as IQ 103—it is possible, using factor analysis, to discover which particular component factors of intelligence are responsible for a given child's ranking high or low on any test.

Hoefstaetter factored the scores of a group of children who had repeatedly been tested from two months of age to almost eighteen years of age and found that up to the age of fourteen months (with a peak at about ten months), one specific factor was responsible for variance in scoring, and thereafter abruptly diminished in importance. A second factor shot to prominence at about age two and a half, waning more slowly. From age four to six, a third factor rose in influence, and from seven years onward was the most important ability in determining a child's overall test score. Wallach says, "These findings support the generalization that whatever is being assessed by 'intelligence' tests is structurally or qualitatively different in infancy, early childhood, and middle childhood."

And before we leave the subject, you might turn back to page 13. T. G. R. Bower's comments on children's perceptual abilities will now have more meaning.

CHAPTER 13

PERCEPTION

In what form does a child acquire information from the environment? How does his mind process it into concepts? In the preceding chapter emphasis fell on cognitive change itself, on developmental stages and sequences, rather than upon the agents and architects of that change. So it is appropriate now to consider some of these in more detail—notably, perception, language, and how information is processed.

In attempting to do this, however, one immediately runs into a linguistic barrier. Although our bodies, like all organisms, habitually synchronize many simultaneously occurring and reciprocally operating events, we cannot verbally describe such activity. Our language allows us to speak of only one thing happening at a time. You will therefore have to make a special effort—as if working your way through a game of three-dimensional ticktacktoe—if you are to keep the following three chapters synchronized in your mind. Remember: perception, language, and the mechanisms of information processing are thoroughly intertwined and concurrent in their operation. It is only an arbitrary choice that starts us off with a discussion of perception.

According to one dictionary definition, perception is "physical sensation interpreted in the light of experience." The eyes, for example, respond to the light waves that strike them but the person does not see—in the sense of comprehension—until his mind has

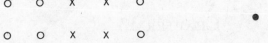

A. GROUPING. The circles and x's at left above are equally spaced; yet they seem to group themselves into four-circle and four-x groups. The dots on the right organize themselves into a hexagon rather than into a square with offset dots.

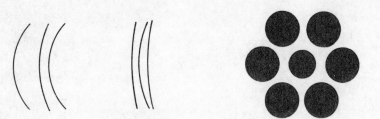

B. CONTEXT. At the left, which inside curve is curvier? At the right, which center circle is larger? In each case, the center figure is the same.

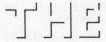

C. CLOSURE. The single lines are unconnected in the figure above, yet you see them as block letters.

FIGURE 17

evaluated and reached an opinion as to the meaning of the raw data provided by his eyes. Only when this has been done can he know where he stands in relation to the environment as it is at any given moment, and act accordingly.

In the early years of this century, most psychologists believed that the nature of what was being perceived was the most important aspect of perception. The individual qualities of a given stimulus were thought to evoke consistent responses in a given individual, those responses being conditioned by the frequency with which the perceiver had experienced the object or situation and the conditions of its presentation—its nearness or farness, its loudness or softness, its brightness or dullness, its contrast with other objects, etc.

Certain universal "laws" of perception supported this belief. Among them is our common tendency to group things that are similar (FIGURE 17A) and to make judgments of reality on the basis of the perceived object's relationship to other things in its "field" (FIGURE 17B). We also tend to fill in gaps, as in FIGURE 17C. Similarly, whenever we see an object that is partially hidden by another object—a house obscured by trees, say—we perceive it as solid and whole.

But it has become increasingly apparent in more recent years that the internal condition of the perceiver exercises tremendous influence upon what is perceived. This can mean a physiological state: a maturational factor such as the nearsightedness of children, a condition that diminishes gradually over their first few years of life; or a transient state common to everyone, such as hunger. It has been found by many experimenters that if you flash pictures of various objects on a screen so quickly that they are difficult to identify, subjects who are hungry will identify pictures of things to eat or drink more quickly and accurately than the other pictures. "Internal condition" can also mean a range of personal factors, from the presence of some special interest on the part of the perceiver to an overall cast of personality that colors an individual's entire attitude toward the world. Here are a series of examples:

Attentiveness to a stimulus varies greatly according to circumstances. Creatures capable of hearing do not perceive sound just because it's there—a fact that was graphically recorded by Raúl Hernández-Peón and two colleagues when they were observing how cats in different states of attentiveness respond to sound. After electrodes had been implanted at a point in the brainstem where sound impulses are processed, the investigators broadcast short bursts of sound at an intensity that was comfortable for humans to hear and presumably for cats, since they remained resting and relaxed. Each burst of sound was reflected in the brain wave pattern shown in FIGURE 18A. (The dots indicate the "click" of sound, and you can see the corresponding attentional peak of brain wave activity.) But when a jar containing two mice was placed in the

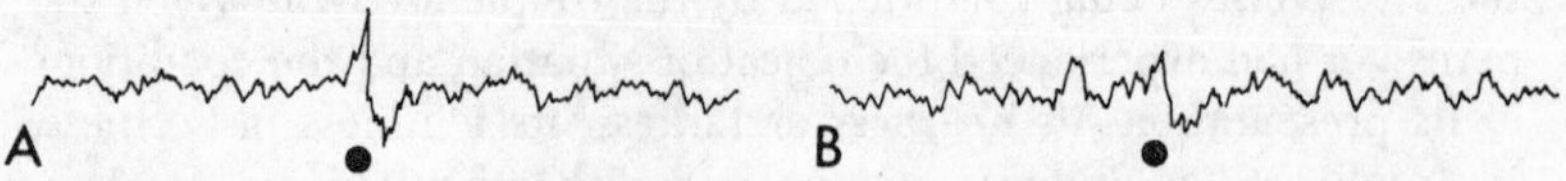

FIGURE 18
The ears hear, but the mind must listen: the two brain
wave graphs above, recorded by Raúl Hernández-Peón, H.
Scherrer, and M. Jouvet show a relaxed cat's attentiveness to
sound (A) and its diminished attentiveness, despite no change in
volume of sound, when a jar containing two mice was placed in
its cage (B). (From *Science*, Vol. 123, February 24, 1956.)

cage, the attentional peak diminished almost to the vanishing point,
as shown in FIGURE 18B. The sound was still there, but the cat's
attention was now concentrated on what it was seeing rather than
on what it was hearing.

Human beings are no different. A clock's striking does not change
in loudness, but while a girl is waiting for her date to arrive it may
sound like Big Ben and when it is time for him to go she may not
hear it at all.

Comparably, people do not necessarily perceive valued objects
as they really are. In a famous 1947 experiment by Jerome Bruner
and Cecile Goodman, ten children from poor homes and an equal
number from rich homes were asked to estimate the size of coins.
The children, all of whom were ten years old, used an apparatus
which included a ground glass screen and a knob at the lower
right-hand corner. Focused on the screen was a circular patch of
light which could be varied in diameter by turning the knob.

The children were first asked to estimate coin size from memory,
then the experimenter held coins (from a penny to a half dollar)
in the palm of his hand so that the child could actually see the
coin whose size he was expected to duplicate on the screen. A
control group of ten children was given the same problem, except
that the objects whose size they were supposed to estimate were
gray discs.

The results correlated with the social value of the objects estimated. The children who were estimating the size of the gray
discs adjusted the circular patch of light so that it was closer to
true size than did the children who were estimating size of coins.

Of these latter, the rich children slightly overestimated the size of the coins and the poor children greatly overestimated size.

Furthermore, the greater the value of the coin the greater the deviation of apparent size from actual size. With one exception—overestimation reached its peak in appraising the size of a quarter and came closer to true size in the case of a half dollar. Because this deviation in otherwise consistent behavior did not characterize adults who were similarly tested, Bruner and Goodman theorized that to children a half dollar had less "reality value" than a quarter. "To a ten-year-old," they said, "a half dollar is almost too valuable to be real." (This was probably true in 1947; it would be interesting to repeat the experiment in the inflated 1970s.)°

To have the approval of others is one of our most basic needs. That it can affect behavior without our being at all aware of the fact was demonstrated by Joel Greenspoon, who is now at Arizona State, in an experiment since repeated by others. He said to each person among a group of seventy-five college undergraduates, "Say all the words you can think of. Say them individually. Do not use any sentences or phrases. Do not count. Please continue until I say stop. Go ahead."

There was no further conversation on his part, but whenever a student in the experimental group first said a plural noun ("eyes," "cars," "cities," etc.) Greenspoon said an encouraging "Mmm-hmm." For the control group, no comment of any sort was made. At the conclusion of the session, the subject was asked questions intended to reveal whether he had tumbled to the purpose or procedure of the experiment; ten students were eliminated; and the responses of the remaining sixty-five were analyzed.

For both the controls and the experimental group, the first plural noun said was about the twentieth word in the series. From that point until the end of the session, the controls said an average of six to fifteen plural nouns within any five-minute period of naming, whereas the experimental group averaged nine to twenty-five. Greenspoon's approving murmur had increased the number of plural nouns said—even though the students didn't realize that it was that particular response that was eliciting approval.

° The Bruner and Goodman experiment was challenged by other psychologists on methodological grounds, but a couple of later variants—one using hypnosis to make the subjects temporarily feel rich or poor—confirmed the Bruner and Goodman conclusion.

The suggestibility of human beings is, in fact, one of the most tested of our frailties. Experiments have ranged from observing the ability of individuals to see things as they are when everyone else in the group reports them as they *aren't* to experiments in which an entire group is beguiled by the authority or prestige of a leader.

One of the latter sort was conducted in 1933 by Ramona Messerschmidt, who is now the chief clinical psychiatrist at the Veterans Administration Mental Hygiene Clinic in Spokane, but was then not long out of school herself. She used a group of six- to sixteen-year-olds and of course did not tell them the purpose of the tests. (They provided their own evaluation. "The majority considered them a new and peculiar series of 'nut tests,'" she says.) Among a series of discriminations was this one:

Carefully removing the wrapping around a small bottle of water, Messerschmidt said, "In this bottle there is something you have never smelled before. I am going to pour some on a piece of cotton, hold it in the air, and begin counting—one count a second. As you smell it, you are to put the number you hear me say on a piece of paper. Remember, all you need is one number, the number you hear me say when you first smell this."

Then she poured water on the cotton, turning her head away from the bottle as if the odor were disagreeable, and counted to 100. The younger children "smelled" the odor on the first few counts. As age of child increased, the number the child wrote down tended to be higher. Not until high school age did some young subjects pronounce the test "a fake"—and that appraisal was by no means unanimous.

(I will have more to say shortly about children's decreasing vulnerability, as they grow older, to the "field" in which they find themselves.)

The social standards of one's culture also affect what one sees and hears. In fact, the term "perceptual defense" has come to be used for the tendency to screen out of awareness words whose use is disapproved in polite society. Elliott McGinnies and Joseph Adornetto measured this tendency by presenting to a group of men a series of words, some of which are "neutral"—eater, anvil, and zebra, for example—and some of which are "taboo"—such as filth, belly, and penis. All words chosen were similar in length, and the neutral and taboo words were paired as to their frequency of usage in the language. The words were flashed on a screen for .01 second, then for .02 second, then for .03 second—and so on, until the subject reported the word correctly. The neutral words were recognized in 67.6 milliseconds (on the average) but it took 75.8 milliseconds for the men to recognize the taboo words.

A variation on this experiment was undertaken by McGinnies and another associate, Howard Sherman, to make sure that the lag was not due to a conscious reluctance on the part of the subject to say the taboo word out loud. In this test, the word that was to be recognized (the "task" word) was neutral. But it was sometimes preceded by a neutral and sometimes by a taboo "pre-task" word. If the task word was not recognized during its initial .01 second exposure, the pre-task word was shown again, followed by exposure of the task word for .02 second. The investigators found that the viewer was slower to recognize the task word (which, remember, was neutral) whenever the pre-task word was taboo.

The leading exponent of the theory that perception and personality are very closely correlated is Herman A. Witkin (who intended to be a biologist but was deflected by a course on animal behavior that so captured his interest that he switched to psychology). Since 1942 he and his colleagues at the State University of New York's College of Medicine have exhaustively studied the ways in which individuals with different personality traits perceive the same things.

He began with a battery of perception tests that were designed to reveal the ease with which a given individual isolates a particular item from its "field." The item may be three-dimensional—as when the subject enters a dark room, sees at some distance a luminous frame which in fact is tilted to one side, and is asked to align a luminous rod to an upright position. The viewer can use his own upright body as his point of reference or he can use the visual field; if he uses the latter, his "upright" rod will also be tilted.

Another test is two-dimensional. The viewer is shown a simple geometric figure and then is asked to find it again when it is embedded in a more elaborate figure. (See FIGURE 19.)

If, in the first case, the subject aligns the luminous rod with the tilted frame and, in the second case, has difficulty finding the simple shape within the elaborate one, Witkin calls him "field-dependent." Conversely, if he aligns the rod according to the posture

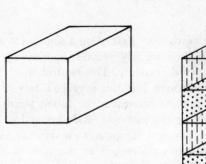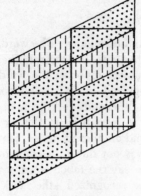

FIGURE 19

Can you locate the simpler shape within the more elaborate one? In Herman Witkin's experiments, the dotted areas were orange and the dashed areas were red, which made discrimination even more difficult than in the figure above.

of his own body or if he can spot the simple shape within the complex one, he is "field-independent." These are only two of many visual perception tests used by Witkin. He has found that people are quite consistent in their mode of perceiving, whether they are matching colors or hunting embedded figures, aligning luminous rods or trying to keep themselves upright when their visual field is swaying.

The other half of Witkin's project required the same subjects to take tests known from clinical use to reveal personality traits. Among them was the Draw-a-Person Test: people unconsciously reflect their self-image in the size and placement of the person they draw, in the degree to which the figure has male or female characteristics, in the extent to which one part of the body is emphasized. Then there is the Thematic Apperception Test (TAT), in which a series of pictures like the one in FIGURE 20 are presented, and the subject is asked to make up a story about the scene. Another such test asks the subject to tell what he "sees" in a series of very ambiguous shapes. The kind of story he tells or the imagery suggested by inkblots similar to the one in FIGURE 21 indicate such qualities in the individual as assertiveness, hostility toward others, self-esteem, ways of handling anxiety, etc.

Witkin's conclusion, after years of such testing and making com-

FIGURE 20

What is the relationship between the women? What are they
thinking about? Pictures used for the Thematic Apperception
Test have an ambiguous quality in order to encourage children
to interpret the scenes in highly personal ways. (Illustration
No. 12F from *Thematic Apperception Test* by Henry A. Murray.
Copyright 1943 by the President and Fellows of Harvard
College. Reproduced by ‘permission of Harvard University
Press.)

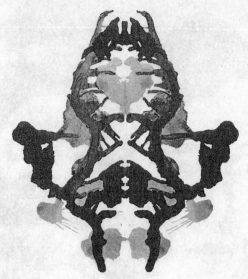

FIGURE 21

Some people see an X-ray in Holtzman Inkblot Y above; others see dancers. People with similar personality traits often interpret ink blots in the same way. (Inkblot Y from *Holtzman Inkblot Technique.* Copyright © 1958 by The Psychological Corporation, New York, N.Y. All rights reserved. Reproduced by permission.)

parisons between the ways that his subjects perceived things and the kinds of personalities they had, is that field-dependent people tend also to be passive in dealing with the environment; are unfamiliar with and afraid of their own impulses and have poor control of them; and lack self-esteem. In contrast, people who can successfully separate the parts from the whole or themselves from their setting when they are perceiving something tend to be initiators and organizers; people who try to change or control social and environmental forces; people who are aware of their own impulses and successfully master them; people who think well of themselves.

There is another important finding in Witkin's work. Although he observed tremendous variations of behavior on any one test, some children performing better than adults, in general children are far more influenced by the structure of the surrounding field than adults are. Around age ten, however, a sudden and dramatic change occurs, and between the ages of ten and thirteen children develop virtually their full adult capacity for separating an item from its context (if they are going to have it). Witkin suggests, therefore, that field-dependence is a developmental first step, and that its persistence into adult life indicates an arrest in progress toward emotional maturity. Many of the personality traits typical of the field-dependent adult are echoed in the behavior of young children—submission to authority, for example, or difficulty in controlling impulses.

To say that the young child is field-dependent does not mean, of course, that he can't isolate *any* parts from the whole. As the work of Robert Fantz and others has made clear, newborn babies can see pattern; that is, they can distinguish a figure from its background. But it takes children a long time to learn to pick out the details within a pattern, to note the subtleties of a perceived scene, or—and this is very important—to correctly relate its various parts to each other.

Until children are well into the school years, their attention is caught by objects or scenes that are strong and simple—big bold strokes, bright clear colors, sharp contrasts, and similar overstatements. They need more clues to what they're seeing, hearing, tasting, or touching than adults do. That is, much more of a building must be visible if they are going to recognize it—understandably, for they haven't seen many buildings and therefore aren't as able as adults to infer a church from a steeple or a service station from a revolving sign seen through some trees.

In an excellent review of research on the developmental course of visual perception, Clark University's Joachim Wohlwill notes that young children have a marked tendency to follow continuous linear paths in the perception of shape, which of course results in awareness of general outline rather than internal detail. He cites a study that was done years ago in Germany in which children were shown a series of pictures of familiar objects, the first in the series being a simple outline but each following picture having more internal detail. With each addition, the youngsters were asked to point out what details had been added. Only 36 percent of four-year-olds could spot the additions, in contrast to 88 percent of eight-year-olds.

When children do become aware of details, they tend not to perceive them as parts-of-a-whole but as separate entities—smaller
"wholes." This behavior was documented by William A. Miller, who
tested the perception of third-graders by asking them to describe
the pictures in their own school books. In each picture there were
twenty to twenty-six constituent items whose perception was important to an understanding of the pictured scene. The children
identified (on the average) fewer than a third of the items.

Some of these items were generalized in nature; they set the scene
of the story or carried the theme—as in a picture of a table laid with
food and with a jack-o'-lantern centerpiece. Yet only half the
children viewing that picture mentioned Halloween and only 10
percent said anything about eating. In general, they saw the various
segments of the picture in isolation, not as parts that contributed to
a larger unity.

A similar inability to relate parts to each other is apparent in
children's progressive ways of copying the geometric shape in Fig-
URE 22. As recorded by Arnold Gesell and Louise Ames, children
of about four make the vertical and cross lines quite separately
(FIGURE 22A). By age six, they have all the lines in, but they can't
make them intersect properly (FIGURE 22B).

Another example comes from the work of Lauretta Bender, a
child psychiatrist with much institutional experience and also the
mother of three children. She has found that children under six
have great difficulty relating two parts of a drawing, especially
when one of the parts is oblique or overlaps the other. For example,
seven-year-olds can copy the forms shown in FIGURE 23A and 23B,
but not until they're about eleven can they reproduce 23C.

Interestingly, young children do better than adults when it comes
to recognizing things despite changes in position that put the object above, below, or sideways to the viewer. That's because, as
many more observers than Piaget have noted, children tend to ignore spatial orientation in their response to form. But the other side
of the same coin is that they have great difficulty in discriminating
between forms that are mirror images or up-down reversals of each
other. This tendency, of course, markedly affects a child's ability to
learn to read.

Helen Davidson, one of the Terman group at Stanford, once
tested this perceptual behavior by showing shapes similar to those
in FIGURE 24 to a group of children, picking one shape as a standard

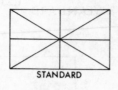

STANDARD

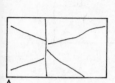

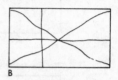

A

B

FIGURE 22

Children are commonly past six years old before they can copy
the geometric shape at the top above. The lower sketches indicate how four-year-olds (left) and six-year-olds (right) typically
do it.

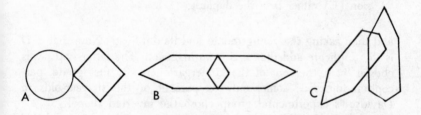

A   B   C

FIGURE 23

These, "the Bender figures," are much used by psychologists
in tests of children's perceptual abilities. Seven-year-olds can
usually copy A and B, but not until a child is close to eleven
can he make a good copy of C. (From "A Visual Motor Gestalt
Test and Its Clinical Use" by Lauretta Bender, from *American
Journal of Orthopsychiatry.* Copyright, The American Orthopsychiatric Association, Inc. Reproduced by permission.)

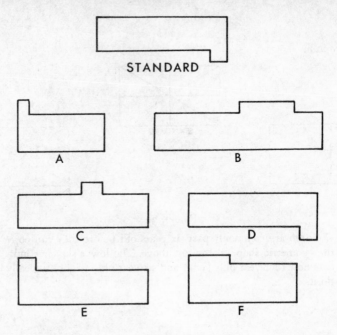

STANDARD

A

B

C

D

E

F

FIGURE 24

Which of the shapes above is the duplicate of the standard? If you were five years old, you would probably pick the inversion (E) rather than the duplicate (D).

and then asking the youngsters to find its duplicate. Note that 24D is the duplicate and that 24E is an inversion. The latter—24E—was chosen by 94 percent of the kindergarteners. By first grade, perception improves—some; only 62 percent of the six-year-olds in Davidson's experimental group chose the inverted shape!

As for inverted letters,° confusion of "p" with "b" and "q" with "d" is conquered by the average child during the first-grade year, but he has trouble with reversals—"b" and "d," "p" and "q"—up to about the age of eight.

° J. A. Deutsch, commenting on his three-year-old son's early recognition of letters, says, "He learned to write a capital A readily and would point it out whenever he saw it. On one occasion when he was looking at a book he discovered a V. 'Why is the A not crossed?' he asked.

"He discovered how to write L, but wrote it as a mirror image: ⌐ . He could make an H and an E, but both were frequently tilted: ⊥ Ǝ ."

Deutsch makes the point that the child was very fussy about the letters he made. He would scribble over those that didn't meet some self-determined standard—but he did not see the wrongly oriented letters as wrong.

An experiment specifically directed toward finding out which letters of the alphabet present the greatest perceptual problems for children was recently carried out by Cornell's Eleanor Gibson. She most ingeniously created a set of twelve letter-like forms, structurally compatible with actual letters of the alphabet, and then created twelve variants of each. FIGURE 25 shows this artificial alphabet. Take the top line as an example: the first three variants shift straight lines to curves; the next five rotate the standard figure by varying amounts; the next two are "slant" or "tilt" transformations; and the final two involve breaks or closures of lines.

Gibson tested 165 children aged four to eight, using the apparatus also shown in FIGURE 25. She placed one of the standard forms on the top row and asked the children to find its duplicate among the twelve variations assembled in random order in the second row.

On break and close transformations (in the English alphabet, "c" versus "o"), even four-year-olds did well, and by the age of eight the children were making virtually no errors. Line to curve transformations (as in "v" versus "u") were a bit harder to spot, but the error curve dropped off rapidly with age. Inversions and reversals (as in "m" versus "w"—which is also a line to curve transformation—or as in "d" versus "b") followed a similar pattern.

It is fortunate, however, that slant and tilt formations are not important in learning to read print—for Gibson's young subjects were still making great numbers of errors on the slant and tilt figures at age eight. So it's just as well that few children, having learned to recognize "G," are required to recognize such handwritten versions as ᏅᏗ or ᏋᏗ until middle childhood.

The inversion and reversal problem affects children's initial ability to read a page of text too. The New Zealander Marie Clay, as part of her research for her Ph.D., observed one hundred children between the ages of five and six as they began to read, and noted every possible combination of scanning: left to right along a line; right to left; top to bottom; bottom to top; and snaking movements across a page, in which one line was read left to right, the line below was read right to left, the next line left to right, and so on. This last approach is really a very sensible and economical method, if one looks at it as a time-and-motion-study engineer would.

Another of Clay's beginning readers was equally systematic: he used the center fold of the book as his focus and read right

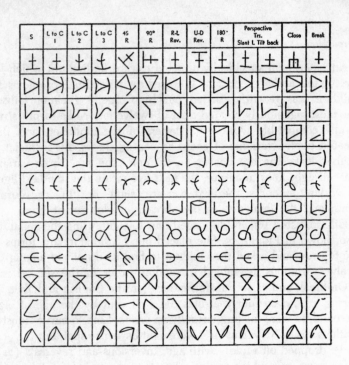

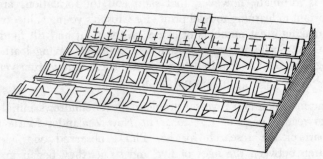

FIGURE 25

Eleanor Gibson's "artificial alphabet" is constructed according to the same graphic principles as the English alphabet. To test the skill with which children discriminate the subtle variations among letter shapes, she asks her subjects to match a given symbol to its duplicate on the display rack; and has found that even at age eight it is difficult for a child to distinguish between an upright letter and a similar one that is slanted or tilted. (Reproduced with permission of the author.)

to left on a left-hand page and left to right on a right-hand page. And a third child followed the pattern blocked out in FIGURE 26. Of this reading of the text, Clay remarks with gentle irony, "The child shows flexibility of approach, and who is to say whether the child or the author is constructing better English sentences?"

THE TEXT   HOW THE CHILD READ THE TEXT

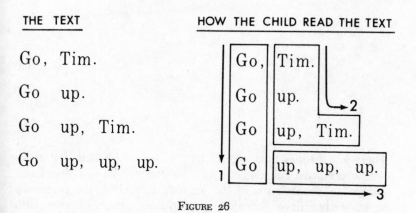

Go,   Tim.

Go   up.

Go   up,   Tim.

Go   up,   up,   up.

FIGURE 26

But first things first. Before we take children farther on their journey into literacy, perhaps we ought to consider how they learn speech? The next chapter will therefore focus on the uses and development of language, and I'll return to reading a bit later.

CHAPTER 14

LANGUAGE

There are theories galore as to how speech originated, but there are no primitive languages to test the theories on—no "fossil languages" as counterparts of the imprints in rock or the fragments of bone that have provided geologists or anthropologists with their knowledge of prehistoric life. There are still some Stone Age peoples in existence—modern remnants of very primitive cultures, hidden away in the world's backwaters—but none is without language, and all speak highly complex languages.

The extraordinary diversity of the world's languages also argues for ancient origin of speech. English and German, for example, have been separate languages for over two thousand years, yet they are still very similar in many respects. Think how much longer ago language *itself* must have originated. In order to account for present diversity, given such a slow rate of change, one has to go back 300,000 to 500,000 years.

A persuasive theory about the development of human speech has been put forth by the Cornell University anthropologists Charles F. Hockett and Robert Ascher. Extrapolating from other evidence that man differs from other primates in degree rather than in kind, they suggest that human speech evolved from the call systems of the gibbon-like creatures who are thought to be the ancestors of both men and modern apes.

In linguistic terms, call systems are "closed" languages: a given utterance is always composed of the same units of sound, and signals just one thing. Such calls are fixed action patterns characteristic of all members of a species. (Owners of cats, if attentive to their pets' "language," can discriminate a mother cat's hunting cry from the croon she utilizes when coaxing her kittens to follow her, and these calls occur at the appropriate time without prior practice.) Human languages, on the other hand, are "open." We learn to combine a rather small set of sound units into utterances that may never before have been said or heard, and our fellows understand these novel utterances perfectly well. How did this transition come about? Hockett and Ascher propose the following:

Let ABCD represent the call that means "food here" and let EFGH represent the call that means "danger coming." (These are arbitrary symbols; the actual number of sounds that might be present in either call are not represented.) A gibbon, finding food but at the same time seeing a tigress in the vicinity, would have to emit one call or the other. But suppose that one of our prehuman ancestors and his band discovered how to make and hear *blended* calls—ABGH, say. If the sounds in this composite were to become established as a call meaning "food here but danger coming," that band of prehumans would have accomplished two things— one of immediate value to them and the other of long-range value to us.

They would have acquired a new call; limited in its usefulness, to be sure, because it could still be used in only one special situation, but nevertheless a valuable addition to their previous repertoire. In addition, however, they would have invented for *us* a system in which parts of meaningful utterances could be used in new combinations. ABCD would still mean "food here," but so would the AB part because of its inclusion in the composite ABGH meaning "food here but danger coming." Likewise, EFGH would still mean "danger coming," but the GH alone would also mean "danger coming" because of its inclusion in the composite ABGH. Therefore, the CD and EF parts of the original calls could take on individual meanings, too. CD could mean "no danger," EF could mean "no food," and in time CDEF could mean "no danger and no food."

It would not require a tremendous number of initial calls to provide the base for an "open" language system—once the user had acquired the habit of building composite signals out of meaningful parts. But this ability would have been no small accomplishment. It requires intelligence to infer the meanings of parts and the patterns by which the parts are combined, the clues being the acoustical properties of the calls heard and the behavioral contexts in which they are uttered. Therefore, once the first primitive steps in the direction of "openness" had been taken, natural selection would have favored those prehumans with greater brain capacity.

To repeat from Chapter 2: It was long believed that early man first developed the cortex that so distinguishes him from other living creatures and then used the resultant intellectual ability to make the tools that have given him superior control over his environment. The prevailing anthropological theory now, however, is just the reverse: that tool use came first, and that man's big brain was a response to that practice. This belief is based on modern discoveries of skulls dating back almost two million years, all of them in deposits containing tools, but with brain size gradually increasing over the centuries until a threefold enlargement had occurred and *Homo sapiens* had arrived.

Hockett and Ascher also argue that human beings' vocal apparatus developed especially for speech. The chronology of evolution permits this hypothesis—if one assumes that mutations in the muscles and organs of the throat and mouth were concurrent with those that eventually created the human brain. Common sense certainly suggests that it would have been useful, and perhaps even necessary, for emerging man to be able to talk about the making and using of tools.

A number of linguists believe that human beings have a genetically determined predisposition for language. The idea was enunciated by Noam Chomsky of the Massachusetts Institute of Technology, and has most notably been developed by Eric H. Lenneberg of Cornell and David McNeill of the University of Michigan. Here are some reasons for their belief, from a paper by Lenneberg:

1. All languages, different though they are in detail, are phonetic systems built upon a relatively small number of sounds within a relatively narrow range of those that the human throat can make; all string those sounds together to form meaningful utterances; and all are characterized by syntactical rules that govern the order and arrangement of the component parts.

Lenneberg says, "The absolutely unexceptional universality of [these three traits] and the absence of historical evidence for their slow cultural evolvement lead me to suppose that we have here the reflection of a biological matrix which forces speech to be of one and no other basic type."

2. Language development follows a regular chronology for all children everywhere—from babbling to short words to short sentences, with concomitant increases in complexity. Lenneberg believes that this sequence is as maturational in character as walking, and walking is controlled by genetic factors.

3. Children's speech is *not* a "mechanical playback" of adult speech. They bring something of themselves to it, from the very beginning. To call their speech wholly imitative is wrong, Lenneberg says, because their articulation differs from that of adults, they combine words in unique ways, and they make up words. They ask questions that have never been asked before ("What does blue look like from in back?") and make statements that have never been stated before ("I buyed a fire dog for a grillion dollars.")

That word "buyed," incidentally, is other evidence for nonimitative speech. Like the use of "foots" as the plural of "foot" or the use of "gooder" as the comparative of "good," it indicates that the child is fitting his own language system into the one he was born into. Instead of deriding his error, his parents should accept with joy this evidence that he has been clever enough to figure out the principles that govern the language system he hears around him. That he hasn't yet learned which particular words have irregular forms is, by comparison, a small point.

4. Furthermore, his precociousness at this one job—learning a language—is inconsistent with the rest of his mental powers. Three-year-olds, for example, are cognitively very immature (as Piaget has shown)—yet they have a "feel" for syntax long before they can possibly understand the rules or benefit by teaching. Lenneberg and those who think like him do not claim that human beings are genetically programmed to learn a particular language, just that they have an inborn readiness for language *structure*.

An experiment that amplifies this last point (with entertaining as well as enlightening results) was undertaken by Harvard's Roger Brown, using sixteen children aged three to five. He showed them several pictures, each containing a pair of hands doing something to a substance on a surface or in a container. What was being done would properly be named with a verb (like cutting or kneading); the substance would properly be described with a mass noun (like fabric or dough); and the container, surface, or tool with a particular noun (like table, bowl, or knife). When the first picture was shown to the child, a nonsense word—*niss, sib,* or *latt*—was used in such a way as to indicate whether it was a verb, a mass noun, or a particular noun.

"In this picture," Brown would say, "you can see *sibbing.*" Then he'd present the other pictures and ask the child, "Now show me another picture of *sibbing.*" If the word was to be a mass noun, he'd point out "some *sib*" in the first picture, and ask the children to find "more *sib*" in the other pictures. In the case of particular nouns, he'd say, "There is a *sib* in this picture . . . Can you show me another *sib?*"

Of the sixteen children, ten equated *sibbing* with what was being done in the pictures; twelve identified "some *sib*" with the substance shown; and eleven pointed to the surface, container, or tool as examples of "a *sib.*"

"In the first trial with the first child," Brown reports, "I showed a picture of cloth being cut by an odd tool, said there was a *sib* in the picture and asked the child if he could show me another *sib.* While I was still fumbling around with the other three pictures, my subject swung around and pointed to the steam valve on the end of the radiator. 'There's a *sib*,' he said. And indeed the pictured tool looked very like the steam valve.

"In another case, when using *latt* as the nonsense word and a picture of hands manipulating a bulky substance protruding over the rim of a container, I said to the child, 'There's some *latt* in this picture.' He immediately replied, 'The *latt* is spilling.' And it was."

At older ages, too, our unconscious awareness of the rules of syntax affects behavior, W. A. Epstein is among those who have verified this fact by comparing the ease with which a group of individuals learned two strings of nonsense syllables and then two strings of English words arranged in meaningless sentences. He found that it was much easier for his subjects to learn and remember

A haky deebs reciled the dison tofently um flutest pav.
than to learn
        deebs haky the um flutest reciled pav a tofently dison

And, of the English word mixtures, this one
  Wavy books worked singing clouds to empty slow lamps.
was easier to learn than
  worked clouds slow empty to wavy singing books lamps
In each "easier" case, the words were arranged according to the rules of grammatical structure of the English language.

Language is popularly thought of as a system of communication, a way of sharing ideas and information with others; and indeed it is. We and everyone else in the same language community codify our experiences into words—arbitrarily chosen symbols that we have all agreed to use in the same way—and put those words together to make meaningful utterances.

But this use of language may be of less importance than its role in controlling thought. Language is to thought what a catalyst is to a chemical reaction: it starts it, speeds it up, facilitates the progression of a process that would go extremely slowly or perhaps not at all without it. Here are some examples of its function in this second role:

It is generally agreed that children have an innate ability to see a figure—a triangle, say—as distinct from its background. This is an ability they share with other mammals. But to learn the distinctive identity of that shape, to recognize it as different from some other shape, is an increased skill of such magnitude that only the primates seem capable of doing it. Rats, for example, can learn that food is to be found behind a black door labeled with a white triangle or behind a white door labeled with a black triangle, but since these discriminations must be learned separately it seems clear that rats cannot go beyond the discrimination of figure from ground. Children and chimpanzees, however, are not confused by the dark-light reversal; once they have found a reward in a box marked with a black triangle, they can find a reward in a box marked with a white triangle.

But then the human species forges ahead. In a famous series of experiments, Yale's Louis W. Gellerman compared the perceptual behavior of a little boy and a little girl, both two years old, and that of two young chimpanzees. The problems were the same for all subjects: to go from a starting chair to a panel upon which two geometric shapes were displayed, choose one, and (if the choice was correct) collect a cookie or a bit of fruit as a reward. The trials took place every morning at eleven, when it was presumed that the subjects would be beginning to get hungry. On this matter of motivation, Gellerman noted that the chimps seemed to be more eager for food than the children—but the children nevertheless outperformed the animals.

There were two perceptual bridges that the chimps could not cross. After having learned that a triangle was the correct choice, the children—but not the chimpanzees—realized that they were still seeing a triangle when it appeared as at left in FIGURE 27A and with its sides bulged and rounded as at left in FIGURE 27B. What the children had learned was the concept of triangularity; they had discovered that *three-sidedness* was the heart of the problems that were being set them.

And how had they done this? Gellerman credited their use of language, which occurred *before* the action implied took place and which he viewed as their way of organizing their behavior. On first seeing the triangle, the little girl—obviously a precocious child—said, "There's a A!," and when she later saw it in the outline form of dots she said, "That's a funny A, isn't he?"

In another series of problems, testing the ability of the children and the chimpanzees to discriminate forms from their backgrounds, the little boy made nineteen successive errors. But he hesitated a great deal on the eighteenth and nineteenth trials, and then on the twentieth he pointed to the correct form and said to himself, "Over here, huh?" He made no further errors, chanting, "This way, this way, this way," as he approached the correct symbol.

And, for another example:

The Russian psychologist Alexander R. Luria and his colleagues at the University of Moscow have done many experiments whose object is to understand the role of speech in mediating thought, and through thought, behavior. In each, the child is asked to press a bulb to signal a perceptual discrimination. The bulb is connected by flexible tubing to a paper-covered moving drum upon which an inked stylus makes a record of the bulb-pressings—a technique similar to that used in medical diagnosis for recording brain waves or heartbeats.

One such experiment uses pictures of a red airplane on a yellow background and a green airplane on a gray background. The figures are perceptually dominant, and three-year-old children can easily learn to press the bulb with the right hand when they see the red plane and press the bulb with the left hand when they

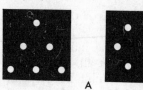

A   B

FIGURE 27

Louis Gellerman found that children were more successful than chimpanzees in identifying as triangular the left figure in each pair above; that is, human beings are more capable of realizing that the key fact about triangles is their three-sidedness rather than details of configuration.

see the green plane. But not until they are five or older can they normally do the same thing when the experimenter asks them to respond to the perceptually less important element in each picture, the yellow or gray background.

However, the result is quite different when the younger children are told to press the bulb with the right hand when the yellow-ground picture is shown "because planes can fly when the sun is shining and the sky is yellow"; and with the left hand when the gray-ground picture is shown "because when it's raining planes can't fly and have to be stopped." In the overwhelming majority of cases, three- and four-year-olds are then able to "see" the backgrounds instead of the figures. The use of language facilitates perceptual discrimination.

A comparable exercise demonstrates how speech controls motor responses at different states of development.

If one asks a two-year-old to squeeze a bulb, he can follow directions; but he cannot stop on command. It's the same problem one faces when trying to persuade a toddler to take his stockings *off* while he is engaged in pulling them *on*. An adult's verbal instructions can start an action but cannot stop one already begun.

However, what if you rig your apparatus so that the child's own activity produces a signal that ends the action? Give him the job of pressing a bulb but arrange the apparatus so that a light will go off or a bell will ring when he presses. Then, 75 percent of children aged two to three can not only initiate the action but voluntarily terminate it when they see the light go off or cease to hear the bell. The heard or seen signal has served to coordinate the experimenter's verbal instructions and the child's motor response.

Finally, suppose you ask the child to press the bulb when the light goes on. A child under three can't do this at all, because you have asked him to *anticipate* action . . . to inhibit his response until a future event occurs. Nor will older children perform much better. Look at FIGURE 28A. This is the record of a little girl aged three years nine months; you can see that she pressed the bulb without reference to the light's going on and off. But after she was told, "When you see the light go on, say 'Go!' When you say 'Go!', press the bulb," her behavior changed as shown in FIGURE 28B.

Again, behavior was controlled by a perceived signal: when the child ceased to hear the word "Go!" she stopped pressing the bulb. But this time it was an internally initiated, self-given signal. As children grow older, speech becomes increasingly internalized. Eventually it is enough simply to *think* "Go!"; the thought alone will start or stop an action. This is why the University of Minnesota's James Jenkins once referred to language as "the queen of all the response systems"—because it can be extended to cope with any other kind of behavior.

(I should add at this point that linguists are not half so certain as psychologists that language controls thought and, through it, behavior. There is a small intramural controversy here—one that the linguists hope to resolve as they learn just how children *do* internalize their language.)

Now let's consider the developmental chronology of human speech, as you might observe it in your own baby.

At three months or so, he begins to babble: verbal play, a trying-out of every sound he can make. Interestingly, most of his first sounds do not appear in adult speech. O. C. Irwin and H. P. Chen once kept a vowel and consonant frequency count, using phonetic symbols, and found that infants are eleven months old on the average before they have shifted the sounds they spontaneously babble to the sounds they hear about them.

How they do this is a great feat and a great mystery, for the child must learn to discriminate some forty° basic sounds, and all of them will be pronounced with slight differences by speakers

---

° The exact number of basic speech sounds, or phonemes, is disputed because linguists use different methods of differentiating and recording them.

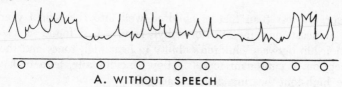

O O   O   O   O O   O   O

A. WITHOUT SPEECH

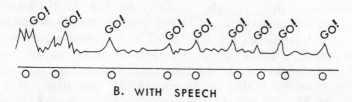

O O   O   O O   O O O   O

B. WITH SPEECH

O = LIGHT GOING ON

FIGURE 28

Asked to press a bulb when a light goes on, young children have great difficulty coordinating observation and reaction, as the upper graph shows. When speech is added as a mediator, Alexander Luria has found, performance improves dramatically (lower graph). (Adapted from *Role of Speech in the Regulation of Normal & Abnormal Behavior* by Alexander R. Luria. Copyright © 1961 by Pergamon Press, Ltd. Reproduced by permission of the Liveright Publishing Corporation.)

within any given group and sometimes even by the same person. (Next time you're at a party, ask the other guests to say "fork," "marry," or "wash" and listen for the differences.)

One clue as to the auditory cues that aid young children in this difficult task comes from the work of George A. Miller and P. E. Nicely. They suggest that what the child hears is not initially a particular sound, but what the linguists call a "feature"—the characteristic way in which various sounds are made. *T, k,* and *p,* for example, are recognized first as belonging to an organically similar class of sounds; the second step is to discriminate one from the other.

There is also some evidence that children are prone to recognize some sounds more readily than others. (Genetic predisposition, again?) The general auditory acuity of very young children is measurably less than that of children well into the school years; and at least one investigator—Sibyl Henry—has found a clear relationship between children's ability to hear high tones and their perception of consonant sounds. (Boys, incidentally, tend to have more high-tone hearing deficit than girls.)

"An adult does not always need to hear completely what is being said, because his experience can fill in many sounds that his ears miss," Henry remarks. "However, the more limited knowledge and experience of the child may result in the misinterpretation of sounds that his ears have failed to distinguish accurately."

In general, however, children can discriminate all but the most difficult sounds—in words like "little" and "pickle," for instance, which sound much alike at the end—by the time they are five years old. This was one of the findings of a 1957 survey of almost five hundred three- to eight-year-old children by the University of Minnesota's Mildred C. Templin. As for their ability to articulate these sounds themselves, she found that:

► By age three they could correctly say 93 percent of vowels and 65 percent of simple consonants (as in "pig" or "bed");

► By age five they were up to 85 percent correct on simple consonants;

► By age six they were scoring 88 percent on doubled consonants (like *ch* in "chip" or *wh* in "whistle");

► And by age seven they scored 94 percent on triple blends (like the *skr* sound in "scratch" or the *mpt* in "prompt").

Overall, the average score at age three was 53.3 and at age eight was 94.9—which means that the average American's ability to articulate correctly the basic sounds of his language is half-developed by age three and virtually at the adult level by age eight.

And what about the development of meaningful speech?

Somewhere around nine months of age, babies begin to produce real words, although it is unlikely that they comprehend this young that their words have meaning. ("Mama" doesn't count as a bona-fide first word until it is abundantly clear that the baby is referring to one particular person when he says the word.) However, babies of this age seem to *understand* words, perhaps with the help of the accompanying intonation or gestures. By ten months most children can follow instructions such as "Show me the ball," or will lift a foot when Grandma asks, "Where are Baby's toes?"

The big step, at twelve to fifteen months, is the child's discovery that words refer to things. As he and his mother go about their daily business, she names objects, people, animals, events. "See the dog, Billy," she says; and Billy forthwith finds himself engaged in a number of mental exercises. He must connect the utterance "dog" with the specific dog referred to. But since his mother does not always use the word to describe the same dog, he must also form a hypothesis about the categorical nature of what is being named when he hears the word. Then he must test his hypothesis by naming a few dogs himself. If he says "Dog!" when he sees Lassie on TV, his mother will murmur approval; but if he says "Dog!" when he spots the neighbor's cat sunning herself on the porch steps, he will be corrected—thus firming up his dog category and starting one for cats.

As one might expect from this initial emphasis on naming things, children's early vocabularies are heavily weighted with nouns. According to a study made in 1930 by Dorothea McCarthy of the University of Minnesota's Institute of Child Welfare, nouns compose 50 percent of the beginning speaker's vocabulary, but by age five are down to 19 percent. Verbs and pronouns double in proportion during the same period of time, and the interjections that make up some 16 percent of a toddler's speech—"Oh!", "Ouch!", "Ooh!"—are down to 1 percent before he's five.

To attempt to specify the "average" child's—or adult's—total vocabulary is tricky business. Not only must one differentiate between vocabularies of use and vocabularies of recognition, but in addition there is tremendous variation within age groups. Mary Katherine Smith once found that the vocabularies of six-year-olds can range from fifty-five hundred to thirty-two thousand words, and that within a single school system the highest scoring first- and second-graders knew more basic words than did the poorest student in every grade level up to and including the eleventh grade.

So I will summarize the various studies on vocabulary size by using the comparatives cited by Benjamin Bloom in a survey of children's intellectual achievements at given ages. He says that by age six, children have 50 percent of the vocabulary they will have at age eight and at age eight have 50 percent of the vocabulary they will have at age eighteen. Again, the importance of the early childhood years looms large.

The way children learn to put their words together to form sentences was the subject of an early study (1926) by Madorah Smith of the University of Iowa's Child Welfare Research Station. She noted, as have many others, that most children begin speaking in one-word "sentences," amplified by gestures. When a toddler says, "Mama!" he can mean "Mama, come here!" or "Mama, look!" or "Mama, give!" But he soon gets the knack of sentence structure, and many two-year-olds say things like "What's that?" or "I write paper." (Use of prepositions like "on" is still beyond a child of this age.)

The very young child doesn't really converse. Even at three, and in company, much of his talk is monologue, a running commentary on what he's doing. At play in a nursery school sandbox, he says: "I am making cake. I make something out of sand. I want some. I want some more. Let me pat."* But now listen to a five-year-old in the same play situation: "Let's fix this road up. See, let's make a ditch along the road. Have a big hole, see. Hey, get your hand out of the way." This child is clearly using language to share his thoughts and wishes with others.

After she had recorded these and many other utterances of children aged two to five, Madorah Smith tabulated the average number of words, by age, in children's sentences. So did Dorothea McCarthy. (Women seem to have more tolerance than men for this kind of finicky research.) Both investigators found that four or five words constituted the average sentence of a five-year-old. But Mildred Templin, compiling the same kind of records approximately thirty years later, discovered that the newer generation of children spoke in longer sentences, five-year-olds on the average using six words and up to twelve on occasion. This is probably due, she thinks, to the personalized attention to each child which characterizes the "permissive" mode of child-rearing that has been fashionable since the mid-1940s (you have to talk to them a lot)—

* This kind of discourse, according to Piaget, is descriptive only; it reflects the child's egocentric nature. Not so, says the Russian psychologist L. S. Vigotsky; it is self-directive. The child is communicating with *himself*. The two men have been fighting this battle for forty years, but have acquired partisans in the United States only recently—Piaget's work having been unappreciated here in the 1930s and Vigotsky's work having been suppressed in Russia because it didn't adhere closely enough to that of the revered Pavlov.

and also to the presence of television in most homes from about the same time.

McCarthy and Templin are only two of the many investigators who have observed the developing language patterns of children and have come to the same conclusions about three important points. Whether you are measuring discrimination of speech sounds, articulation of those sounds, growth of vocabulary, or development of sentence structure:

1. Girls are ahead of boys by about a year—until around age eight.

2. Children from upper class homes are ahead of children from lower class homes—at all ages. ("Upper class homes" are defined in these studies as those in which the father's occupation is professional, managerial, or clerical; "lower class homes" are those in which the father's occupation is semiskilled, slightly skilled, or unskilled.)

3. By the time children go to kindergarten most have mastered the basics of language. Templin found that about half the remarks of three-year-olds are grammatically correct, and McCarthy noted that "the development of the sentence is practically complete by age five." The school years, in short, are used for polishing and perfecting—for making the child's language conform to generally accepted standards of "good English"—rather than for building the linguistic structure itself.

Writing is a fairly recent invention; the Sumerians of 3100 B.C. are credited with the creation of the word-syllabic system that we use today. Writing is not necessary to the preservation of a culture, for primitive peoples pass on orally their accumulated wisdom to each new generation. But writing *is* necessary to the advancement of a civilization. Even five thousand years ago, mankind's accumulated knowledge was sufficiently specialized and record keeping was sufficiently complex• so that human memory and oral transmission (both notoriously fallible) were poor vessels for the storage of that knowledge. Today, the world's libraries are jammed and new knowledge pours out at such a rate that the only way to keep it until someone needs it is to put it in writing.

The ability to read is therefore central to the educational process to which those of us who live in modern industrialized nations expose our young. That this skill is at the core of our culture

is witnessed by the emotionalism that surrounds the regularly recurring controversies over methods of teaching reading—which, in
this country, have swung in a kind of cyclical fashion for the
past seventy years between teaching methods based on the way
words sound and on the way words look.

Stress on phonics was dominant in the early years of this century, but when reading research showed that adult readers' eyes
move along a line of text in a series of jumps, taking in several
word shapes at a single glance, educators thought it made sense
to teach children to read in the mode they would use as adults.
From the 1920s onward, therefore, word recognition—the "look-
say" method—was a favored teaching technique.

Then, in the 1930s, Rudolf Flesch's *Why Johnny Can't Read*
had such impact on the public that parents pressured the schools
to use more phonics-oriented methods. A number of variants have
been developed, the most interesting in many respects being a
beginner's alphabet (See FIGURE 29) from which children shift to
the standard English alphabet in second or third grade. The 1967
publication of *Reading: The Great Debate,* a well-publicized and
readable (but controversial°) book by Jeanne Chall, will probably
further encourage instructional emphasis on the relationship between sounds and letters.

It is a shame that so much polarization of attitude has occurred,
for quantities of research have shown that some children learn
better with one approach; that other children learn better with the
other approach; and that most children learn to read regardless
of the method used. In 1967, to give a recent example, the results
of a very large comparative study coordinated by Guy Bond for
the U. S. Office of Education were published. In these, first-grade
programs using word recognition approaches were contrasted with
programs using phonetic approaches. The results have comforted
neither pedagogical camp, for in tests of spelling, vocabulary, word

° Rudolf Flesch wrote as a "concerned layman," but Mrs. Chall, a professor
at Harvard's School of Education, has written a quasi-scholarly book. Intended
to be read by the general public, it also reviews and evaluates a half century
of research on reading methods and results. It is this latter aspect of the
book that has aroused the ire of some other professional educators. They
say that Mrs. Chall's inclusion of scholarly material as well as her own status
as a professor gives the book a stamp of authority which makes her conclusion
more convincing to the public—but that the research does not support her
enthusiastic endorsement of a phonics-oriented "code-breaking" approach.

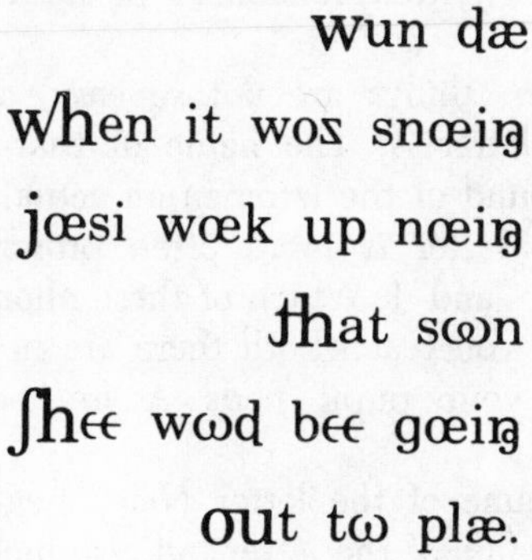

wun dæ

when it woz snœiŋ

jœsi wœk up nœiŋ

that sœn

ʃhεε wɷd bεε gœiŋ

ɷut tɷ plæ.

Figure 29

This sample page of text uses the Initial Teaching Alphabet (ITA), in which letters with several sounds are replaced by symbols for specific sounds. Proponents of the system, which was developed in England, say that children have no difficulty shifting to the standard English alphabet after cutting their teeth on ITA. (From *Josie and the Snow* by Helen E. Buckley, illustrated by Evaline Ness [Initial Teaching Alphabet Edition]. Copyright © 1964 by Lothrop, Lee & Shepard Co., Inc. Reproduced by permission of the publisher.)

meaning, and paragraph meaning children trained by either method did equally well.

My own opinion, offered in both a spirit of conciliation and because I think that the paragraphs which follow will support it, is that equal attention should be given to helping the child master sounds *and* shapes; more, that this is a requirement which grows out of the structure of the English language itself.

Keeping in mind that in learning to read the essential job is to associate printed symbols with words that one has already learned to speak, listen to Roger Brown on the subject of letter sounds:

"If our writing were consistently phonetic, you would simply teach first-graders the letters of the alphabet corresponding to each sound, give them a little practice in analyzing words into sound elements, and they would have reading vocabularies as large as their speaking vocabularies. The child would spell out each new word, recognize the result as one of his familiar speech forms, and understand the written version as he understands its spoken equivalent.

"In fact, however, things are not so easy, and this is clearly illustrated by the letter A. The name of that letter is *ay*. This is sometimes the sound of the letter in an actual word (as in "ate" or "ape") but the letter is more often pronounced as a short vowel (as in "at" or "and"). Which of these phonetic values should you teach? Even if you teach both there are horrible errors to be anticipated when your pupil finds A in "boat," "peak," and "beauty."

"As for B, the name of the letter (*bee*) begins with the most common phonetic value of the letter but also includes a vowel that is not ordinarily associated with the letter (as it is not in "but" or "bill"). Then, ought one to tell children about "doubt" and "debt" in which B has no sound?

"Some letters have names which do not even contain the sound most commonly associated with the letter. The sound of H is usually that heard in "he," but that sound is not contained in *aitch,* the name of the letter . . ."

And so on. But the problem is not just that the English *alphabet* is inconsistent in its phonetic values. In addition, English *words* are only in part based on the principle of single letter-single sound correspondence. They are also constructed on another system—the use of "meaning units."

When a reader sees words like "followed" or "eating," it is the function of the suffixes that is the most important thing about these letters. The addition of "-ed" and "-ing" changes verb tenses, just as "-al" changes nouns into adjectives and "-ly" changes adjectives into adverbs. When "nation" becomes "national," we change the sound of the *a* in the first syllable, and when "origin" becomes "original," we change the stress—but these sound changes are secondary to the basic fact about those words and thousands of others, which is that a given prefix or suffix preserves their meaning. (And we should give thanks to our unknown forebears who worked out the system; think of how many fewer words we have to learn.)

As a result, beginning readers must learn to recognize, in such words as "seeds" or "sails," that the single letter "s" is both the symbol for a sound and for a meaning unit. In case you're thinking that this is not so difficult, because the meaning unit—the "s" that pluralizes—always comes at the end, consider the case of "under" and "undo"; or think about the word "ringing," in which the meaning unit is a three-letter grouping tacked onto an identical three-letter grouping that *isn't* a meaning unit.

And keep in mind, please, that at the same time that a six-year-old child is being asked to make such distinctions as these, he is having to wrestle with the visual problems inherent in discriminating between graphic shapes that are confusingly similar. To recapture some sense of *that* problem, turn back to the pictures of Eleanor Gibson's artificial alphabet and ask yourself how easy it would be to learn words and sentences composed of those forms. Essentially, this is what the beginning reader is asked to do. The shape of the letters is immaterial; it's discriminating among them and finding correspondences with spoken language that is difficult.

Marie Clay's close observations of the reading practices of five- to six-year-old children led her to the conclusion that the characteristic approach is "intuitive, irrational, and illogical." Beginning readers depend upon auditory memory of the text and upon their own expectations of word sequences or grammatical structure in spoken language.

When the text says, "Come to breakfast," the child may read, "Come and have your breakfast"—a substitution that is perfectly acceptable from a linguistic standpoint. Clay found that over half of word-substitution errors are of this type. It is the sense of the material that the child is after; it may take him a year of practice to discover that each word or sentence carries a *precise* message.

As children make progress in the visual identification of individual letters or words, the probabilities of successful guesswork further improve. Here is Marie Clay's record of the code-breaking effort of a child who got stuck on "after" in the sentence, "Look after Timothy":

"It wouldn't be 'at,'" he said. "It's too long." [Visual matching of word lengths.]

"It wouldn't be 'hats.'" [Linguistically awkward; "Look hats" doesn't make sense.]

"And it wouldn't be 'are,' it's too long too." [Visual matching, again.]

The child finally gave up—but note that two of his guesses correctly identified the word as one beginning with *a* and that all three guesses had two letters in common with the word he was (pardon the pun) after.

Cornell University's Gabrielle Marchbanks and Harry Levin recently tested a group of one hundred kindergarten and first-grade children in an effort to find out which cues they use in recognizing words. They showed the children a nonsense word like *cug* and then asked them to pick out the word most like it from the following array: *arp* (same overall shape); *che* (same first letter but other letters and shape different); *tuk* (same second letter but other letters and shape different); or *ilg* (same third letter but other letters and shape different).

They found that the first letter was the cue most utilized— that is, *che* was most often picked—and that the last letter, as exemplified by *ilg*, was the second most utilized cue. For the younger children, there was great competition between the first and last letters, a fact that is consistent with young children's lack of spatial orientation and their tendency to read from right to left. *Arp* was the least-chosen word, from which Marchbanks and Levin conclude that overall word shape is the least-used word identification clue among beginning readers.

It may be that letter discrimination is a helpful preamble to reading words by shape. Fewer visual cues would be needed as the child progressively learns the sequential probabilities linking the various letters in a written language, and more and more words could be read at a glance.

Marie Clay's summary is a good one. She says that children learn to read by "manipulating a network of cues and relationships. Cues exist along several dimensions which parallel in written language some of the dimensions that are already well-developed in the child's spoken language. As new dimensions are added—such as letter knowledge, word knowledge, letter-sound associations, and syllabic awareness—the chances of detection and correction of error are increased . . . Good readers succeed not by making few errors but by learning how to detect and overcome them."

The overall process is akin to the learning of a sport such as tennis. Body position and coordination of limbs are uniformly awkward at first; next, you experience a gradual but uneven improvement—the forehand swing is better than the backhand, say; and then, all of a sudden, everything meshes and you've become an accomplished player.

CHAPTER 15

INFORMATION PROCESSING

It is typical of young children to label as "dogs" all objects that have four legs and move. In time, they learn to differentiate dogs from other creatures that have four legs, and one breed of dog from another. So it is too with all other objects and events in the world around them: originally "global" and undifferentiated perceptions become more detailed and discriminating, the net yield being a tremendous amount of specific information.

This would be a vast cognitive overload if it were not for a simultaneous process, the increasing ability of a child to fit these specifics into abstract concepts. In other words, at the same time that Billy is learning to differentiate dogs from cats, he is learning to group both into the category of "animal."

The two processes are equally important, for the mature individual copes successfully with his world in proportion to the amount of specific knowledge he has of it, yet at the same time he would function at a tremendous disadvantage—in fact, he might not be able to function at all—if he had to dredge up from memory each individual encounter with his environment. He would be in the unhappy position of a person with a lot of money, all of it in pennies.

So how does the growing child go about this dual process of expanding his detailed knowledge of the universe and compacting this knowledge into some efficient and usable form? How, to repeat the analogy, does he convert the pennies into dollars?

When a hungry rat stands facing a black door and a white door, behind one of which is food, its characteristic pattern of choice is trial and error. Sooner or later (sooner if it's a bright rat, later if it isn't), the percentage of correct choices will begin to rise above the level of chance (50 percent) on a learning curve, and will thereafter build up at a slow but steady rate. Psychologists of the stimulus-response school say that learning has resulted because one of the initially random responses of the rat was rewarded by food and each such reinforcement has further strengthened that particular response. Learning, in this view, builds up via many small increments.

An illustration of this kind of learning may be found in B. F. Skinner's laboratory work with pigeons. Skinner bypasses the stage during which one waits for an animal to make a response which can then be reinforced. If he wants to teach a pigeon to peck at one card rather than another, he programs each step of the behavior —beginning with the reward of a kernel or two of grain whenever a free-moving pigeon turns its body or head or takes a step in the direction of the wall where the cards are posted. (Because the pigeon's spontaneous behavior, when in the desired direction, must be rewarded instantaneously, Skinner-does not rely on the human hand to throw out grain. He uses a bell, whistle, or metal "cricket" in the Pavlovian way. The pigeon becomes conditioned to the sound as the reinforcer and the grain as the immediately following reward.)

By stages, then, the pigeon's behavior follows the direction set by the trainer. Eventually Skinner has the pigeon poised in front of the cards. Any upward movement of the head is reinforced and rewarded, likewise any peck at either card. And so on: to peck one card rather than the other comes next, and pretty soon the pigeon "knows" the difference between, say, a ten of diamonds and a three of spades. This is only the beginning. Pigeons can learn extremely fine discriminations, and will continue to peck at whatever they have learned to peck without requiring constant reinforcement. In fact, they will peck hundreds of times between rewards, so long as reward comes at periodic intervals.

Incidentally, a bizarre World War II project grew out of these experiments, one that Skinner himself describes as "a crackpot idea, born on the wrong side of the tracks intellectually speaking"—but one whose rationale he still defends.

Pigeons are lighter, less bulky, and more reliable than the radio-guidance equipment that was available to missile designers in the late 1930s. So Skinner taught dozens of pigeons to peck at a moving image projected on a wire-gridded glass, and they became part of proposed three-pigeon, seven-pigeon, and nine-pigeon missile guidance systems. (See FIGURE 30.) A lens in the missile's nose projected an image of the target on the screen; pecking indicated that the missile was on course, diminished pecking indicated that the missile was drifting off course; and automatic steering equipment then made the necessary correction. (Yes, pigeons *can* peck fast enough to keep a missile on course when traveling at a rate of six hundred

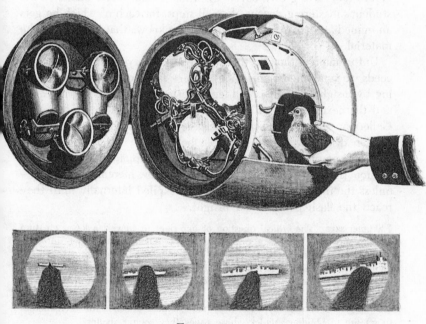

FIGURE 30

B. F. Skinner's pigeons that never went to war were trained to ride in the nose of a guided missile and there peck at an image of the target on a gridded screen. Automatic steering equipment adjusted the missile's course in response to the rate at which the pigeons pecked.

miles per hour!) Luckily for all those pigeons, however,* the committee of scientists in wartime government service who were asked to evaluate Skinner's project turned it down. Skinner recalls his final demonstration, so:

"One can talk about phase lag in pursuit behavior and discuss mathematical predictions of hunting without reflecting too closely upon what is inside the black box. But the spectacle of a living pigeon carrying out its assignment, no matter how beautifully, simply reminded the committee of how utterly fantastic our proposal was. The merriment was restrained but it was there, and it was obvious that our case was lost."

The training technique used on the pigeons has had wide application to human learning, however. Programs for the teaching machines that have grown out of work like Skinner's are based on the student's mastering dozens of small steps, for each of which he gets an immediate reward: awareness that he knows that segment of the material.

Unfortunately, though, the underlying theory—that learning proceeds via small increments—doesn't very satisfactorily explain learning by insight. Insight is sudden: one moment you haven't a clue, and the next moment all the pieces have fallen into place. (In the Gellerman study discussed in the preceding chapter, the little boy's sudden discovery of the principle behind the correct choice is a perfect example of insight.) To learn in this apparently single-jump fashion is inconsistent with a theory of slow-increment learning—unless the increments are somehow stockpiled internally until they reach the flash point called insight.

* Skinner says, "The ethical question of our right to convert a lower creature into an unwitting hero is a peacetime luxury. There were bigger questions to be answered in the late thirties." He mentions other nations' alleged efforts of the same type as his Project Pigeon: programs to train dogs to blow up tanks, seals to blow up submarines, and sea lions to cut mine cables. It has also been rumored, he says, that one of the Powers intended to (or did) use swarms of bats with time bombs attached to their bodies to set fire to buildings under whose eaves they sought shelter.

A more benign exploitation of animals is credited to the British, who are said to have sent their own submarines through the English Channel, releasing food to the surface. Gulls, who can easily see submarines from the air, learned to follow them. Whether a given submarine was British or German was, of course, immaterial to the gulls—but not to human spotters on land. When they knew the British submarines were not in the vicinity, an offshore flock of gulls took on a very special significance.

This is essentially what modern S-R theory proposes—the presence of internal "mediating responses" which are created as offshoots of basic S-R reactions. The belief is that some portion of the initial response remains as a nervous-system residue, links up to another stimulus, and leads to a response that differs from the original one. Because this new S-R linkage is internal, its overt expression would not seem to be a consequence of the initial stimulus—and the expressed response could appear to come out of the blue.

To demonstrate the existence of mediating responses, Tracy and Howard Kendler and Doris Wells employed a three-part discrimination test that is much used by psychologists to measure rate of learning. First, the subjects are required to learn a discrimination based on brightness: to choose a white box, say, rather than a black one. Next, they are given a problem based on height; this time the correct choice is a tall box rather than a short one. The third, and telling, problem combines both dimensions—brightness and height —while at the same time reversing *one* of the previously learned choices. Let's say the reversal shift occurs on the brightness dimension, and the correct choice is now a tall black box.

The Kendlers, who are now at the University of California at Santa Barbara, theorized that the speed with which their subjects learned this third problem would indicate the kind of learning mechanism used. Their reasoning was as follows:

1. If learning occurs as a result of a unitary S-R reaction, the habit to choose white would have to be extinguished before the habit to choose black could be established—and therefore the rate of learning the third problem should be slower than the rate of learning the second problem (in which no previous learning had to be eliminated).

2. If internal mediating responses are present, however, the third problem should be learned faster than the second problem—because the entire second problem is new, whereas only *part* of the third problem (the reversal from white to black) is new. To choose a tall box is still a correct choice, and this knowledge could be transferred via the internal mediators—a short-cut that would speed learning.

Other experiments had shown that the first learning pattern is characteristic of rats—either they lack mediating responses, or single-unit S-R learning predominates. But human learning follows the second pattern. So we must possess mediating responses. If so, do we have them from birth? Or how early are they acquired?

The Kendlers and their colleague first tested a group of five- to six-year-olds on discrimination problems like those described above. They found that children who were fast learners during the practice period performed on the actual tests like adults would, whereas children who were slow learners during the practice period performed on the tests like rats would.

Then the three investigators tested a group of three- to five-year-olds. The learning pattern of these nursery school children was an exaggerated version of the kindergarteners'. Some showed clear-cut positive transfer from the brightness and height discrimination problems to the reversal-shift problem, and others showed equally marked negative transfer. The variability was so extreme that the Kendlers believe they have located a developmental watershed. They therefore suggest that infants learn, like rats, via unitary S-R associations; but that mediating responses begin to form somewhere around the third year of life, with subsequent rapid growth in the child's ability to learn by insight.

Cognitive theorists disgree. Any kind of unit with an S at one end and an R at the other, hidden or not, puts the learning process on too mechanistic and rigid a basis to suit people like Harry Harlow. He would agree that trial and error learning usually precedes learning by insight, and that adult learning differs from that of children, but insists that the neurological mechanism—whatever it is—must permit the organism to acquire general patterns of response rather than specific linkages.

He says, "By the time a monkey has run 232 discriminations and followed these by 112 discriminations and reversals, he does not possess 344 or 456 specific habits, bonds, connections, or associations. He does have a generalized ability to learn *any* discrimination with the greatest of ease; he has *learned how to learn efficiently* in the situations he frequently encounters."

Harlow calls this ability a "learning set," and has demonstrated its development by recording monkeys' learning behavior throughout a long series of similar problems. In one series, for example, the monkeys were required to choose one of two objects. In another, the object's position was the clue to the right choice. In a third series, the job was to identify the one object out of three which differed from the two others. In each series, as many as a hundred individual discriminations were required.

Harlow's unit of measurement was the percentage of correct responses on each monkey's second trial—this figure being the amount learned on the *first* trial. FIGURE 31 shows a given monkey's learning pattern at the beginning and end of a series. The lower curve, a record of the first six attempts to learn a particular problem, is a typical trial and error pattern—slow but steady. The upper curve records the same monkey's performance on the first six tries at solving a later problem of the same general type. It had indeed learned how to learn. Learning was not only faster (97 percent versus 53 percent, on the second try) but more accurate (99 percent versus 78 percent, by the sixth try).

"The learning set," Harlow says, "transforms the organism from a creature that adapts to a changing environment by trial and error to one that adapts by seeming insight." In other words, insight is

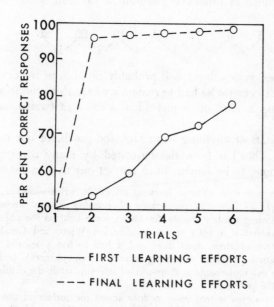

FIGURE 31

When men or monkeys start to learn a problem, their first efforts are by slow trial and error (lower curve). But once they have formed what Harry Harlow calls a "learning set," their performance on a similar problem speeds up spectacularly (upper curve).

not really a bolt from the blue; it simply reflects the learner's mastery of the principles that govern any systematic task.° Insight is predictive. By acquiring a hypothesis against which prospective action can be tested, the learner is freed from the slower process of attending to each detail of each problem that comes his way.

You can test the utility of such short-cut learning by duplicating an experiment done by the University of Michigan's George Katona. Give two friends the following series of numbers to be memorized:

$$5\ 8\ 1\ 2\ 1\ 5\ 1\ 9\ 2\ 2\ 2\ 6$$

See that one of them learns it just as printed above; wait a week; and ask him to recall it. He is unlikely to be able to do so. When you put the same problem to the other friend, however, explain the principle of organization: that there is a difference of 3 and then 4 between groups of numbers. Diagram it for him, so:

A week later, your subject will probably be able to remember the series. That's because he had to remember only three numerals with a relationship to each other instead of a chain of twelve unrelated numerals.

Twelve units of anything is, in fact, too much for our minds to cope with. This has been demonstrated by many investigators—although some, to be honest, have not set out to demonstrate that

° No one has ever seen either a learning set or an S-R association (unitary or mediating); in fact, the psychology of learning is way ahead of its physiology. Among the few studies that throw some light on the physiological processes involved is a 1964 report by Sheldon White and Gerald Plum. They set sixteen children, aged three and a half to five years old, a series of discrimination problems (choosing between two pictures) and photographed their eye movements at three-second intervals while the children were working on the problems.

The children's eyes moved more rapidly across the surface of the pictures *just before* they solved each problem. This behavior, White and Plum say, is reminiscent of the side-to-side head movements that rats are often seen to make just before they successfully learn a maze. Some "rat psychologists" have felt that these scanning peaks signify the animal's final adoption of a hypothesis; i.e., that it is demonstrating insightful learning. So too with the young subjects of White and Plum. They showed no appreciable rise in percent of correct choices until they suddenly "got it"—and the moment before successful choice was made was accompanied by heightened eye movements.

fact, or have offered some other explanation for their subjects' failure to learn material that in truth was simply more than their brains could handle in (pardon the mixed metaphor) one gulp.

Take rote learning: of the alphabet, the multiplication table, or the spelling of new words. Children are generally believed to learn these and similar tasks as a result of repetitive drill. The psychological theory behind the belief is that one saying of A, B, C, and on to Z, or a single recital of "one times two is two, two times two is four," etc., establishes only a thin and tentative connection between contiguous items, and that repetition is required to strengthen the linkages. And indeed it *is* true that both as children and as adults we often require repeated exposure to a list of words or a section of text before we can confidently say that we know it.

But does that circumstance prove that repetition is necessary for learning? No, says the educational psychologist Irvin Rock of Yeshiva University: there are too many exceptions to the rule. Children often understand and use correctly a new word after one telling of its meaning; adults often remember the name of a stranger after one mention of it; and even in laboratory experiments where subjects are required to learn long lists of nonsense syllables, they remember one or two of them after one try.

Might it not be, Rock suggests, that the learner is simply being asked to learn too much, and that what he is really doing when he engages in repetitive drill is to learn some additional part of the material with every repetition? And if that's the case, why not abandon boring drill, and instead undertake to learn smaller amounts of material each time one tries?

Rock did a series of experiments in which subjects were required to learn a list of eight paired nonsense syllables—like FAX-SOQ or GEY-NUR—under different sets of circumstances. Among them were these:

1. Subjects were shown the same eight pairs of syllables until they learned them.

2. After each try, pairs that subjects had not learned were removed from the list and replaced by different pairs.

The result? Both groups learned at the same rate, requiring on the average about eight trials to learn eight pairs of nonsense syllables. Whether a given pair had been presented to them once or seven times was immaterial. In other words, those in Group 1 did not familiarize themselves somewhat with all the syllables and gradually commit them to memory. They learned them sequentially, but in one shot, like the subjects in Group 2.

(This is not to devalue repetition as a tool of *memory*. In fact, the group that had learned by the traditional method of repetitive drill was retested some weeks later, and remembered best those syllables out of the eight pairs that they had learned first and therefore had repeated with each subsequent try. The technical term for this experience, incidentally, is "overlearning.")

During the experiment itself, Rock says, "interference" accounted for the subjects' learning only one or two of the eight pairs with each try. As far back as 1885, he notes, the great German psychologist Hermann Ebbinghaus had discovered that the longer you make a list the more time is required to learn any single item on it. A list of ten items might require 52 seconds, or a little more than five seconds per item, whereas a list of thirty-six items might require 792 seconds, or twenty-two seconds per item.

The implication is clear: in rote learning, set a child, or set yourself, the job of learning only a few items at one session. The next time you tackle the same material, repeat those items that have already been learned (as insurance against forgetting) and then go on to learn a few more. But don't try to memorize a lot of material at once. You may end up by learning none of it.

In perception, too, we have an astonishingly small capacity for recall. Test this ability in yourself by having someone toss down varying numbers of marbles or beans or pennies and check your ability to enumerate the number on the table after you take just one quick look. Unless you are extraordinary, your accuracy curve will plunge sharply downward whenever more than five objects are on the table. After hearing a list of numerals read, few of us can jot down from memory more than seven or eight of them. And the same is true of letters or words: the recall of six to eight, from a randomly chosen list, seems to be our limit.

Harvard's George A. Miller once discussed this brake on our mental powers in a paper with the beguiling title of *The Magic Number Seven, Plus or Minus Two*, but before I quote from it, it is necessary to consider some important concepts from cybernetics. Cybernetics, a twentieth-century science, is the study of automatic control systems; and it defines "information" in a rather specialized way.

A message put into a communication system has to be transformed—as when, for instance, the sound of a voice is converted into

electromagnetic impulses for radio transmission—and then recon-
stituted by the hearer. The meaning of the message is unimportant
when one is considering the transmission process; what matters is
that one particular message should be picked out as correct. Therefore, "information" is defined as the choice of one message from a
pool of possible alternative messages.

The simplest such choice is one that is made between two possibilities which are equally likely—a coin toss, say—and the cybernetics
people have consequently chosen to use the amount of information
produced by this kind of choice as their basic unit of measurement.
They call it a "bit." When a motorist approaches an intersection and
sees that the red light rather than the green light is glowing, he has
processed 1 bit of information.

As the number of equally likely choices rises, the amount of information that must be processed also rises. The rule is that every
time the number of alternatives increases by a factor of two, 1 bit
of information is added. (Four equally likely alternatives produce
2 bits of information; eight equally likely alternatives produce 3
bits; sixteen alternatives, 4 bits; and so on.)

Often, of course, the varying possibilities are *not* equally likely
—but once you know their probabilities of occurrence, you can figure out, by logarithmic calculation, how many bits of information
are carried by any message, and therefore must be processed by
the receiver of that message. It has been estimated, for example,
that the amount of information carried by each numeral is 3.3 bits;
by each letter, 4.7 bits; and by a one-syllable word, about 10 bits.

A second term used by this new science of communications theory
is "channel capacity." Like pipes that transport water, channels that
transmit messages have a finite capacity. In the case of the human
brain, channel capacity has been reached when a person can no
longer discriminate accurately among a number of stimuli. Suppose,
for example, that you are asked to discriminate two to fourteen
tones. The information input in this situation ranges from 1 to
3.8 bits. It has been found by testing, however, that most people cannot accurately discriminate more than six tones. This means that the
average person's channel capacity for such a job is about 2.5 bits.

In the Miller paper previously mentioned, the channel capacity
for many different discriminations is given. For loudness of sound,
it is 2.3 bits (about five discriminable degrees of loudness); for
saltiness or sweetness, 1.9 bits (about four different concentrations

of salt or sugar in water); for discriminating the size of squares, 2.2 bits (about five alternatives); for brightness, 2.3 bits (again, about five clear-cut discriminations). All, note, fall in the same range. It appears that we possess a rather small capacity for making judgments along one sensory dimension.

Frequently, of course, we have to discriminate among two or more sensory dimensions at the same time—loudness and pitch, perhaps. It would be a help to perception if we could add the 2.3 bits channel capacity for loudness to the 2.5 bits channel capacity for pitch and thus expand capacity to 4.8 bits. Alas, what actually happens is that people who are asked to discriminate loudness *and* pitch bog down somewhere around the level of 3.1 bits. The same pattern characterizes efforts to judge sugar-salt compounds. If their separate channel capacities could be doubled we'd be able to process 3.8 bits of information—but we can't; our channel capacity in this instance is 2.3 bits. The same is true of discriminations of hue and saturation. In each case, the addition of more variables increases the overall channel capacity of the discriminator—but by a progressively smaller amount. This is another way of saying that the more things we have to discriminate, the less accurate we become.

Well, then, how do we process more information than, in a sense, we have the equipment to handle? The single word "dog" carries 10 bits of information, and we process thousands upon thousands of such words. How on earth do we do it?

George Miller once asked one group of people to memorize lists of words or numerals which were built from thirty-two alternatives (that is, drawn from a pool of twenty-five letters of the alphabet and seven numerals) and another group to memorize lists built from eight alternatives. The first set, of course, contained a vastly larger amount of information than the second set. If our brains were like our backs—whose carrying ability absolutely determines the weight of the material that may be loaded upon them—the lists built from thirty-two alternatives (a much heavier "load") should have taken much longer to learn than the lists built from eight alternatives.

But that's not what happened. What made the lists easy or difficult to learn was their *length*. Shorter lists were learned faster than longer ones, regardless of the fact that they carried differing amounts of information. Six items are easier to learn than twelve:

again, our memories are limited by the number of units they can process. So, if we daily handle a bigger load of information than the packages provided for the purpose seem to have room for, as we obviously do, there is only one logical explanation: we must increase the carrying capacity of the packages by consolidating, miniaturizing, or otherwise recoding the information we store in them.

Miller makes an analogy with the learning of Morse code. A man just beginning to use Morse hears each dit and dah separately. Soon he is able to hear these sounds as letters, then as words, and eventually as entire phrases. "The dits and dahs are organized by learning into patterns," Miller says, "and as these larger units emerge the amount of message that the operator can remember increases accordingly. He has simply learned to increase bits per chunk."

This is why language is such a boon to mankind. First, young Billy compresses all the attributes of the family beagle—its size, shape, structure, coloration, sound, smell, behavior—into the single word "dog." To this he adds the differing attributes of collies, terriers, poodles, dachshunds, spaniels, and mongrels of all sorts—and stores this information too within the same small word. ("Dog" does double duty; it can be an individual label or a category.) Meanwhile, he is doing the same thing for cats, cows, horses, hamsters, monkeys, bears, and so on. Then he increases the bits per chunk by storing all his information about these creatures inside the word "animal." And eventually he combines all *that* information with the information stored in "plants," "fish," "birds," "reptiles," and "insects," and calls the whole lot "living things." It is a wondrous system.

The conceptual relationship of "living thing" to "animal" or "animal" to "dog" is that of a superordinate to a subordinate class. As we have already seen in Piaget's work, very young children have difficulty with this concept. Remember the confusion over which would be longer—a necklace using the brown beads or a necklace using the wooden beads? Here is another example, from a study by Jerome Bruner and Rose Olver. They asked a group of six- to twelve-year-olds what the following words had in common: bell, horn, telephone, radio, newspaper, book, painting, education.

A typical six-year-old's response was: "In an education you learn how to do painting, you read books and gradually you learn how to read newspaper, how to use radio, how to use telephone, horn, and bell." The child had taken one element and run all the others in on it. He had used all the words given him, and probably felt proud of the accomplishment. But he certainly had not reduced the amount of cognitive work that either he or the receiver of his message had to perform. Eight words had grown to thirty-one!

A twelve-year-old, however, summed up the eight words given him by saying, "They all communicate ideas." *He* had mastered the superordinate concept.

Bruner and Olver conclude, "Might it not be the case that [cognitive] development consists of finding techniques for being simple with respect to information?"

CHAPTER 16

THE MEASUREMENT AND INHERITANCE OF INTELLIGENCE

The greater one's intelligence, the faster and better one does all the things we've just been discussing: perception, comprehension and use of language, remembering, recalling, reasoning.

Look back to the account of the Kendlers' kindergarten and nursery school studies; and then consider the findings of an experiment done by Sonia F. Osler and Myrna Fivel of Johns Hopkins. Six-, ten-, and fourteen-year-old children, half with average IQ's and half with high IQ's, were combined in each test group. All saw 150 paired pictures, one of each pair being an example of the same class of things. The concepts represented by the pictures got harder: for one group, the correct choice was a bird; for the next group, it was an animal; and for the third group, it was any living thing. When a child made ten consecutive correct choices, it was assumed that he was using the appropriate concept as his guiding principle in making choices.

When the "game" was over, Osler and Fivel checked the records of the "winners"—those who *had* made ten consecutive correct choices—to see how they had responded on the ten trials *preceding* the final all-correct ten. Children were classified as sudden learners if six or more out of these ten penultimate trials had been wrong, and the other children were classified as gradual learners.

The two psychologists discovered that there were sudden learners in all age groups, and that the increasing difficulty of the three concepts (the first subordinate to the second and the second sub-ordinate to the third) did not affect the incidence of sudden versus gradual learning. The one thing that set the sudden learners apart from the gradual learners was that they had the higher IQ's. As was true of the Kendlers' younger subjects, superior intelligence correlated with the use of the faster learning technique—insight instead of trial and error.

What *is* intelligence? It's a trait we intuitively recognize in those of our fellow men who have smaller or larger amounts of it than is usual. But we are only a little closer today to locating its source or identifying the physiological form it may take than was the case five millennia ago when some unknown genius in Mesopotamia or the Caucasus invented the wheel.

One can say, simply, that intelligence is "the ability to learn." But there's more to it than that. The part of Webster's definition that comes closest to expressing its essence is this phrase: "the degree of one's alertness, awareness, or acuity." An unusually in-telligent baby is not necessarily an exceptionally early walker or talker, but he will have an exceptional amount of dynamism, perceptiveness, and drive. He will explore his surroundings with uncommon vigor, and respond in an especially sensitive manner to the people around him. He has something *extra*. In the words of Helen Davidson, after testing the early-reading abilities of chil-dren with mental ages of four years old, "The average four-year-old is appreciably superior to the dull five-year-old, but bright three-year-olds are very superior to the other two groups." In short, to be of superior intelligence is to have the cognitive equivalent of superb physical health. It improves the quality of everything you do.

There is no reliable way to measure intelligence—because nobody knows precisely what it is. Part of it is inherited and part results from environmental experience, part of it is general and part is specialized. But is it the general level of mental ability that is the inherited part, with environmental influences responsible for the making of this child into a good violinist and that child into a good mathematician? Or is it the specific abilities that are inherited —motor facility, say, or easy use of symbols—and does environment then act upon these, melding them into a given child's general level of intelligence?

Current thinking favors the second view. The work of various psychologists, notably a group at the University of Southern California headed by J. P. Guilford, indicates that intelligence is *not* unitary in character (and more evidence will be given later in this chapter). Guilford has even proposed a "structure of intellect" similar to the Periodic Table of Elements which, a century ago, helped chemists understand the relationship of different elements. It also indicated (by gaps in the chart) which elements remained to be found, and Guilford expects his "structure" to serve the same purpose. He predicts that more than ninety separate factors of intelligence will in time be located. At present, however, no generally used intelligence test measures ninety, or even twenty, different factors of intelligence, and until that day comes the measurement of intelligence will continue to be as imprecise as it is now.

In 1904, at the urging of France's Minister of Public Instruction, a commission was formed to find ways to teach mentally retarded children in the public schools. Staff work for the study was done by Alfred Binet, a young psychologist, and Theodore Simon, a physician. They constructed some tests, administered them, and kept careful records of the problems that normal children of given ages could solve. From these records came the concept of rating children by mental age. (Its relationship to chronological age was indicated in the quotation just above from Helen Davidson.)

In later years, as testing continued and it became apparent that mental age often changed relative to chronological age, psychologists began to measure intelligence by the following formula (using the "100" to eliminate decimals):

$$\frac{\text{Mental age}}{\text{Chronological age}} \times 100 = \text{Intelligence quotient}$$

Thus, if a child's mental age is twelve and chronological age is ten, his IQ is 120.

Binet's material was the basis for intelligence tests developed in this country in 1916 by Lewis Terman of Stanford University; and, with periodic revisions, the Stanford-Binet tests have been the most commonly used measure of intelligence ever since. Relative newcomers, favored by many, are the Wechsler Intelligence Scale and the Wechsler Intelligence Scale for Children.

As a result of such tests, it has been determined that about 13 percent of Americans have IQ's between 65 and 84 ("dull normal"), about 70 percent have IQ's between 85 and 114 ("average"), and 13 percent have IQ's between 115 and 134 ("highly intelligent"). At the extremes, about 2 percent have IQ's below 64 ("feeble minded") and another 2 percent score above 135 ("superior" or "gifted").

There are valid reasons, of course, for comparing the mental abilities of individuals within groups that have to work, study, or live together; and presently available tests *do* provide useful general measures. But during the past few test-happy decades in American life, the ratings that result from such tests have been accorded far too much weight in the evaluation of persons. The kind of parents who worry about their six-year-old's eventual admission to Harvard are too likely to wear his IQ as a badge of shame or glory. Even teachers sometimes consider children with high IQ's as "better" than those with low IQ's—as if, somehow, the IQ rates a child's intrinsic worth.

The plain fact is that the IQ score simply reflects a child's performance on tests which measure some portion of his ability to reason, to solve problems, to understand the meanings of words, to use symbols—and, incidentally, to take intelligence tests. The British psychologist Philip E. Vernon a few years ago summarized some research undertaken in Great Britain because so many ten- and eleven-year-olds were receiving "black market" coaching to prepare them for the tests that would determine their admission to college preparatory-type secondary schools. It was found that such practices "raised" the IQ from five to fifteen points.

"Our curiosity about the [mental] function of the child should begin, not end, with the tabulation of what he can and cannot do," said the child psychiatrist Leon Eisenberg in a paper read at a 1966 symposium on child care at the University of Chicago. "Does a child fail an item because he cannot reason or because he has not accepted the task as relevant to him, because he has not been able to sustain his attention for the time required for the mental operation [or] because he lacks the vocabulary to comprehend the question asked of him?"

Then Eisenberg reported on an experiment done in his clinic at Johns Hopkins:

Children afflicted by hyperkinetic behavior disorders—which means that they were physically active to an abnormal and uncontrollable degree—were separated into two groups. One group received a drug that reduces impulsiveness, the other group received an inert pill. Then they were given a maze test whose results have been found to correlate with IQ tests that depend on verbal ability, and their test results were compared to their IQ ratings. Those in the lowest IQ group did over twice as well as the children who had not received the drug, and *all* the children in the experimental group improved their performance somewhat.

Eisenberg asks, "Did we increase 'intelligence'? Or did we, by a drug that diminished impulsiveness, 'reveal' the IQ that was 'really' there? Clearly the answer depends on what we are prepared to include in our definition of intelligent behavior."

So, next time you get tense and defensive because the Mortons' Douglas but not your David has been put into a special accelerated class for gifted children, remember the words of Herbert C. Birch. He recently said, "Any [intelligence] test is a measure of achievement and not a measure of capacity, and the notions of capacity we derive from it are inferences. In short, intelligence is an inference deriving from differential achievement and not a measurable thing in itself."

A host of circumstances contribute to this "differential achievement" among people. A particular child's intelligence depends upon (1) the combination of genes he happens to inherit from his two parents; (2) his physical well-being during fetal and early postnatal development; and (3) the social environment in which he is raised. Let's take them in order—beginning with heredity.

Studies of children raised by adoptive or foster parents consistently show that the child's mature IQ correlates more closely with that of his natural parents than that of his adoptive or foster parents. Twin studies, likewise, show much greater correspondence of scoring patterns between identical twins (whose inheritance is the same, since they grew from the same fertilized egg) than between fraternal twins (who develop from eggs that happened to be fertilized at the same time).

A typical twin study was recently done by R. C. Nichols of the National Merit Scholarship Corporation. This organization, as every educated American parent knows, administers a large college scholarship program for which qualifying tests are given during the junior year in high school. In 1962 these tests were taken by 596,241 high school juniors—which is a nice big pool of research subjects. From this pool, the tests written by 1169 sets of twins were compared. Slightly over half of the twins were identical, the other fraternal—but all twin pairs were of the same sex, all pairs had been raised together, and all pairs had had as nearly as possible the same environment.

When there is perfect correlation between the performance of any two individuals or groups being compared, it is expressed as 1.0; when there is no correlation, it is expressed as 0. The higher the intermediate ratio, the closer the correlation is. On the 1962 Merit Scholarship tests, the ratio of fraternal twins whose scores were alike was .64 (boys) and .66 (girls). For indentical twins, however, the comparable figures were .90 (boys) and .91 (girls). Environment makes a difference—indeed it does, as we'll show a bit later on—but within the normal range of a single cultural pattern the larger factor is the inherited one.

There are various statistical methods employed which estimate the genetic component in general intelligence; it is believed to be approximately 70 percent. Nichols computed the "heritability ratios" for the youngsters in his sample, and found that it was .72 for boys and .74 for girls. (In these calculations, their being twins was immaterial. The heritability ratios of *individuals* were being estimated.) These ratios were based on each pupil's total score, however—a composite of his scores on five subtests (English usage, mathematics, social studies, natural sciences, and vocabulary). So Nichols went a step further, and computed heritability ratios on the subtests. Among the boys, the range was from .27 (English usage) to .80 (mathematics); among the girls, from .50 (natural science) to .75 (vocabulary). This finding supports the theory that intelligence is a composite of specific abilities which are inherited independently of each other. And indeed these particular ratios *do* tie in nicely with other research which indicates that boys excel girls in spatial intelliegence and ability to solve problems, whereas girls excel boys in word fluency, rote memory, and reasoning ability.

In 1922 Lewis Terman began a study of thirteen hundred California school children whose average IQ was 150. These brilliant children were followed along over a thirty-year period, and by the 1950s it was clear that the gift of intelligence can be the key to success in life. Ninety percent of Terman's subjects had gone to college, and 93 percent had graduated (a higher percentage than for the nation as a whole). Their grades were higher and they were more active in extracurricular affairs than the average college student. Most of them married; and their divorce rate was lower than that of the general population of California. In 1940, when they were thirty years old on the average, their earned income was twice the national average. In 1940, and again in 1952, they were given specialized "concept mastery" tests, in which they not only scored as far above the average adult as they had scored above the average child in the 1920s but in addition they scored higher in 1952 than in 1940—indicating that they were still learning.

Then Terman and his associates decided to test the intelligence of the offspring of these uncommonly intelligent adults. Their children were also highly intelligent; but the average IQ in the second generation was only 127, whereas that of the first generation was 150. Why—if intelligence is inherited?

According to Mendelian laws—and assuming that intelligence, like stature, is influenced by many genes—a person of very high intelligence has received a relatively rare combination of genes from his or her parents. Even if such a person marries someone of equal intelligence, the chance of their children receiving the same combination of two sets of genes is small. Furthermore, although persons of very high intelligence are likely to marry spouses of above-average intelligence, it is improbable that their partners in marriage will be of equally high intelligence. (This was true in the case of Terman's grown-up gifted children.) This phenomenon was observed by Sir Francis Galton in pre-Mendelian times. Galton's "filial law of regression" says that children of exceptional parents—whether in intelligence, height, or any other multigenic trait—tend to drift back toward the average of the population, in large part because the rare combinations of genes of the parents are statistically unlikely to recur in the children.

Intelligence is thought to be affected by at least seventy genes, according to the calculations of N. E. Morton—but nobody has pinpointed them.

Something should probably be said at this point about racial differences in the inheritance of intelligence—especially between American whites and Negroes. That the average Negro has a lower IQ than the average white is a fact; it is roughly 85 or 86 as against 100. But the extent to which this difference is due to genetic factors rather than to environmental factors is unknown. In a recent review of studies on racial differences in behavior, James

Spuhler and Gardner Lindzey say, "There is probably no area of psychological investigation that has been accompanied by greater passion and more strenuous activity and yet has led to less in the way of definitive findings than the study of intellectual differences between races."

They use as an example of the investigative problem some data gathered over fifty years ago but still valid—the scores made by draftees from twenty-three States on the Army Alpha Intelligence Test during World War I. Using this material, one can compare how whites and Negroes as subgroups varied from the high and low scores of the total group of draftees, and thus ascribe calculated proportions of this variance to genetic or environmental factors. But what happens when, all according to statistical Hoyle, you do it?

Spuhler and Lindzey say that data from ten States support the "conclusion" that genetic factors are the most important cause of the variance in score, and data from thirteen States support the "conclusion" that environmental factors are most important. Furthermore: "If we make all possible groupings and comparisons, these paired observations from twenty-three State samples can . . . provide exactly 44,152,005,855,224,745 different estimates of the proportion of the variation in Alpha scores due to genetic factors."

Nor do more recently given tests settle the question. In 1966 Audrey M. Shuey reviewed 382 studies comparing the intelligence of whites and Negroes, and about all that can be said with certainty is that there is almost three times more variance of intelligence among individuals *within* racial groups than there is *between* the groups themselves. If one makes the necessary statistical adjustments to control socioeconomic level, the average difference between whites and blacks is about 11 points, which is the same average difference that one finds among children in the same family.

There are genetic differences among races, of course—just as there are genetic differences among individuals within races. But nobody knows whether any of the genes that are different in American Negroes, African Negroes, Orientals, American Indians, Polynesians, and whites of European ancestry are genes that affect intelligence. They may do so; again, they may not. Until such time as it is possible (if it ever is) to provide absolute equality of environmental experience for representative samples of different

racial groups, it will be impossible to prove either that there are
no innate intellectual differences among the races of mankind or
that there *are* innate differences.

The educational psychologist Arthur R. Jensen has said, "Racial
variations have been identified in just about every anatomical and
physiological characteristic anyone has chosen to study, and it
would be surprising indeed if the brain alone were exempt from
this generalization. But the relevance of physiological differences
to behavior will still have to be proved in the psychological realm
by psychological techniques.

". . . Further research will contribute little more to our understanding of human differences and will have only meagre educational implications if the emphasis is placed solely on differences
in [standard] intelligence test scores, which reflect only an undifferentiated composite of abilities having unknown weightings in
the total scores. Perhaps our greatest hope of achieving equality of
educational opportunity lies in the possibility of finding significant
patterns of individual differences in the development of abilities
and in taking advantage of these differences to create the optimal
interaction between pupil and instruction."

He cites a 1965 study by Gerald S. Lesser, Gordon Fifer, and
Donald H. Clark, in which the mental abilities of four groups of
youngsters with distinctly different genetic backgrounds were compared. The children were Chinese, Negroes, Jews, and Puerto Ricans, all attending public schools in New York, one group of each
ethnic background being middle class and the other group being
lower class. The mental abilities tested were verbal ability, reasoning, numerical ability, and skill in handling spatial concepts.

The middle class children, predictably, scored higher than the
lower class children, but regardless of socioeconomic background
the children's scores followed the pattern shown below:

	Rank-order			
	Verbal	Reasoning	Number	Space
Chinese	3	1	2	1
Negroes	2	3	4	4
Jews	1	2	1	2
Puerto Ricans	4	4	3	3

Jensen says that there is no way of inferring from these findings
what the relative contributions of heredity and environment might
be. These distinctive patterns of ability could be due largely to

distinctive cultural influences pervading all social classes within each ethnic group. But he also reminds us that a number of investigators have obtained heritability estimates on special abilities by factor analysis, and that "special abilities show almost as high heritability as general ability, with about 70 percent of the variance [among individuals] attributable to genetic factors."

Speaking of Jensen brings to mind the publicity that followed the 1969 publication of his paper, "How Much Can We Boost IQ and Scholastic Achievement?" He was widely quoted as having said that Negroes are innately the intellectual inferiors of whites, with predictable results: some Southern whites immediately demanded that school segregation be maintained, some economy-minded Northern legislators proposed the abolishment of Head Start programs, and militant black students at Berkeley demanded the firing of this "racist" professor.

Jensen, of course, didn't say that Negroes are intellectually inferior to whites; a social scientist would never make such an unequivocal statement. What he did say was that "various lines of evidence . . . make it a not unreasonable hypothesis that genetic factors are strongly implicated in the average Negro-white intelligence difference. The preponderance of the evidence is, in my opinion, less consistent with a strictly environmental hypothesis than with a genetic hypothesis which, of course, does not exclude the influence of environment or its interaction with genetic factors."

The way that this statement, and the rest of Jensen's paper, was summarized in the popular press is an interesting case history of the social mischief that can be done by oversimplification, so I'm going to review its main points:

First, what is "intelligence"? At the beginning of this chapter, I defined it as "the ability to learn"—a definition that is, I believe, the one most laymen use. It is also, I suspect, the one that the white citizens groups and the legislators read into Jensen's use of the term. Then I went on to say that IQ tests measure only a *portion* of any individual's intelligence, specifically his "ability to reason, to solve problems, to understand the meanings of words, to use symbols— and, incidentally, to take intelligence tests."

Jensen, however, uses a different definition. Intelligence, he says, is "the capacity for abstract reasoning and problem solving." And since this is indeed the mental ability that IQ tests best measure, he is being quite consistent when he equates IQ scores with intelligence. Learning ability, Jensen says, is something else again. It spans a wider range of mental powers and comes in two versions. There is, first, "associative learning ability," in which learned material is recalled in essentially the same form as when first presented. We exhibit associative learning, for example, when we memorize lists of numbers, learn to spell, or remember someone's name because we identify the person with the place or company in which we usually see him. "Conceptual learning ability," on the other hand, requires us to mentally manipulate incoming information, elaborating or transforming it into abstract concepts before we use it. It is this ability that equates, in Jensen's thinking, with "intelligence"; and, like other special abilities, some 70 percent of it is inherited.

Two main themes run through his paper. It annoys him that so many social scientists still believe "in the almost infinite plasticity of intellect," that they persist in an "ostrich-like denial of biological factors in individual differences," and that the role of genetics continues to be slighted in scholarly studies of intelligence. Too much contrary evidence has accumulated lately, he says, to support a purely environmentalist view of how man's intellectual skills develop—so it's foolish and wasteful to base our educational programs on the assumption that if we control environment we also control intellectual achievement.

The second point is related. The educational goal of our schools, and hence the pedagogical approach, is the same for all children: to develop their capacity for abstract reasoning. But if this capacity is largely innate, children who lack it are at a great disadvantage when they go to schools structured for children who *have* it. Jensen says that those who don't, or can't, "show that they 'understand' the meaning of $1+1=2$ in some abstract, verbal, cognitive sense [are] in effect not allowed to go on to learn $2+2=4$." But the same children might very well learn how to manipulate numbers and a host of other basic scholastic skills, he says, if teaching techniques were employed which did not require cognitive and conceptual learning—techniques based on associative learning, for instance. Children so taught would not turn out to be jurists or astronauts or corporation presidents, but at least they wouldn't be high school dropouts with a built-in sense of failure.

Jensen is probably overoptimistic about the potential of teaching techniques based on associative learning, but nobody can quarrel with his assertion that alternative teaching methods of some sort should be available when a second- or third-grader is clearly unable "to reason, to solve problems, to understand the meanings of words, to use symbols—and, incidentally, to take intelligence tests" as well as his classmates can.

But this plea for greater recognition of innate differences in intellectual ability and for more variation of educational goals and teaching methods in order to better build on those differences was not the "public message" of Jensen's paper. It was the ten pages (out of more than a hundred) in which Jensen talks about the relationship of race to intelligence that lay readers and the popular press were interested in. This material was specific, not general; was easy to summarize; and it discussed a taboo topic, one that is charged with emotion for most Americans.

In those pages, Jensen said that the conceptual learning ability ("intelligence") of lower class children—a category into which most Negro children fall—is less than that of middle class children, and also that the conceptual learning ability ("intelligence") of middle class Negro children is less than that of middle class white children. His later recommendation that associative learning should be stressed in instructional programs for children with low innate capacity for conceptual learning was therefore inevitably interpreted by readers as a recommendation that Negroes should be taught by different methods than whites.

Now, it may be that Negroes as a group do have less inherent conceptual learning ability than some other genetically-distinct group, just as boys are inherently less fluent with words than girls. (Sex, don't forget, is a genetic distinction, too; and one that is much easier to define than race.) But such findings should not lead one to the conclusion that Negroes as a group ought to be schooled in one way and whites in another, or that boys ought to be schooled in one way and girls in another. Schooling happens to individuals, not to "Negroes," "whites," "boys," or "girls," and a great many individuals do not behave according to group norms. It is an unarguable fact that some Negroes are better at abstract reasoning than some whites, also that some boys are more fluent than some girls.

Because he was addressing himself to other social scientists, Jensen mentioned but did not stress the distinction between statistical studies of populations and actual differences among individuals.

This, however, is a distinction that laymen have trouble making, and it is easy to see why many readers found it simpler to lift out of a tediously long scholarly exposition just the parts that deal with the group performance of Negroes on IQ tests, and the possible genetic component in the scores. They overlooked the existence of individual variations and the influence of environment, which can make a whopping difference.

Both Jensen and the editors of the journal that published his paper must have known that this outcome was a possibility. Which poses a nice problem: in a country devoted to freedom of the press, how should scholars handle those "not unreasonable hypotheses" which can be socially inflammatory?

CHAPTER 17

HOW ENVIRONMENT AFFECTS INTELLIGENCE

Insofar as the inheritance of intelligence is concerned, the results of the World War I Army Alpha Intelligence Test were about as inconclusive as any data could be. Not so the test's correlation with environmental factors. A clear relationship exists between the draftees' test scores and annual per-pupil expenditures by the States where these young men went to school.

For example, Kentucky's per-pupil expenditure in 1900 was $4.57; its white draftees scored 48.6 on the Army tests; and its Negro draftees scored 32.4. In Illinois, however, with a per-pupil expenditure of $13.46, white draftees scored 66.7 and Negro draftees scored 47.9. James Spuhler and Gardner Lindzey say, in their modern review of these tests, "On the average, the scores of the white draftees were elevated 1.51 alpha units and those of Negro draftees by 1.48 alpha units for each dollar of yearly expenditures on schools."

The kind and quality of formal education available to a child is only one of numerous environmental variables that can affect intelligence—but, in terms of timing, a child's school experience is way at the end of a list that begins with the chemical environment in which the organs and tissues of a not-yet-born baby are developing, and includes the child's birth experience and his diet in early infancy. Here are some examples that illustrate this intimate relationship between "mind" and "body":

Cretinism is a rare condition resulting from absence or non-function of the thyroid gland. The cause is unknown. Children so afflicted are dwarfed physically as well as mentally, but dosages of thyroid hormone often normalize bone growth and improve mental function.

The importance of *early* treatment (either for cretins or for individuals with less acute forms of thyroid deficiency) has been emphasized by John Money and Viola Lewis in their study of a group of hypothyroid patients whose progress they followed over a period of years. The patients were twice given IQ tests: when their condition was diagnosed and medication prescribed, and again five to eleven years later. At second testing, their IQ's had risen on the average about ten points.

Money and Lewis could not find a correlation between this IQ change and the age at which hormone therapy began, IQ level at the start, or the length of time that the patient had been taking thyroid hormone—but they *did* observe that those patients who had begun treatment before rather than after the age of two and a half had had higher IQ's, at the time of first testing, by an average of fourteen points.

What a lack of thyroid hormone does to the developing brain tissue of babies may be the same thing it does to the brains of rats. Other mammals including man are still confined to the uterus when their brains are at the developmental stage characteristic of rats at birth, hence rats are good subjects for brain research if one is seeking clues as to what goes on in the maturing human or other mammalian brain in the period just before birth.

J. T. Eayrs, of the Institute of Psychiatry at London's Maudsley Hospital, has exploited this developmental difference by removing the thyroid glands of young rats on the day they were born, then sacrificed* them at regular intervals thereafter to see what internal changes had occurred. He found that their craniums had been stunted in growth whereas the brain tissue inside those bony shells had grown at normal rate.

His first tentative conclusion, then, was that the symptoms of cretinism may (in part at least) be attributable to a compression of brain tissue and a rise in intracranial pressure. This increased

---

* In accounts of animal research, scientists often avoid the word "kill"—but so do other humans who raise animals for commercial use. People who raise minks for ladies' coats, for example, "harvest" the pelts.

pressure could interfere with blood circulation sufficiently to reduce the supply of oxygen to nerve cells—which require far more oxygen than any other cells in the body—and cause the anoxic condition which is known to cause brain damage in human babies.

Another change in the brain tissue of the rats without thyroid glands was in the size of blood vessels in the cortex. They occupied the same space as in normal rats but there were fewer of them and they were larger. A consequence of this condition is a reduction in the intake of essential cell nutrients by capillary action between cell membranes: a system composed of a large number of small vessels presents a greater capillary surface for such metabolic exchange than a system of similar volume but made up of fewer and larger blood vessels.

Finally, in rats without thyroid glands, the neurons in the part of the brain that controls sensory-motor activity were smaller than those of normal rats, with shorter and less-branched dendrites.

The animals so handicapped were—like human beings in the same fix—more sluggish, less aware of minor changes in their environment, and in learning situations made many more errors than their normal littermates. Furthermore, the number of errors they made during a fixed number of trials was directly related to the age at which they had lost their thyroid glands. When Eayrs postponed the operation beyond the tenth day of life, the effects were negligible. Restoration of thyroid hormone (via medication) helped improve the performance of the early operated rats, but they never matched their normal littermates. The brain damage suffered in this very early period was, in short, irreversible.

Eayrs' conclusion: "If it be permissible to extrapolate from rat to man on the basis of the relative stages of cerebral development, a critical period for the influence of thyroid hormone in man would be expected to occur during the latter stages of [fetal] development. While these findings reinforce the need for early postnatal treatment, they might equally be regarded as providing a case for [prenatal] diagnosis."

Something of the latter sort *has*, in fact, been done. Thyroid hormone can be transmitted from mother to unborn child through the placenta; and in the case of two women both of whom had borne two cretinous children, a group of researchers at the University of Michigan's Medical School—headed by E. A. Carr, Jr., and W. H. Bierwaltes—prescribed large doses of thyroid hormone for the women during subsequent pregnancies. Both gave birth to apparently normal children, although one child later showed some signs of thyroid failure.

This kind of therapy is never undertaken lightly, partly because one cannot be sure that the developing baby will be a cretin and partly because a dosage large enough to help the developing baby may cause *hyper*thyroidism in the pregnant mother. In human biochemistry, balances are very delicate.

Less hazard attends vitamin dosage given at one remove, and can be of substantial benefit in cases where the normal diet is deficient in vitamins. Ruth Harrell, E. R. Woodyard, and A. I. Gates once gave vitamin supplements to over six hundred poverty-stricken expectant and nursing mothers, and a non-nutritive pill to a group of controls. Several years later they tested the IQ's of the children. Those whose mothers had received the vitamins had IQ's on the average eight points above those whose mothers had received no dietary supplement.

And what is the effect of too little food and of the wrong kind—upon mother, baby, or both?

There is currently under way a world-wide effort to answer this question, and not for humane reasons alone. As the underdeveloped countries begin to industrialize, fewer women breast-feed their babies, and millions of infants are now being fed from extremely early ages on milk substitutes of so little nutritional value as to constitute near-starvation. Although the physical health of those who survive is often later improved by school feeding programs, there is a growing belief that severe undernourishment in babyhood does such irreparable damage to the brain that the survivors of present practices will be mentally marginal if not downright defective. If that is true, and if such feeding practices continue unchecked, the prospect for the future of mankind is not encouraging.

The Cornell pediatrician Myron Winick has recently reviewed much of the work in this field, beginning with an appraisal of the animal studies. Although findings vary in detail, the broad outlines are clear: first, malnutrition in infancy restricts the growth of brain cells and alters their structure; second, the younger the deprivation occurs—that is, the closer in time to the period of most rapid brain growth—the more intense the effect and the less susceptible to later reversal.

For an example of this second point, consider what happens to rats born of malnourished mothers and themselves raised on inadequate diets. They are much worse off than rats born to malnourished mothers but themselves adequately fed, or than rats born to well-nourished mothers but themselves undernourished. The "doubly deprived" rats are not only severely stunted in overall growth but in addition have less than half the normal number of brain cells. "It is as though prenatal malnutrition has . . . made them hypersensitive to postnatal undernutrition," Winick says.

There are far fewer human studies, but one in which he participated (with Pedro Rosso of the University of Chile) compared the physical and chemical composition of brain tissue from ten well-nourished babies, who died in accidents, and nine malnourished babies, who died of that condition. The brains of the second group contained far fewer cells than those of the well-nourished children of similar age; in three, the count was as low as that of the "doubly deprived" rats.

None of these studies prove, of course, that brain *function* is damaged by malnutrition. Animal studies indicate that specific intellectual abilities are affected, some of which improve after proper feeding and some of which do not. An example of the latter is the finding that pigs malnourished in infancy but well fed later are less curious as adults and don't do as well in maze problems as pigs that ate properly as piglets.

With respect to human beings, one should remember that a malnourished child is almost invariably one whose total environment is bad for optimum physical or mental development: housing is poor and so is hygiene, the family structure is unstable, cultural deprivation is acute. That's why no one can say that subnormal performance on IQ tests at age five is due *just* to physical damage from malnutrition that the brain may have suffered during its prenatal formation and immediately postnatal development. But it is equally impossible to eliminate poor nutrition as a contributing factor in many cases of mental retardation. Here are two examples of studies, one done in the United States and emphasizing maternal nutrition and prenatal care, the other done in South Africa and emphasizing infant diet and home environment, which show how all these factors interweave:

Pregnant women from poor and underprivileged environments

do without the monthly medical checkups that middle and upper class women take for granted. Hilda Knoblock, Benjamin Pasamanick, and others of a research team at Ohio State have for some time been studying the effect of such pregnancies upon children's intelligence—and they have found that its development is fraught with peril.

When they checked thirty-four years of admissions records at a State institution for feeble-minded children, they discovered an odd fact: an uncommonly large number of these youngsters had been born in the winter. Heat was the only seasonal factor they could think of that might affect children conceived in the summer. So they compared admission rates year by year with the recorded temperatures of the summers when these children had been conceived; and, believe it or not, more mentally defective children were born during winters that followed exceptionally hot summers.

Knoblock and her colleagues think it possible that these babies' mothers may have reduced their protein intake during a period when it was "just too hot to cook anything"; or, perhaps, excessive heat affected their hormone balance. If either event transpired during the eighth to twelfth fetal week, when the molecular organization of the baby's cortex was taking place, permanent impairment of the infant's brain could have resulted.

This possible relationship of hot weather to prenatal development raised the question: Was this a problem of the poor or of the general population? Examination of Baltimore's seasonal variations in birth rates, according to race and census tract, for a five-year period, provided a clue. The birth rate was about the same the year around among the well-off middle and upper classes, but it decreased significantly between February and May among the poor. Did that mean that they engaged in less sexual activity during the hot summer months? Or that the babies then conceived were less viable? Probably both, the researchers think. But whatever the cause of this "noxious effect of heat stress," one thing is sure. The poor—lacking air conditioning, medical advice, and dietary supplements—cannot escape it.

Another medical corollary of inadequate prenatal care is a high rate of premature births or complicated and difficult deliveries. What effect do these circumstances have upon a child's mental powers? Knoblock and her associates have kept records on 492 full-term babies and 500 babies defined as premature because they weighed under five pounds at birth. Of these, a subgroup weighed around three pounds. When these children were between three and five years old, nine hundred of them were given intelligence tests. Look at the relationship of birth weight to mental defects:

	Percentage of children with mental defects	
	White	Negro
Full-term controls	3.5	6.6
Larger prematures	7.4	11.0
Smaller prematures	17.7	27.0

In a reverse kind of study, one in which children's IQ's were known but not the circumstances of their fetal growth or birth, the same investigators found that 93 percent of the mothers of children with IQ's below 50 had had complications of pregnancy.

Another study that was continued long enough to permit some conclusions as to the effects of poverty was begun in 1955 by two South African researchers, Mavis Stoch and P. M. Smythe of the University of Cape Town. For eleven years they followed the progress of forty children from the lowest socioeconomic level of society, twenty of whom grew up in poor but not grossly deprived circumstances and twenty of whom experienced cruel neglect and severe malnutrition as babies.

Although the home conditions of the undernourished group greatly improved in later childhood, they came into their teens weighing about ten pounds less and measuring three inches shorter (on the average) than the controls. Their IQ's were lower; they showed less initiative in play situations; and they tested lower in motivation. Furthermore, their behavior on certain nonverbal tests "resembles that found in some brain-damaged children; that is, a defect of visuomotor ability and pattern perception."

Stoch and Smythe make the point that this could be due either to organic brain damage or to the inactivity and lack of energy associated with malnutrition. An apathetic baby is less receptive than an alert one to the sights and sounds around him, and a low level of activity during the sensorimotor period of learning might indeed affect his intellectual development as did the sensory deprivation of dogs raised by Ronald Melzack (Chapter 4), William Thompson, and Woodburn Heron (Chapter 6).

In addition, as Herbert G. Birch reminds us, "Good evidence exists that the nature of the mother's response and the degree to which she [is] a developmental stimulus to the infant are, in part, functions of the child's own characteristics of reactivity. Since one of the first effects of malnutrition is reduced responsiveness of the child to environmental stimulation, the value of the child as a stimulus to the mother is reduced and may serve to diminish her responsiveness to him.

"Thus, apathy can provoke apathy, and so contribute to a cumulative pattern of reduced adult-child interaction. If this occurs, it can have consequences for stimulation during infancy, for learning, for maturation, and for the development of interpersonal relations. The end result of all of these interferences can be, and most predictably would be, the development of significant backwardness in later intellectual performance."

Speaking of adult-child interaction brings to mind a prophetic but unappreciated psychological experiment of almost forty years ago—to which the final chapter has just been written.

In 1938, long before John Bowlby wrote his famous monograph on the effects of maternal deprivation, Harold Skeels and several University of Iowa colleagues reported on a project which they had undertaken as a result of an "unbelievable" event witnessed by Skeels. He was then a consulting psychologist to two State institutions, an orphanage and a nearby hospital for the mentally retarded. Among the youngsters admitted to the orphanage in the early 1930s were two little girls, thirteen and sixteen months of age but in developmental age only six and seven months old. In fact, they gave such overwhelming evidence of retardation that they were almost immediately bundled off to the mental hospital.

About six months later, when making his rounds there, Skeels spotted two alert, smiling, apparently normal toddlers—and could not believe that these were his two hopeless cases. He gave them intelligence tests and found them well within the normal range; but he still couldn't believe that this improvement was real, so he left them in the hospital. He tested them twice again, at approximately twelve-month intervals, and their rating of normal intelligence held steady. What had happened? The only circumstance that distinguished their lives before and after admission to the hospital, he found, was that the women inmates at the mental hospital had adored the babies; had cuddled them, played with them, and provided for them an intense one-to-one adult-child relationship.

So he and three associates then set up an experimental project involving the transfer of more orphans—they were called "house guests"—to the mental hospital. There were thirteen children in this experimental group, ranging in age from seven to forty months, with an average IQ of 64 (which was the main reason that Skeels could withdraw them from the orphanage—they were considered unadoptable). At the same time, a contrast group of twelve children were chosen. They were matched to the others insofar as possible in age, sex, medical histories, and family background. However, their IQ's were higher; the average was 86.7. As potentially adoptable children, they remained in the orphanage.

The "house guests" lived in the mental hospital from six months to over four years, and at varying intervals were returned to the orphanage. Eleven of them were subsequently adopted, the other two grew up in the hospital. Two and a half years after their first transfer back to the orphanage, the children were given intelligence tests—and it was found that the group's average IQ had risen to 95.9. (And that of the eleven who had been adopted was up to 101.4!) The reverse had happened in the case of the contrast group, the children who had never left the orphanage: the average IQ of these youngsters had dropped to 66.1.

When, in 1938, Skeels reported these findings, other psychologists scoffed. In fact, he and his colleagues "were very nearly drummed out of the American Psychological Association" (to quote a man who says that he overstates the professionals' sense of outrage only a little). That's because it was then an article of faith that intelligence was a trait comparable to, say, stature. Children were born with a certain potential which subsequently developed to whatever genetic limit had been set on it. IQ changes of a few points were acceptable, but gross changes of this nature? It was recognized, of course, that stature could be stunted by severe malnutrition, but social deprivation was not seen in an analogous role relative to intelligence —and it was a shocker to have a group of young psychologists out in Iowa make such an assertion. Something had to be wrong with their experiment, since their conclusions were so obviously wrong.

Nor has Skeels's follow-up study of the same children received the attention *it* deserves—but for a different reason. In the intervening years, numerous studies have demonstrated the relationship of intelligence to the environment of rearing; therefore, the follow-up study now falls into the category of "confirming evidence." There are penalties in science, as in other human endeavors, for being ahead of your time!

Anyway, beginning in 1961, Skeels—who is now with the National Institutes of Health in Bethesda, Maryland—began an attempt to trace the children on whom he had reported in 1938. Astoundingly, he managed to find all thirteen of the children in the experimental group and the surviving twelve in the contrast group, who by then were between twenty-five and thirty-five years old.

He found that those in the experimental group had all finished high school and a few had gone to college; most are married; and all are self-supporting. Their average income is $4224. By comparison, four of those in the contrast group are in institutions for the mentally retarded, only one has gone beyond eighth grade, most are unmarried, and those capable of holding jobs work on a hit-and-miss basis as dishwashers or groundsmen. One is categorized simply as a "floater." Their average income is $1200.° The experimental group averaged 28.5 IQ points *above* their initial scores of thirty years earlier, and the contrast group averaged 26.2 points *below* their childhood scores.

Now, perhaps you have been wondering how—if some 70 percent of intelligence is inherited—the environment could make such a tremendous difference in IQ? (This, of course, is one of the reasons that Skeels's 1938 report was so severely criticized by other psychologists.) Arthur R. Jensen has a good answer. He says that one should regard environment as a "threshold variable," and explains as follows:

"For a particular mental ability, realization of genetic potential depends upon the presence of certain environmental influences. Beyond some threshold level of favorable environmental influences, however, further increases do not make for appreciable increments in ability.

"An analogy is the effect of diet on physical stature. When the diet is deficient in certain vitamins and minerals, growth is stunted, but when the minimal daily requirement is provided, growth will be normal and further supplements to the diet will produce no appreciable effect."

If the bulk of a population sampled in a heritability study is above

---

° In his 1966 report, Skeels also makes a significant economic point. Basing his figures on the monthly per capita costs for care in Iowa institutions since 1933, he says that the children in the experimental group cost the State a total of $30,716 whereas those in the contrast group have to date cost the State a total of $138,571—"and for at least four of the cases costs to the State will continue at a rate now in excess of $200 a month for another twenty to forty years."

the threshold value on the relevant environmental variable, the heritability estimate will be very high, he says; and, conversely, heritability estimates will be low for people raised in exceedingly poor environments—because that environment prevented the full development of those individuals' genetic potential.

And the younger the child, the greater the effect of environment upon his genetic potential. Here are two cases in point, both of them studies of children with roots in the rural South:

In 1951, E. S. Lee, having followed the progress through the Philadelphia schools of several groups of Negro children, reported that those born and raised in Philadelphia maintained about the same IQ scores throughout the elementary grades whereas newcomers from the South raised their IQ's in proportion to the child's age when the move North was made.

Although I find it difficult to think of a Northern urban ghetto as an "enriched environment," these are nevertheless the facts: children whose parents moved to Philadelphia before the child in question was six years old gained an average of 6.5 IQ points by the beginning of ninth grade; children who entered the Philadelphia schools at fourth grade level gained an average of 3 IQ points during the following six years; and those who came into the system at the sixth grade level raised their final scores by an average of 2 IQ points.

The other study was done much earlier, by Lester Wheeler. In 1930, he tested over eleven hundred East Tennessee mountain children in grades one to eight. He found a steadily dropping IQ: from an average of 94 at age six to an average of 73 at age sixteen. He blamed the drop primarily on the fact that standard IQ tests are designed for children with urban middle class backgrounds. Ten years later he repeated the tests on a new generation of Tennessee school children—children whose experiences were more like those of urban middle class children because of changes that had occurred in the region. Roads had been built, allowing the mountain people more access to "outside"; tiny school districts had been consolidated, bringing such benefits as better-trained teachers and school libraries; more industry had been attracted to the area, providing steadier work, more income, and better nutrition for the population. And this time the average IQ at age six was 102 and the average IQ at age sixteen was 80.

You will have noted immediately that despite the gain in average IQ, the decline-with-age persisted. This dropping IQ is, in fact, a well-documented developmental trend among lower class children. What causes it?

Environmentalists ascribe it to steadily dwindling opportunities, because of social and economic circumstances, to learn the kind of things that IQ tests measure. There is also the "shallow foundations" effect: the less one has to build on, the less one can add as the building period progresses.

Those who give more weight to inherited components of intelligence, however, say that people of low socioeconomic status are in that category at least in part because innately below average intelligence prevents their learning how to do the jobs that command high pay and high prestige in a modern industrialized society—jobs that require the same mental abilities that IQ tests measure.

Wheeler's findings in Tennessee, therefore, would be explained by environmentalists as indicating that the damping effect of the total environment outweighed the elevating effect of such improvements as had occurred in the ten year period between the two studies. Arthur Jensen and those who think like him, on the other hand, would say that the overall rise in IQ reflected the passage of that particular population over an environmental threshold, but that the age-related decline in IQ indicated the presence in a highly inbred population of inherited limitations in mental ability.

Your guess as to which explanation is correct is as good as mine. In any case, the main point of the preceding paragraphs is that enriched environments can boost the IQ's of lower class children by amounts inversely proportional to their age. If those same IQ's slide downhill later in life, at least the children start higher and their IQ's don't drop as low as those of individuals who were more culturally deprived during the preschool years.

From all the material in this and the previous chapter, you can see why intelligence is no longer thought of as something that children *have* (like blue or brown eyes or Type O blood) but as something they *grow* (like straight backs or friendliness). The potential for growth is in the genes, but the intellectual stature that is eventually achieved depends upon a series of interactions with the environment. If the early interactions are pleasant and productive, the child will reach out for more, progressively enlarging his capacity for noticing and remembering things, and for making use of the information thus acquired. Intelligence, in short, is *a mode of behavior*—a reflection of the child's total experience in life.

That, at any rate, is the belief of a good many modern psychologists; and among the studies that support it is one that was published in 1958 by Lester Sontag, Charles T. Baker, and Virginia Nelson of the Fels Research Institute in Yellow Springs, Ohio. These investigators had watched and studied the development of well over a hundred children as they progressed from nursery school to the sixth grade, and here are some findings relevant to intelligence:

Throughout the years, they observed, a given child's IQ scores may follow an essentially level course; may take brief downward or upward detours and then return to the level; or may make a decided shift. These sudden shifts, when they occur, most frequently take place at around age six. The more usual course is the level one, with a gently upward-moving trend. About half of the children in the study lost or gained more than 15 IQ points in the course of their first ten years of life. Boys tended to gain more than girls, and their IQ's also stabilized later than girls'; but for the entire group, the IQ had stabilized by age eleven.

Over the years that these children were observed and tested in many school, home, and experimental situations, a large body of data was assembled which could be cross-checked as desired. For example, take the group of children who gained most in IQ points between ages six and ten. Did they have different qualities of personality than the children of the same age who lost the most IQ points during the same period?

The investigators went over the records of those particular children and found that at age six these were among the qualities that had been noted in the two groups who were to perform so differently during the next four years:

Would Have IQ Gain

Self-confident in play situations, often bossy, quite competitive; comfortable with strangers; self-propelled much of the time, initiated activity and didn't require adult encouragement in order to stay with it; resisted or ignored demands of others (including parents) if didn't consider them appropriate; took punishment in stride, regained equanimity soon.

Would Have IQ Loss

Uneasy with children of same age, shy with strangers; passive and conforming in play situations, likely to withdraw when games got too competitive; anxious and fearful when adults tried to promote independent behavior; not much persistence in problem solving, requiring steady praise or other reward; punishment by parents a shattering experience.

Therefore, Sontag and his colleagues concluded that "aggressiveness, self-initiation of activity, and competitiveness are the dimensions of personality, at age six, which best predict future IQ change during the elementary school years."

And the degree to which a child has these qualities does not come out of the blue on his sixth birthday. If your five-year-old Jennifer, for example, has developed a passion for collecting worms, despite your repeatedly telling her that little ladies don't *like* worms, should you follow your inclination to flush them down the toilet while she's at kindergarten? Think again: you may be nipping the genius of another Madame Curie.

You worry about her domineering ways, too. Last time her cousin Kathy came to visit, Jennifer wouldn't let Kathy decide anything. Of course, Kathy isn't a very forceful child—but Jennifer shouldn't be allowed to boss her around as much as she does, should she?

Come to think of it, though, it *is* hard to keep Kathy entertained. She drops any activity if she can't do it on the first try, unless you stay right with her and keep her going. And remember how she behaved last Easter? When Jennifer and Tommy found some Easter eggs before she did, Kathy came back in the house. Said it was too cold and hunting for eggs wasn't any fun, anyway.

Tom, of course, will be the death of you yet. He's only four, but he sneaks the eggbeater out of the drawer and whips soapsuds all over the kitchen floor; he refuses to leave the dials on the TV alone, no matter how often you slap his hands; and five minutes after you tell him that he *must* stay in the back yard, he's out on the front curb watching the cars go by. How, you wonder, can you make him obey? Maybe what you should be wondering is how you can help him safely handle his obvious fascination with machinery.

Such children, in short, may not be easy to live with, they may not seem to need you as much as more passive and less self-reliant children would, and they certainly don't promote household tranquility—but they are probably the ones who are going to be on the Honor Roll in high school.

CHAPTER 18

CULTURE AND CASTE

Each human society, over the thousands of years of its group experience, has accumulated a stock of beliefs and expectations about the world we live in, and how best to make existence in it orderly. These assumptions of what is best determine how we dress or ornament ourselves, what we eat, the kind of goods we make or value, how we get our mates and rear our children, how we define sin, whether we worship gods or God. This customary behavior—patterned for us by others of our kind, living and dead—is our culture. We transmit it to our children in a thousand ways, explicit or implicit, during the early years of their lives, when they are most highly motivated to learn and most vulnerable to our teaching. The psychiatrist Otto Rank once said, and truly, "Every generation uses children for its own purposes."

As the varying cultural patterns of the world's peoples attest, young humans are enormously adaptable; and older humans are exceptionally faithful to the ways of their forebears. A baby can learn to sleep upright and tightly swaddled, or prone and without a cover. If his mother elects not to carry him in a sling on her back during the day and keep him in her bed at night, he adjusts very well to spending long solitary periods in his crib or playpen. As a newborn, he feeds whenever he is hungry or according to some externally imposed schedule, and grows into a pattern of eating once a day or five times a day—not because such behavior is best in any absolute sense but because it is customary in his culture.

His dexterity can be channeled into the shaping of a spearhead or into the playing of a piano; his visual acuity can mature as an ability to discriminate among many colors or among many patterns; and his intelligence can manifest itself as a knowledge of weather signs and portents or as comprehension of a written language. He can be taught to view the world as benign or malevolent, and can—with equal ease—become a member in good standing of a society that is basically gentle and cooperative or one that is belligerent and competitive. In short, the reality that Piaget says the child gradually encompasses in the course of cognitive growth is not an objective and universal reality, but reality as it is perceived by the culture of which he is a part.

When Wayne Dennis spent a year as a visiting professor at the American University in Beirut, Lebanon, he had an uncommon opportunity to investigate the social values which different cultures inculcate in their young. The group he studied included 120 American children (whose parents were U.S. government employees, University faculty, American businessmen based in the area); 240 Arab children; 60 Armenians (most of whose families had emigrated to Lebanon after World War I); and 60 Arabic-speaking Jewish children (of families that have lived in the Near East for centuries, but have preserved their ancient culture and religion). The children ranged in age from five to eleven; except for the Arabs, some of whom attended local public schools, all went to private schools maintained for their particular national or cultural group.

Dennis asked each child to tell him about two recent occasions when he or she had been praised, by whom, and for what reason. His tabulation of their responses is an illuminating reflection of the behavioral standards of the different societies in which these children were growing up. (See next page.)

All the children were praised for helping their mothers. But in addition the Near Eastern children were praised most for academic achievement; for being polite, quiet and obedient; and for helping the unfortunate. The American children, on the other hand, were praised most for creative activity; for excelling at sports and games; and for helpful acts to people *other* than their mothers.

When you add to this last item the fact that 25 percent of the praise given American children came from other children and only

	Americans	Arabs	Armenians	Jews
Schoolwork (doing it well, getting good grades, etc.)	5%	28%	31%	41%
Helping mother (with housework, running errands, etc.)	25	26	15	22
Helping father	6	2	0	2
Helping brother or sister	9	4	3	5
Helping playmates	8	0	1	2
Helping unfortunates (giving alms, etc.)	0	9	12	3
Being quiet, polite, or obedient	6	14	12	9
Excelling at sports or games	6	2	3	2
Giving or sharing (with friends or relatives, not in the sense of charity)	9	2	8	3
Creative activity (making a dress or boat model, undertaking some unassigned project, etc.)	13	2	8	3

5 percent from their teachers (whereas the Near Eastern children were praised almost entirely by adults), you see in microcosm one of the characteristics of American culture about which foreigners frequently comment: our tendency to engage in cooperative activities, to organize into groups for common effort in some cause, to be "joiners."

It is unlikely that these children's parents or teachers realized that their selective approval of certain behaviors was in effect a choice. Cultural standards are so deeply ingrained that (so long as we remain in the culture that produced them) we forget that what we reward or punish in our children is not behavior that is right or wrong in any absolute sense, but behavior that is merely ours and of our time. Each new generation modifies its cultural inheritance, to greater or less degree, and in due course yesterday's "right" may become today's "wrong"—or vice versa.

An entertaining account of such a shift within our own culture and in our own time has been provided by Yeshiva University's Martha Wolfenstein, who compared the advice given American mothers in various editions of *Infant Care*, a widely distributed publication of the U. S. Department of Labor's Children's Bureau. She found that the pamphlet's hypothetical 1914 mother and hypothetical 1914 baby had virtually nothing in common with their 1945 counterparts.

In 1914, when *Infant Care* was first published, babies were born with strong and dangerous impulses and would "rebel fiercely" when these impulses were thwarted. But thwarted they must be, for children in whom they were not controlled were sometimes "wrecked for life." Thumb-sucking and masturbation were the worst of these impulses; in fact, mothers were told to tie the child's feet to opposite sides of the crib and pin his nightgown sleeves to the sheets in order to restrain him. Rocking horses and even swings were frowned upon; they were too stimulating to erogenous zones. (This, don't forget, was the period when the American public was first feeling the impact of Freudian theory.)

Other infantile impulses needed curbing too. Since babies don't know when they've had enough to eat, the mother was not to rely on the child's appetite as a guide to feeding him. She was not to play with the infant. ("A young, delicate, and nervous baby needs rest and quiet.") She was to distinguish carefully between his legitimate needs and his selfish wants; if he cried and wasn't ill, in pain, hungry, or thirsty, she was to ignore him. ("When the baby cries simply because he has learned from experience that this brings him what he wants, it is one of the worst habits he can learn.")

The 1914 mother was also seen as having strong impulses, and she was asked to deny these as severely as she denied those of her child. Certainly it would be hard not to cuddle a baby fresh from its bath. Certainly it would be hard to let it cry itself to sleep in its crib. But the conscientious mother would put her child's welfare before her own wishes. There are frequent references in the 1914 *Infant Care* bulletin to the maternal virtues of self-control, wisdom, strength, and persistence.

By 1945, however, all had changed. That year's version of *Infant Care* told the mother not to make a fuss if the baby put his thumb in his mouth or happened to touch his genitals. ("See that he has a toy to play with and he will not need to use his body as a plaything.") The dichotomy between needs and wants was gone: "Babies want attention; they probably need plenty of it." Mothers should *enjoy* their motherhood: nursing is no longer a duty, it brings joy and happiness; introducing the baby to solid food will be "amusing"; plenty of time should be allowed for the baby's bath or "it won't be the fun for either of you that it should be."

These changing recommendations on how to raise a child are not in themselves especially significant, for the majority of mothers have always picked up crying babies (sometimes feeling guilty about doing so) or have played peek-a-boo with them when they're fretful. The publications of governmental bureaus are never radical or innovative, however, and therefore document the general mood and spirit of their time; in the case of *Infant Care,* a change in our underlying assumptions about the nature of children and of society.

Because the ways of one's culture are wholly learned, it is possible to change a people's cultural behavior within a single generation—but it hasn't often happened that a conquest of one nation by another was so complete or the vanquished people were so demoralized that their traditional culture has perished. The Indians of the Americas, for example, have preserved many of their ancient ways despite bloody conquest by Europeans. Only in circumstances such as were experienced by the black Africans who were brought to this country as slaves has a new culture replaced a traditional one within a few years. That change was possible because the cultural lifeline between generations was cut. Individuals from a variety of African cultures were transported to an alien land from which there was no escape; once here, had little or no contact with other members of their own culture; and were subjected to environmental pressures so extreme that there was no withstanding them.

This may also be the basic situation of a newborn baby. Although Benjamin Bloom was referring to the development of individuals and not to the acculturation of a people, his following comments seem applicable in either context. He has said that the young infant is both plastic and helpless in the face of the environment in which he lives—he knows no other—and can therefore be directly affected in a one-way direction by its pressure and demands. That is, the *baby* is altered or affected by the environment and is relatively powerless to affect or alter *it*. Its force upon him is further increased if many aspects of it are similar and mutually reinforcing. Bloom says, "Perhaps the notion of *consistency* is what distinguishes a powerful learning environment from one that is only moderate or ineffectual in its consequences."

There have been quantities of studies, some of which are mentioned in other chapters, which relate such environmental variables as amount and kind of social interaction or parental practices of child-rearing (amount of freedom permitted the child, for example) to the child's personality. There have also been studies relating the family's social status, parental occupations, or educational backgrounds to a child's general intelligence. But in most of these, the presence of many mutually reinforcing factors has been implied rather than shown. That's why a study by R. M. Wolf (cited by Bloom) is of interest. Wolf picked out thirteen different factors describing the interactions between parents and children, which various other investigators had related to the development of general intelligence; rated the home situations of 60 fifth-graders according to these thirteen factors; then compared those ratings to the children's IQ's.

The thirteen factors divide into two groups. Those that characterize the home itself (irrespective of the presence of a child) are: emphasis on use of language in a variety of situations, opportunities provided for enlarging vocabulary, emphasis on correctness of usage, quality of language models available, availability of books, availability of other learning supplies. Those factors that describe parental response to or pressure on the child directly are: nature of intellectual expectations of the child, nature of intellectual aspirations for the child, amount of information possessed about the child's intellectual progress, nature of rewards given for intellectual accomplishment, opportunities provided for learning in the home, opportunities provided for learning away from home (excluding school), nature and amount of help provided for the mastery of intellectual tasks.

Wolf found a multiple correlation of .76 between these factors and the children's IQ's, whereas correlations of .40 or less are characteristic of studies relating parents' educational backgrounds or social status to their children's IQ's. In other words, parents having had a college education or their possession of a high income do not necessarily promote the growth of intelligence in their children; it's the overall emphasis within the home on intellectual activities that matters. Such an atmosphere *can* be created in homes of any economic or social status. This is not to say (as the following paragraphs will indicate) that poor or low-status families are as likely to produce high IQ children as are college graduates in comfortable circumstances—only that the advantaged position of the latter must be used in the service of those attitudes and interests which produce intellectual growth if the children's inherited potential is to have maximum development.

The Wolf study illustrates environmental consistency as provided by just one institution of society—the family—and as related to just one dimension of personality—intelligence. Now let's consider an environment that includes agencies other than the family and a different trait of children, school achievement.

During the past ten or so years many programs of "compensatory education" have been undertaken by the Federal government, local school systems, and private agencies. Their primary object has been to enable disadvantaged children to catch up to their better-off contemporaries in academic skills. It is now generally conceded that such programs have failed to accomplish that goal; too many of the children who have participated in them continue to lag behind national norms—and by a progressively greater amount as they grow older. In the urban Northeast, for instance, minority-group sixth-graders (mostly Negroes and Puerto Ricans) are 1.6 years behind majority-group sixth-graders; in the ninth grade are 2.4 years behind; and in the twelfth grade are 3.3 years behind.

These figures come from a massive survey coordinated in 1965 by James S. Coleman of Johns Hopkins University, under the auspices of the U. S. Office of Education. The study was undertaken at least in part because leaders of the civil rights movement have blamed the poorer school achievement of Negro children on the allegedly inferior education that is offered them by a predominantly white society. Hence it came as a surprise when the study (covering 4000 public schools enrolling 645,000 children) found that the differences in pupil achievement cannot be explained by differing class sizes, curriculums, teacher ability, materials, or quality of physical plant. It is true that schools attended by Negroes are somewhat poorer overall° than schools attended by whites—but they

° The Coleman report emphasizes the fact that regional differences are extreme. In the well-populated States of the Far West, for example, almost every child—black or white—attends a high school with a remedial reading teacher. In the well-populated States of the South, however, only 46 percent

are not *sufficiently* poorer to account for the failure of their pupils to achieve at the level of whites.

The conclusion has to be that school achievement depends upon forces over which the schools have little or no control. The Coleman report says, "The principal way in which the school environments of Negroes and whites differ is in the composition of their student bodies, and it turns out that the composition of the student body has a strong relationship to the achievement of Negro and other minority pupils. A pupil attitude factor—the extent to which an individual feels that he has some control over his own destiny—appears to have a stronger relationship to achievement than do all the 'school' factors together. Minority pupils, except for Oriental Americans, have far less conviction than whites that they can affect their own environments and futures. When they do, however, their achievement is higher than that of whites who lack the conviction."

The above paragraphs should not be read as an indictment of compensatory education or the multitude of "enrichment" programs which have breached the walls of city ghettoes for thousands of deprived children. Their lives are incredibly constricted, geographically as well as culturally, with no link to "outside" except through the fantasy world of television. *Any* broadening of experience is therefore a net gain. The Coleman report says that Head Start children come to school with better motivation than youngsters who have not had the preschool experience provided by that program. It also emphasizes the fact that minority-group children are more affected in a positive way by good teaching and by good school facilities than are majority-group children. (Twenty percent of the achievement of Negroes in the South is associated with the particular schools they go to, whereas only 10 percent of the achievement of whites in the South has this relationship.) Thus: improving the education offered a minority-group child may increase his academic achievement more than a similar improvement in the schooling offered a majority-group child.

But the sad fact seems to be that compensatory and enrichment programs as we have known them in the recent past cannot overcome the weight of the *total* environment in which most minority-group children live. In retrospect, it was unrealistic and even naïve

---

of Negroes and 65 percent of whites have such help available at school; and in the sparsely settled areas of the Southwest the figure is 4 percent for minority-group children and 9 percent for majority-group children.

to have expected that a few hours in school or occasional excursions to museums and day camps would tip the scales against the multitude of powerful and mutually reinforcing factors—poverty, ignorance, disease, danger, and despair—to which such children are exposed for years before they *enter* school and for more hours in any day than they *attend* school.

Regardless of the "goodness" or "badness" of a social environment, however, those who live in it develop a life style that serves the essential purpose of helping the individual anticipate the behavior of his fellows and by conforming to it become one of them. Depending on degree of variance from the general norms of the dominant national culture, these varying life styles become identifiable subcultures. In the United States, some subcultures have endured for a long time—for example, those of the Pennsylvania Amish and New York's colony of Hasidic Jews; those of the Southern mountain whites and the American Indians who live on reservations; and that of the rural or ghettoized urban Negro. Whether the hippies of the 1960s will remain as a definite subculture remains to be seen. Americans are a mobile people, and only in the case of prolonged social isolation is any environment "pure" for the establishment and maintenance of just one life style.

Another division characteristic of most societies is that of caste. Webster defines caste as "a system of social stratification characterized by hereditary status, marriage within the group, and social barriers rigidly sanctioned by custom, law or religion." India's castes are perhaps the best known, but the United States has them too. All Negroes, and in some circumstances Jews and Catholics, are members of castes. There are caste overtones among what sociologists and politicians call "the ethnic groups." These are the first and second generation descendants of immigrant groups against whom social barriers were erected when they first arrived in the United States ("ROOM FOR RENT—IRISH NEED NOT APPLY") and who remain clannish in proportion to the length of time since their arrival.

A third kind of division is by social class, but I will reserve a discussion of class differences until we have considered how children learn their identity as members of a distinctive social group. That will be the subject of the next chapter.

CHAPTER 19

ACQUIRING SOCIAL-GROUP
IDENTITY

At what age does an American child learn that he is a Protestant, a Catholic, or a Jew; a Japanese-American, a Mexican-American, or an Irish-American; a white or a black? And what do these labels mean to him?

The young child's first job, as indicated in earlier chapters, is to differentiate himself from other individuals—to become "I", an independent person with an independent self. To do this takes at least three years; in fact, its essential achievement somewhere around the fourth birthday has been nicely documented by the husband-and-wife team of Kenneth and Mamie Clark who are at New York's Northside Center for Child Development. In a series of studies, they presented pictures of white children, Negro children, lions, dogs, hens, and clowns to groups of both white and Negro children of nursery school age, and said to each child, "Show me which one is you."

At age three, a sizable fraction of children—in one group, almost 18 percent—picked the animals, thus indicating failure to identify themselves as distinct persons. But at age four, hardly any children equated themselves with hens or lions. By then, they not only knew that they were persons but also (if dimly) that boys differ from girls and that white persons differ from black ones.

When the Clarks recorded the responses of the Negro children according to the degree of pigmentation in the child's own skin, they found that the picture of the Negro boy was chosen by 56 percent of the dark-skinned three-year-olds; by 52 percent of those with medium-brown skin; and by 36 percent of those with light skin. Furthermore, the pattern was consistent as the children grew older (although the percentages changed so that the choices of the white boy diminished for all three groups). This indicated to the Clarks that Negro children develop their consciousness of self-as-different-from-others on the basis of a concrete physical trait (observed skin color) and *then* acquire their awareness of race in its social-caste connotation.°

That this awareness is established by age five, in both whites and Negroes, has been recorded in numerous studies. One of the best—and also one of the most readable—was done by the cultural anthropologist Mary Ellen Goodman, now a professor at Rice University in Houston, and the mother of two children. Her subjects were 103 four- and five-year-olds attending nursery schools in a northeastern city.

And if you are thinking that such *young* children couldn't possibly be aware of the social implications of belonging to a given race, Goodman has disturbing news. Adults just don't catch the cues. "Because Americans like to believe in the 'purity' of childhood," she says, "we ignore or selectively forget matters which are distasteful. Precocious sexuality shocks us and so does precocious raciality."

The cues, however, are there. They can be as public as a child's first use of skin-color labels when describing someone, or his observed interest in the color and texture of a playmate's hair. They can also be as private as those that emerge during sessions of doll play with a trained observer. The mother of one little Negro girl, for example, said that her Joan never judged people on a basis of color—yet in play sessions set up for the Goodman study the child repeatedly described dolls or pictures of people as "white," "brown," or "colored," and at one point said, "The people that are white, they can go up. The people that are brown, they have to go down."

Joan, like most other four-year-olds, had already passed the first stage of racial awareness—"the dawning and sharpening of consciousness of self and of others in terms of racial identity"—and

° This, of course, is the definition of "race" that matters in contemporary America, it being perfectly obvious to everyone that some "Negroes" have much lighter skin than some "whites."

was well into the phase of establishing attitudes about race. During this phase, children are learning how other people place whites and Negroes on various scales of value. In fact, some of Goodman's not-yet-five-year-old white children were showing "unmistakable signs of the onset of racial bigotry"; and many of the Negro children were showing with equal clarity, and unease, that they knew they were "marked."

Of the total group of 103 children, 24 percent of the white children and 40 percent of the Negro children had *high* awareness of racial characteristics and the favorable or unfavorable implications of racial membership. And even among the 15 percent of whites and 15 percent of Negroes with *low* awareness there was some differential valuing of people in terms of color.

The story was essentially the same with six-year-olds studied by Eugene and Ruth Horowitz, who lived for a time in a rural area in one of the Border States and recorded the emergence of many social attitudes among the children of the district. This was a section in which there was great cleavage between the races and between the sexes, one in which social roles were firmly fixed. There was no confusion in any citizen's mind as to how one was supposed to behave if male or female, black or white, young or old; and the local folkways allowed very little deviation from the prescribed patterns.

Among the tests given to white first-graders by the Horowitzes was a series of pictures in which the child was to indicate which of the pictured individuals did not "belong" in a given set. A set might include three white boys, a white girl, and a Negro boy; or three white girls, a Negro girl, and a white woman. In the first case, the viewer could exclude the Negro boy (which would indicate awareness of race) or the girl (awareness of sex); in the second case, he could exclude the Negro girl (awareness of race) or the woman (awareness of age).

Result? However the assemblage of pictures varied, race awareness was the dominant social attitude. In the case of the set first mentioned, 59 percent of first graders said that the Negro boy didn't belong, and 15 percent said that the girl didn't belong. Other social attitudes of the children, in order of importance, had to do with the sex, age, and socioeconomic status of other people.

Children's awareness of membership in ethnic groups (whether national or religious in character) develops a bit more slowly, but is well-established by about age seven. Eugene L. Hartley, Max Rosenbaum, and Shepard Schwartz recorded the development of this kind of self-recognition among children attending a settlement house in the Bronx, one that served a heterogeneous population of Jews, Irish, Italians, Puerto Ricans, and Negroes.

They found, first, that three- and four-year-olds, their concepts of themselves as persons so newly achieved, do not think in group terms. If asked, "What kind of people live around your house?", children of this age typically say, "Aunt Bessie and Grandpa." They are past six before the answer is, "Italians" or "Jewish." If asked, "What are you?" the answer of a four-year-old is, "I'm Carol," or "I'm big"; but a year and a half later the same child will say, "I'm Catholic."

To find out what these ethnic labels mean to a child, the investigators asked their younger subjects "Are you Jewish?" (or whatever the proper label was), and collected a rich harvest of marvelously irrelevant answers (by adult standards). Samples:

"Are you Jewish?" "No, I'm only four. I'll get Jewish."

"Are you Catholic?" "No, I'm Richie."

"Are you American?" "No, my father is American. I'm a girl."

And then, to see at what age children understand that one can have two labels at once, the children were asked such questions as, "Can you be Catholic and American?" or "Can you be Negro and Protestant?" Among the younger children, there was great confusion on this point. Some said that one *can't* be Negro and Protestant or Catholic and American; others said just as firmly that one *can* be Jewish and Catholic.

From about the age of seven, however, children use ethnic labels much as adults do, and know that religious and nationality affiliations can be compatible. But they still don't apply these concepts to themselves with the same understanding that adults bring to the awareness. For example, an eight-year-old girl of Italian-American parentage whose widowed mother had recently married an Italian national, said, "I'm just Italian now. I used to be American . . . four weeks ago. I used to have a different father."

One of the most impressive of the studies of children's attitudes on race and religion was done by Marian Radke, Helen Trager, and Hadassah Davis. They examined 250 youngsters aged five to eight, in six different public schools in Philadelphia. The group included Protestants, Catholics, and Jews, as well as whites and Negroes.

The three women showed them pictures similar to Figure 32, in which a Negro child is shown watching a game in which the players are white. The child can be perceived as a passive bystander or as a latecomer about to join the group. There were also scenes showing children leaving a synagogue or church, and classroom pictures in which the absence of some children was explained as due to a religious holiday. While looking at these scenes, the children were queried as to what was going on or what might happen to the child or children in the scene.

Of the playground scene, for instance, each child was asked,

FIGURE 32

"Will the children on the field ask the boy to play?" Marian Radke and her associates found that even kindergarteners are aware of racially based patterns of exclusion: 43 percent of white five-year-olds and 35 percent of Negro five-year-olds said, "No," in answer to the above question. At the same time, 36 percent of the whites and 49 percent of the Negroes answered, "Yes," to the question "Does the boy want to play?" (From "Social Perceptions and Attitudes of Children" by Marian Radke, *Genetic Psychology Monographs*, 1949. Reproduced by permission of The Journal Press and Dr. Marian Radke-Yarrow.)

"Will the children [on the field] ask the boy to play?" The "no" responses rose steadily with age, as shown below:

	White children	Negro children
Kindergarteners	43%	35%
First graders	67%	46%
Second graders	75%	60%

A related question, "Does the boy want to play?", brought these percentages of "yes" responses:

	White children	Negro children
Kindergarteners	36%	49%
First graders	21%	49%
Second graders	22%	34%

The psychological defenses are being constructed, as you can see: on the part of the Negro children, that one doesn't want what one can't have; on the part of the white children, that the Negro child has a choice.

"There was expressed conflict among a few of the older children," Marian Radke says. "They stated that discrimination against Negroes is 'not fair' or 'not nice.' Perhaps the most sophisticated statement was from a white second grader who said, 'He isn't playing because they won't let him play. If he was a white boy they would let him play. Even if he is colored they should let him play. What's different about him? Maybe he was born in the night and they was born in the day.'"

Similar conflict in the Negro children expressed itself in rejecting white in one answer and reaching out for white in the next, as when one Negro child said, "No, he don't want to play. I don't like white people"; and then, "He isn't playing 'cause he wish he was white."

This same yearning appears in other studies. Mary Ellen Goodman, for example, found that "the idea that whites are 'prettier' is a majority opinion." Most young Negro children prefer white dolls, white playmates, white teachers—for the excellent reason that whiteness is equated in their minds with "good" and blackness with "bad."

Goodman says of her four- and five-year-old Negroes, "Our high-awareness children are almost conscious of the dilemma in which they are placed by being unable to like some of the most striking aspects of themselves, their families, and their friends . . . They squirm, literally and figuratively, as they talk with us about matters which clearly focus on race and color.

"We do not use pointed words, but they do, and they recognize the nature of the topic to which we have led them . . . There is a kind of desperation in Tony's cry of 'Brown—brown—brown!' as he throws down the picture about which we have been talking, and talking too long for his peace of mind. The matter is becoming more and more personal and personally threatening.

"He and others must have felt like Barbara, who obviously did not enjoy being asked to tell which doll or picture looked most like herself, and her parents. And finally she said so, with intensity and exasperation. 'Don't ask too many questions!' she said. '*I can't stand it!*'"

Awareness of one's religious group identity follows much the same course as awareness of one's racial identity—that is, the early phase is one of perceiving objective features that are associated with a given group, and only later are the members of the group rated on a value scale.

For example, when Marian Radke asked one of her five-year-olds to tell her what "Jewish" means, the child promptly answered, "Jewish is pickles." Another child of the same age distinguished between Catholics and Protestants by saying, "Catholics write in first grade. Protestants print." By the age of seven, however, children are beginning to classify members of religious groups as individuals about whom evaluations are made. "Sometimes other people's mothers don't like Protestants to play with Catholics," one little girl remarked.

In this particular group of children, anti-Protestant attitudes increased from 5 percent among kindergarteners to 37 percent among second-graders; anti-Catholic attitudes from 11 percent to 24 percent; and anti-Jewish attitudes from 16 percent to 36 percent. Radke and her colleagues summarized their findings by saying that children, between kindergarten and second grade, become increasingly *aware* of group conflicts, patterns of exclusion, and forms of derogation; and at the same time grow more *accepting* of these attitudes.

Jewish children are twice as likely as those of any other group to identify themselves as Jewish, and Negro children are least likely to give themselves a religious label. "For Negro children the most

potent group factors are racial," Radke comments, "and the differen-
tiations along religious lines are dwarfed or obscured by comparison."

Now, what influences in the environment shape children's social
attitudes?

Mary Ellen Goodman makes the point that it is not a simple
matter of transmission from the older generation to the younger,
but rather that each child generates his own attitudes—absorbing
the raw materials provided by society, in amounts and at a rate
determined by his own personality and circumstances. For example,
a child who has been intelligently and lovingly nurtured and is
therefore basically serene and agreeable is more likely to look
across the color line at members of the opposite race. In contrast,
a child who has not learned to trust people and who feels threatened
by life is more likely to look *down* (if he's white) or *up* (if he's
black)—and there are seeds of danger in either posture. The child's
own perceptual abilities—his acuteness of observation, say—and his
intelligence make a difference too.

The raw materials provided by society consist of what he hears,
sees, and (most important of all) *senses* at home, at school, at
church, and on the street corner. Of these, the home is dominant
because it is while the child is still young enough to be spending
most of his time under his mother's wing that his first awareness
of race develops. What his parents teach him then can have a profound effect on his final attitudes.

Not that most parents believe that they are "teaching" their preschoolers anything about race. The Horowitzes, Marian Radke and
her associates, and Mary Ellen Goodman all agree that parents are
generally quite unconscious of either the general atmospheres they
create or of the specific guidance they provide. Here is a nice
example from the Goodman book; all you have to do is pretend you
are a four-year-old white child named Ian who is playing with his
blocks in the same room where his mother is talking to a friend. The
mother says:

"We want our children to be democratic and get along with all
kinds of people. Then later on they can choose their own friends
. . . So it's good for them to be at the Rodney School.

"But, still, the school isn't what it used to be before they started
taking in such a rough group—so many lower class families. There

used to be hardly any Negroes there. Our children haven't associated with colored except at the nursery school . . .

"We've had them in our home only in the capacity of servants—a cleaning woman now and then. Of course, when they're here like that, the children and I have lunch with them. I wouldn't hurt their feelings and beside I wouldn't have the children get the idea that I minded. We certainly don't want our children to be prejudiced."

As for specific guidance on matters of behavior, here's an example from Eugene and Ruth Horowitz's study. They interviewed parents and children separately as to choice of playmates, and got these parallel responses:

The Mother: "Yes, I used to tell her not to play with some. Just told her, never gave her any reasons. She never played with Negro children, I didn't have to tell her *that.*"

The Child: "Colored people have dirty houses, they're dirty. Mother told me not to play with them because sometimes they have diseases and you get it from them."

The Horowitzes: "Apparently parents give direct instruction and cannot recall having done so. Children at first are well aware of their sources but toward adolescence tend to lose conscious recollection of the origins, and devise rationalizations of various sorts to support them."

In a survey of prejudice among college students, Gordon W. Allport and Bernard Kramer found that racial, religious, or other group prejudices play an appreciable role in the mental life of four fifths of the American population; that contact with minority groups does not diminish prejudice unless the contact is in an equal-status situation (and not always then); that religious training in itself does not diminish prejudice (but may, if it is specifically aimed at tolerance); that the most prejudiced people are the *least* likely to ascribe their attitudes to parental example but are disposed instead "to regard their hostilities as natural and fully justified by the misbehavior of the minority groups they dislike."

Every generation uses children for its own purposes.

In choosing and summarizing research reported in this chapter, I deliberately omitted any reference to dates. Does it surprise you to know that the most recent of these studies was published in 1952 and that the majority date from the 1930s and 1940s? Further, does it surprise you to know that the findings of those studies are as valid today as they were then?*

Yet during the past fifteen years the popular press has done a good job of stressing the common humanity which overlies the group differences among our people. It is impossible, for example, for any literate American *not* to know that there is as much class variation among Negroes as among whites. Nevertheless, middle class white mothers, North and South, still stand at school doors and yell curses at a handful of entering middle class Negro children whose cultural background and behavior is indistinguishable from that of white children already enrolled in the school.

Stores owned by Jews are the preferred targets of ghetto rioters, and Jews are still barred from membership in many a club which welcomes individuals with precisely the same qualifications—so long as they have Christian names or features or church membership. Politicians seek votes by exploiting one group's irrational fears of another group. "Only a black alderman can understand the needs of a black constituency," says this aspirant. "You've worked and saved and invested your savings in this nice neighborhood," says another, "so what right have *they* to come in and spoil it?"

All this, and more, despite the fact that we know—and most of us *do* know—that social conflict, especially racial conflict, is gravely damaging the nation and the quality of our own lives. Humiliating, isn't it, to realize that our emotions so control our behavior? And dangerous.

Not that it must inevitably remain so. We adults are a lost cause, Mary Ellen Goodman says, but we can—if we wish to—build for a better future by changing some of our ways of dealing with our preschool children. Here is her advice, for parents of any race:

1. Be sensitive to the development of the child's awareness of racial differences, and don't dodge his questions.

To a four-year-old, "Color is one of the things about people which he sees and naturally wonders about. He is likely to ask about a good many other things having nothing to do with race, and get an open answer. If he gets the same kind of answer when he asks a question which does have to do with race, then he is

---

* One possible exception, to my knowledge not yet documented by any social scientist, has to do with Negro children's belief that "whites are 'prettier.'" The "Black Is Beautiful" campaign launched by militant Negroes of the late 1960s, if sustained, may well help to ameliorate a Negro child's tendency to rate his attractiveness by white standards.

being told—in terms of general atmosphere—that racial features are just one of the many interesting things about people. This is a constructive and rational view.

"If he gets no answer, or an evasive or emotional one, then the atmosphere tells him that this is a taboo subject"—and he sets it apart in his mind as of special importance, something fearsome perhaps but also something fascinating. "Taboos on racial discussion," Goodman goes on, "do not prevent the development of awareness or feeling, but they do allow for the persistence of confusion, conflict, and inaccuracies."

2. Give him factual and logical answers, specific rather than generalized.

"Why am I brown?" or "Why is Mary black?" are questions too often answered with, "Because God made you [or her] that way." Even four-year-olds can understand a simple explanation of pigmentation, Goodman says, and that all of God's people "occupy a brownness continuum which proceeds without a break from dark brown to the extreme bleach of the extreme blond."

The stress should be placed upon the fact that "there are degrees of difference which *unite people on the same scale* rather than divide them into sharply separated kinds." In fact, it's a good idea to avoid *all* "either-or" classifications of people or their behavior. However you define "nice," Goodman points out, it is good to keep in mind that "nice" and "not nice" are at opposite ends of a scale rather than standing for mutually exclusive categories.

And here's an example of a reply that emphasizes specifics. When Johnny announces that he doesn't like to play with Negroes because they're dirty (and white children are not the only ones who say this), a wise mother can puncture this false generalization by asking the child which *particular* Negroes he is referring to. She can also mention some other Negroes who aren't dirty and some whites who *are*. In doing so, she helps him learn to think of individuals as individuals and not as members of some out-group called "they."

3. Be realistic about the present importance of racial differences, for the child will soon enough find out for himself that they *are* important. But at the same time make it clear that tomorrow's realities can be different. "To see racial reality as a man-made yet still malleable thing is a very sophisticated view," Goodman says. "It is also a rational and accurate one."

And this view, too, can be communicated to a four-year-old. The

Goodman book, *Race Awareness in Young Children,* includes some hypothetical mother-child conversations that suggest, in more detail than I have reported, just how mothers of good will and some sense can put the previous recommendations into practice.

The fourth point is my own extrapolation. Whenever you have had contact with people of another race, ask yourself just afterward whether you were looking *across* the color line. And try to look across, rather than up or down (as the case may be) more often. The outcome could be the building of an "America for everybody"—Mrs. Goodman's phrase—a little faster.

CHAPTER 20

THE MARK OF SOCIAL CLASS

Subcultures and castes, because their members are isolated or excluded from the main body of society, have limited relevance to the behavioral patterns of society as a whole. Just the reverse is true of social classes. Not only do they cut across both subcultural and caste lines, and contain members of all races, all religions, and all ethnic groups, but in addition they have pervasive influence upon all American cultural behaviors.

We like to think of ourselves as an egalitarian people because we have so many things in common: a language, a government, public schools which most of our children attend, standardized goods which most of us consume, sports and entertainments which most of us enjoy. But when one looks more closely at this surface picture of commonality, one finds that social class determines the particular form of language used, the type of legislator one votes for, the kind of school one's child attends, one's taste in clothes and food and books and friends.

Historically, the division was between the aristocracy—monarch, nobles, and priesthood—and the proletariat. Today, in industrialized countries like our own (including those with reigning monarchs), it is the professionals and managers who are at the top of the social heap. Then come the second-echelon executives, teachers, and technicians. A grade below are the clerks and the skilled and semiskilled workmen. Individual variations in background and circumstances strongly influence one's position in these middle brackets: a teacher, for instance, may be upper middle, middle, or lower middle class. But the lower class is distinct and recognizable: it is composed of the unskilled and unemployable.

Because social class is based largely on occupation, it is easier for an individual to move from one class to another than to leave a subculture or caste. But upward mobility is not *quite* as easy as the Horatio Alger legends would have it—partly because occupation is based largely on education, which is based largely on opportunity, which is based largely on class°; and partly because class-correlated behaviors have a stubborn persistence across generations.

For many years the University of Stockholm's Torsten Husén has been interested in the relationship between social class and the utilization of opportunities offered by schooling. He recently reported the findings of a survey which did not start out as a longitudinal study but fortuitously turned into one. The story goes like this:

As a young graduate student in educational psychology at the University of Lund in 1938, Husén took part in a survey of all third-graders in the Malmö schools—a total of some fifteen hundred children. In 1942 a colleague of his supervised a follow-up study to see how the same children had done in school during the intervening four years. In 1948, when the boys in the group came of age for military service and were tested by the Swedish Conscription Board, Husén was a consultant for the personnel selection service of the Armed Forces. Knowing of the existence of these three sets of records of the same group of young people, Husén decided that it would be interesting to check on them again when they had become mature—perhaps at that stage of their lives when they had children of the same age as *they* had been when first tested.

In 1964, then, he undertook such a follow-up study. Amazingly, he was able to obtain information about *all* the 1938 subjects—thanks, he says, to "the uncannily effective public registration in Sweden, which in its turn is due to the fiscal zeal which sees to

° The British civil service of the recent past is an excellent example of this circularity. Until the 1940s, only the upper classes could provide for their children the kind of schooling which prepared young people for Oxford and Cambridge; and well into the 1960s, some 98 percent of Foreign Office jobs were held by graduates of Oxford or Cambridge.

it that everybody is kept track of." He was able to obtain answered questionnaires from over 73 percent of the group. Then he set about comparing their overall records and their 1964 status in life with their 1938 home backgrounds and intervening school performance.

In the 1930s, it should be explained, all Swedish children spent four years in elementary schools, from which the brighter children were transferred at about age eleven to junior secondary schools. From these, the brighter ones went, three years later, to the *gymnasium,* an equivalent of an American high school with college preparatory courses only. The less-bright children, in contrast, remained in the elementary school for six years, after which they transferred to a more vocationally oriented secondary school.

Although a bright child from an uneducated family background could in theory and sometimes in fact did make it to the *gymnasium* (and even to a university, which in Europe is far more selective in its admission policies than American universities), the cards were pretty well stacked against the lower class child. Of Husén's 1938 group, for example, 45 percent of the upper class boys entered the junior secondary school versus 13 percent of the lower class boys, and over half of these latter failed to finish. Of those in the 1938 group who got through the *gymnasium,* 59 percent of the upper class boys passed the examination for university admission whereas only 10 percent of boys from any other class qualified.

During the following quarter century, however, the dual track system of education was replaced by common schools of the American type. The majority of Swedish children now remain in school until age eighteen, and there is no bar within the school system itself to deny university admission to any child who is capable of doing the work. Other sweeping changes have also occurred in Swedish life. There has been a great economic leveling, the lower classes becoming less poor and the upper classes becoming less rich; and the health benefits of a social welfare state have been broadly spread.

In sum, the barriers to a lower class child's rising into a higher class became far less formidable than they were in the 1930s—as demonstrated by the fact that two thirds of Husén's 1938 subjects from lower class homes had by 1964 moved into lower middle or middle class jobs, and 3 percent of them were in upper class jobs. But when Husén asked them what educational aspirations they have for their children, here is how they responded:

Class of home in 1938	Percentage of those who in 1964 wanted their children to attend a university
Professional-managerial	80%
Subprofessional white collar workers	49%
Skilled workers	37%
Unskilled workers	34%

In short, as Husén says, "The aspirations that the parents hold for their children's education are to a strikingly high extent connected with their own social class at the age of ten." These findings again underscore a recurring motif in these pages: that a child's *early* experience establishes behavior patterns which persist throughout his life.

As I earlier indicated (and will shortly amplify), there are distinctive class differences in ways of ordering one's life and household—with corresponding variation in the behavior and personalities of children. Will the fact that Husén's subjects have clung to at least some of their 1938 class-correlated attitudes while actually holding occupations characteristic of different classes make a difference in the future of their children? Or will other influences in society at large counterbalance the effect of one generation's early experience upon the behavior of the second generation? Husén suggests that the children of his 1938 subjects be interviewed in 1993, "to confirm or refute the belief that ability as cultivated by universal education has a much stronger impact than any other factor."

The psycholinguist Basil Bernstein of University College, London, is an influential advocate of the view that language shapes not only thought but social class as well. This is not the same as saying that language indicates the social class to which an individual belongs (as indeed it does); Bernstein believes that the language modes characteristically used by the upper and the lower classes *initiate* and then *reinforce* different patterns of behavior and personality. So let us examine the two modes of language, and see what behavioral consequences might result.

Members of the lower middle and lower classes tend to have smaller vocabularies than members of the middle and upper classes. (Gustav Jahoda tested a group of English boys from working class and middle class homes and found that the former, by age fourteen, had vocabularies half the size of their middle class counterparts.) In using these vocabularies, members of the two lower classes rely heavily on "ready-made" phrases: "Nice day today," "How are things with you?", "It's beyond me," "This tastes good."

In this mode of speech, sentences are short, simple, and often incomplete. Even if grammatically correct, they make little use of the structural variety inherent in the language. Subordinate clauses are rare; the conjunctions "so" and "and" are overused; there is scant and unimaginative use of adjectives and adverbs; and dominant ideas are emphasized by phrases such as "You know?" rather than elaborated by use of additional words chosen to confer shades of meaning. This is a basically stereotyped and condensed form of speech, general rather than specific, limited in range and detail.

The language of the middle and upper classes is just the reverse.

To illustrate, here is a classic love story as it might be told by users of the two language modes. The lower class speaker might say:

"There was this boy and this girl, see? Their folks hated each other, so . . . But the boy and the girl were in love and this priest married them. In secret. Then the boy got into trouble, he killed a guy, and had to skip town. Well, the girl's father didn't know they were married and wanted her to marry another fellow. So she took a sleeping pill and pretended to be dead.

"Everyone thought she *was* dead. A funeral instead of a wedding, you know? The story got around and her real husband believed it too. He couldn't live without her so he took some poison. And then she woke up and there he was dead. It was the same with her. So she stabbed herself. Terrible sad, the end."

The upper class version, however, might go something like this:

"There was once a pair of young lovers who dared not ask their parents' permission to marry because an old quarrel between the two families had become a bitter feud. The young people were nevertheless determined to marry, and persuaded a kindly priest to perform a secret wedding ceremony. On the same day, however, the young bridegroom foolishly allowed himself to be drawn into a street brawl, during which he killed a man. The authorities banished him from the town—a punishment which, of course, meant separation from his bride. He spent the night with her but, as day broke, the couple tearfully parted and he went into exile.

"Shortly thereafter, another young man—handsome, charming,

rich, and altogether suitable—asked for the girl's hand in marriage. Her father approved his suit and could not understand the girl's reluctance. She, unable to persuade her father that she did not find her suitor acceptable and afraid to confess that she was already married, turned once more to the family priest. He gave her a sleeping potion . . ."

The upper classes, as you see, are more long-winded; but Romeo and Juliet seem more like real people, their motives are clearer, and there is some sense of an analytical mode of thought beneath the telling of the tale.

Bernstein does not say that the members of the upper and lower classes speak *only* in these modes, for everyone at some time or another uses prefabricated phrases like "Nice day today." They are especially useful at cocktail parties and in apartment house elevators, for example. But Bernstein does say that:

1. A person who habitually uses the simpler and less individualized mode of language will tend to ignore small and subtle differences among objects, persons, and situations, and thus the perceptual relationships that he forms will stabilize rather early. If the twin processes of differentiation and abstraction must occur together (as was suggested in an earlier chapter), a child whose discriminative powers are low will have trouble with higher-order abstractions. Bernstein says, "The Piagetian developmental sequence from concrete to formal operations may not be inevitable in the case of [such a] child; he may well be limited to concrete operations."

2. It will be difficult for the speaker of such a language to make his wishes or feelings explicit enough either to identify them to himself or to convey them to others. Suppose, for example, that a child is caught taking a quarter from his mother's purse and can't explain the intensity of his desire to have it. If he cannot elaborate his emotion or his intent, either to himself or to his mother, and is forced to settle for "I just *wanted* it, that's all!", he will have such an acute sense of frustration because he couldn't label or describe this particular emotion that he will make fewer efforts in the future to label or describe other emotions.

3. He will become relatively insensitive to emotions in other people, and to individual differences in general. He will find his personal identity within a group of children (children of this class are especially likely to belong to gangs), and will categorize other people on the basis of their status in life rather than on the basis of in-

dividual qualities. For example, he will consider it proper to obey the boss *because* he is the boss, and not because the boss is an admirable person or a good leader.

All this from the way one talks?

Yes, if one agrees with Bernstein that "language marks out what is relevant, and experience is transformed by that which is made relevant." Once a group has chosen to stress one rather than another of the different possibilities inherent in language use, the resulting linguistic form will mold its members' ways of thinking and feeling. Bernstein says, "As the child learns his speech, so will he learn his social structure; and the latter will become the substratum of his innermost experience."

In England, as in Sweden, the past twenty years have given lower class children vastly increased opportunities to attend college preparatory schools and then the university. But the language of those institutions is upper class, and the dilemma of a bright working class boy or girl is whether or not to adopt it.

It is not so simple a matter as a change of accent or an expansion of vocabulary. Because speech is so intimately connected with the family and its social traditions, the child in accepting another mode of speech is repudiating his kin and their ways. Inasmuch as twelve or thirteen is rather young for accepting and mastering the role of "marginal man" (a person caught between two cultures), many such English boys elect to speak one way at school and another way at home. This is simply a device for buying time. The psychological stress remains.

Children from America's lower classes have the same problem. Not only do such children use a form of language that differs from that of their middle class teachers and middle class textbooks, but in addition they find themselves being punished—by the teacher's scorn or their own failure—for having the lower class culture of which their parents approve and in which they were raised. It is not "lack of reading readiness" that is the heart of the problem. It is the assault upon their "innermost experience" that isolates and bewilders them, raises their level of anxiety, and further inhibits their ability to learn the new ways that have been thrust upon them.

Or so Basil Bernstein, most persuasively, says.

In 1951, Esther Milner (now at Brooklyn College) compared the reading ability of children in three Atlanta schools with their parents' social class. She gave tests to all the first graders in (a) a pri-

vate school for children of professional and managerial-level Negroes; (b) a public school with a broad range of lower middle to
upper class whites; and (c) a public school in a white slum. The tests
showed a high relationship between high scores and middle class
homes, low scores and lower class homes—and not just because of
the well-publicized reason that better educated people tend to have
many books in the home, value them, and read a great deal to their
preschool children.

In her home visits, Milner noted several qualities of intrafamily
"climate" that differentiated homes of different class. The middle
class children lived in an environment that was verbally much richer
overall than that of the lower class children. At meals, for example,
middle class parents were permissive about childish chatter: the
child was talked to with mature speech patterns and in turn was
listened to. The lower class children's situation was the reverse. In
fact, one mother said of her little girl, "I do not allow her to talk
when she is eating, it is a bad habit."

Kind of punishment and expression of emotion varied by class,
too. Parents of high-scoring children controlled their youngsters' behavior mostly by verbal prohibition, by withholding privileges, etc.
Parents of low-scoring children spanked or slapped their children.
None of the children liked being punished, of course, but punishment was easier for the middle class children to take because their
parents on other occasions expressed overt affection for them. This
practice, Milner says, counterbalanced their controlling and limiting
role as disciplinarians. Because the lower class parents did not show
affection (it should not be assumed that they did not *feel* it), there
existed in these homes no emotional offset for the psychological
effects upon the children of physical punishment.

This is only one of many similar studies that were carried on during the mid-1940s and early 1950s, their purpose being to relate
the character of intrafamily relationships to the behavior and personalities of children. Although varying in method, emphasis, and
terminology, such work divided home environments into "democratic" and "authoritarian" ones (and in sum played an important
role in sanctioning the permissive style of child-rearing now practiced in most American middle class homes). T. W. Adorno and
David McClelland wrote book-length reports on the subject; a dissertation by Marion R. Winterbottom is often referred to in the

scholarly literature; and Lester Sontag's monograph (cited in Chapter 14) is another example.

Dating from the same period, too, is Alfred L. Baldwin's factor analysis of parental behavior toward four-year-old children. In those of his young subjects' homes in which the authoritarian atmosphere prevailed, Baldwin noted that the children were considered as junior, nonvoting members of the family. Arbitrary decisions were made by the adults, and the children were not allowed to appeal them. The children of such households tended to be quiet, well-behaved, gentle, unaggressive, undemonstrative—and restricted in curiosity and originality.

In democratic homes,* the child was accorded equal status as a person with the adult members of the family. In making decisions, the parents consulted the child, considered his preferences, explained the reasons for the rules, and modified them on occasion to suit the wishes or needs of that particular child. If, in addition, it was the kind of family in which the parents encouraged the child to become involved in whatever they were doing (even if it took the father twice as long to wash the car when Johnny helped), the child was likely to be aggressive, impatient, cruel, and quarrelsome—and curious, outgoing, spontaneous, and full of plans and projects.

"The predominant effect of parent behavior upon the preschool child is to raise or lower his willingness and ability to behave actively toward the environment," Baldwin concluded. To parents of four-year-olds, he offered little hope that they can have it both ways: a quiet, obedient, unaggressive child who at the same time is full of zest for living and learning.

In general, although of course not always, middle class homes are more democratic; lower class homes, more authoritarian.

A dominant thread running through all these reports has to do with the degree of verbal interaction between parent and child. In authoritarian homes, less conversation is necessary: rules do not need to be explained and children's individual preferences do not have to be taken into account. In democratic homes, on the other hand, two-way talk flows like a spring flood. But it seems to create a child who is not only ready to read when he goes to school, but

---

* Baldwin observed that the children of democratic homes are not necessarily, or even often, uncontrolled; an observation which challenges the widespread belief that permissiveness equates with complete lack of restraint.

in addition has more acute perception, better developed concepts, and greater reasoning ability than his less talked to classmates.

Such, at any rate, is the opinion of Robert D. Hess and Virginia Shipman. Their research objective was to see whether American speech duplicates the English pattern that Basil Bernstein had in mind when analyzing language modes, and to observe verbal "teaching styles" of mothers of young children. Their subjects were 160 mothers of four-year-old children. All were good mothers, in the sense that they showed no significant differences in expression of affection or responsibility toward their children; and all were Negroes. But they ranged from a college-educated group whose husbands are executives or professional men (some of whom had annual incomes of $20,000) to a group of poorly educated women on public aid, the majority of whom had annual incomes below $3000.

The investigators first asked the mothers a series of hypothetical questions pertaining to the children's behavior. One of these was, "Suppose your child were starting to school tomorrow for the first time. What would you tell him? How would you prepare him for school?"

A lower class mother replied, "I would tell him to go to school and be nice. I'd tell him to obey the teacher and to be very good."

A middle class mother, responding to the same question, said, "I would remind Portia that she was going to school to learn, that her teacher would take my place, and that she would be expected to follow instructions. Also that her time was to be spent mostly in the classroom with other children, and that any questions she might have she could consult with her teacher for assistance."

To a question about what the mother would do if her child came home from school with a note saying that he had been misbehaving, a lower class mother succinctly replied, "I'd whup him!" But a middle class mother said, "Well, I don't know. I would want to talk to the child and find out why. Then I would decide what to do."

The lower class mothers were more authoritarian ("I'd tell him to obey the teacher"), the middle class mothers more inclined to consider the needs of the individual child ("I would want to talk to the child and find out why"). The middle class mothers were more informative in giving instructions, a practice which requires more precise word choice, greater explicitness in phrasing, and more complexity of sentence structure than do the imperative statements that the lower class mothers tended to use.

Other parts of the Hess and Shipman study, therefore, concentrated on the extent to which the mothers used language to impel their children to action, and the quality of that language. It was found that the middle class mothers used almost twice as many words, twice as many abstract words, and twice as many sentences with complex syntax (for example, subordinate clauses to elaborate the content of the message) as lower class mothers.

In some tests, children performed a given task under their mother's direction, then were asked to repeat it by themselves and tell the investigator why they did what they did. In other tests, mothers and children did independent but similar sorting or choosing tasks. In all cases, the children's ability to discriminate, to describe, to reflect, and to think in a sequential rather than a disconnected fashion correlated with the amount and kind of language used by the mothers to cue their children.

Here are three examples (from taped recordings) of how mothers of different social classes instructed their children:

"All right, Susan," said a middle class mother. "This board is the place where we put the little toys. First you're supposed to place them according to color. Can you do that?"

The child nodded her head.

"The things that are all the same color you put in one section," the mother continued. "In the second section you put another group of colors, and in the third section you put the last group of colors. Can you do that? Or would you like to see me do it first?"

Susan said, "I want to do it." And did it.

In the second phase of the same test, toys were to be sorted by function. One of the lower class mothers began her instruction by saying, "I've got some spoons and chairs and cars, do you want to play the game?"

The child did not respond; and the mother continued, "O.K. What's this?"

The child said, "A wagon?"

The mother replied, "Hmm?", and the child repeated, "A wagon?"

The mother said, "That's not a wagon. Now, what's this . . . ?" Her conversation continued in the same vein for several pages of transcription. Unlike the first mother, who gave explicit information about what the child was expected to do, the second one did not tell the child what the problem was, nor did she offer him support or help in solving it.

The same variance in teaching styles occurred when mothers were asked to teach their children how to put a jigsaw puzzle together.

One said, "This is a jigsaw puzzle, James. You have never seen one before. We take the little pieces out, we put them on the table, and then we have to put them back together. Be sure you see where the colors are and what the shapes are like so you will know where they go."

As the child worked to fit the puzzle together, his mother kept up a running conversation: "Maybe·this piece belongs with that one; see, the color is the same," etc.

A second mother, however, simply dumped the pieces of the puzzle on the table and said to her child, "Now work it."

As the child struggled, trying to find where the pieces fit, the mother kept saying, "Turn it around." In a page and a half of transcript, the mother said "turn it around" fifty-five times.

For a third example of teaching styles, picture a mother and child working together to copy a petal design on a contraption called Etch-a-Sketch. It is a flat box with a screen inside, upon which a picture can be drawn by remote control using two knobs—one manipulated by the mother and the other by the child.° It was typical of the middle class mothers to anticipate an error on the part of the child and say, "Be careful you don't make that line too long"—or give similar warning. Lower class mothers, on the other hand, tended to watch silently as their child made a mistake, then say something like, "You shouldn't have done that."

In analyzing this language and behavior, Hess says, "Consider for the moment only the matter of motivation. Some of those children were faced with new situations which they were taught to master; and I would think that through such experience would come the idea that new situations *can* be mastered. That there are answers if you know how to find them. That there is some order, some reason, some purpose in problems.

"Whereas the other children must have felt that problems do not have solutions, that they have no meaning, that there is a great deal of pressure to do the work but there is no clear route as to how to do it. The child who feels that there is a way and

° This ingenious apparatus is also sometimes used by marriage counselors. to help determine which partner wears the pants in the family.

that he can find it has a profound head start in asking the teacher for assistance when he finally gets to school."

It is true that the laboratory situation in which Hess and Shipman placed their mothers and children was an artificial one; but it is hard to believe that the mothers' basic style of communication would alter at home.

Imagine, for instance, a "real" situation familiar to every mother: the telephone ringing while a child of about two is entertaining himself by banging two pot lids together. In going to answer the ring, the mother might say, "Be quiet"; or she might say, "Billy, will you be quiet for a minute? I want to talk on the phone."

In comparing these sentences, Hess says, "The first message is simple and uncomplicated; it requires no response from the child other than compliance. The second message, however, asks the child to relate his behavior to a time dimension and to consider the effect of his behavior upon another person—all in all, a much more difficult task because it requires reflection and mental discrimination.

"Given these two kinds of communication networks within the family, repeated thousands of times in many different situations in the preschool years, children from the two kinds of families can hardly fail to enter school with quite different capabilities for receiving and processing information . . . for defining the world, understanding it, or developing strategies for ordering it."

CHAPTER 21

ALL MICE ARE NOT
CREATED EQUAL

Benson Ginsburg is a behavioral geneticist with a lively professional interest in wolves. He crosses them with other canines to see which traits of wolf behavior reappear in the hybrids and therefore can be considered to be inherited. He is also involved in a project for Guide Dogs for the Blind, for whom he has modified by selective inbreeding the pedigreed German Shepherd (whose show conformation "was not the best for pounding the pavement day after day—the dog got back trouble," and whose temperamental trait of protectiveness toward its owner plus suspicion of others used to make the transfer from trainer to blind person exceedingly difficult).

But Ginsburg has never lost his early interest in mice, about whose genetic composition so much is now known that one can sometimes identify the specific genes related to specific behavior. The title of this chapter is borrowed from a paper he recently wrote in which he recalled an experience which greatly affected his scholarly viewpoint—and will be a cautionary tale for readers of this book, as well. Here it is, condensed and in part paraphrased:

". . . It proved to be a simple matter to find three inbred strains of mice that differed in their readiness to fight, and to record their behavior in encounters with each other. The study was quite successful, except for one small flaw. J. P. Scott, working at the Jackson Laboratory in Bar Harbor (from which we received our mice), was using the same strains in a similar experiment. He also reported that they differed in combativeness. Unfortunately, however, our most combative strain was his most pacific one.

"In going back over the animal husbandry data, we noted that the young animals in his study were handled by being picked up by the tail when they were transferred, weighed, or otherwise manipulated. Our animals were scooped up in a small box.

"Upon repeating the experiments using the tail-transfer technique on half of the mice in each strain, and treating the other half as before, we discovered that the strain that we had rated most aggressive and that Scott had rated least aggressive developed according to the way it was handled before maturity.

"It turns out that this strain is extremely labile on a number of measures. Several investigators have described it as seeming to be perched on a series of environmental thresholds, so that its development is altered when any one of these is changed. By contrast, another strain that we have tested is very well-buffered; the usual manipulations have practically no effects on behavioral processes.

"There are at least half a dozen strains whose behavior is affected by early handling. But in one strain, the effect is maximal only if handling occurs daily during the entire pre-weaning period; in two other strains, handling must occur during the last half of the pre-weaning period to have an effect; and in two more, the critical period comes during the first two weeks after birth.

"If one were simply to mix all the strains together, regard them as one population of mice, and repeat the same experiments, one would undoubtedly find some central tendency as well as a range of variability. If I were to perform such an experiment and you were then to ask me what happens to the aggressive behavior of 'a male mouse' if it is exposed to periodic mild stress during the first two weeks of life, I could give you an answer based on statistics—but my answer would very likely not apply to your particular mouse."

It is probable, in short, that neither "mouse" nor "man" exists as a unitary biological entity. The hypothetical child whom I have been describing all through these pages is a composite of the thousands of children who have been tested and observed by the scientists whose work I have reported, and may resemble your child or your neighbor's child no more closely than the State you live in resembles the "State" whose geographer is the University of Texas biochemist Roger J. Williams. In a recent book whose purpose is to emphasize the importance of individual differences, Williams averages data gathered from the fifty States and creates this demi-Paradise of diversification:

"The average State," he says, "has an area of 72,000 square miles and a population of over 3.5 million. It has about 1200 square miles of fresh water lakes, 37 miles of salt lakes, and 150 miles of shoreline. Its highest mountains are about 6000 feet high, and some 5000 square miles of it lie in the Arctic regions. It produces yearly about half a million barrels of oil; 300,000 tons of coal; 50,000 pounds of copper; 10 million bushels of wheat; 3 million pounds of tobacco; 1 million bales of cotton; 150,000 tons of citrus fruit; and 9000 tons of pineapples."

In a less whimsical vein, he lists a great many individual differences of physiology that fall within the range of normality:

► In about 65 percent of us, the arteries carry blood from the heart via three branches; in about 27 percent of people, blood flows via two branches; and the remaining 8 percent of people (some sixteen million individuals in the United States) have one, four, five, or six arterial branches. These branches differ markedly in size and hence in blood-carrying capacity. Yet all are "normal."

► The blood itself varies as shown in FIGURE 33.

► Only about 18 percent of people have a body temperature of exactly 98.6 degrees. Among the other 82 percent, some have "normal" temperatures as low as 97 degrees or as high as 100 degrees.

► Whenever direct measurements are possible, the output of each hormone is found to vary, among normal people, through at least a fivefold range.

► When a group of twenty-eight young men with 20/20 vision were tested for their ability to see movement out of the corner of the eyes, their performance ranged from that of a man who could see a simulated airplane move when the speed was only two miles per hour to that of another who could not see movement until the "plane" reached a speed of 91 miles per hour.

Are such variances genetic in origin—in the sense of being absolutely determined with the chromosomes? At one time the answer would have been a firm "yes," but today one cannot be so positive. The biochemical environment of the womb affects the physical development of the fetus, as does the timing of delivery and the amount of trauma experienced by the baby. The early functioning—and through function, the development—of certain organs depends on nutrition and quality of care. It is quite possible that even in matters of physiology there may be parallels with Benson Ginsburg's mice. Environmental circumstances may cause a genetically "labile" individual to depart much more widely from the developmental blueprint in his chromosomes than an individual who is by nature buffered against change.

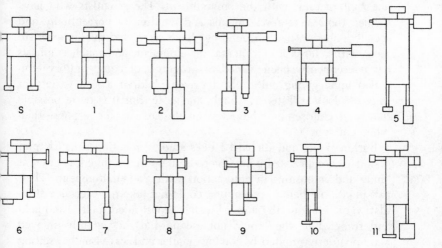

FIGURE 33

These ingenious diagrams were devised by the University of California's W. Duane Brown. The relative amount of eleven chemical constituents of blood is indicated by the size of the eleven rectangles which constitute each "man." The one at the top left represents the proportion of these eleven elements as they are found in what the chemist Roger Williams calls "textbook" blood. But he points out that much individual variance is common.

When the blood of eleven healthy young men was analyzed and the constituents of their blood were measured according to the scales used for "textbook" blood, it became apparent that no one of them had blood like the standard, nor was any individual's blood like that of any other individual. (From *You Are Extraordinary* by Roger Williams, Random House, 1967. Reproduced with permission of the author and publisher.)

There is also, as pointed out in Chapter 2, good reason to believe that there is a genetic component in many of the behavioral variances which in the past have been believed to result primarily from contact with the social environment. But, again, do XYY chromosomes predestine a child to aggressiveness, or does this physical inheritance merely perch the child on an "environmental threshold" beyond which several possible alternatives await the toss of the coin of circumstances?

Intelligence is marked by a quality of alertness in the totality of one's interactions with the environment. The scientists who have studied the effects upon animals and children of perceptually and socially impoverished surroundings have correlated this impoverishment with retardation in mental development, and much emphasis has consequently been placed in programs of compensatory education upon giving culturally deprived children a rich variety of things to look at, listen to, touch, and taste. But it is quite possible that some children may have less innate capacity for response than other children.

Burton White and Richard Held's studies, mentioned in Chapter 3, underscore a related point: there is an optimum time for different kinds and intensities of interaction with the environment. Their two-month-old babies, remember, could not take the excessive stimulation of an over-crib "stabile" which almost filled their visual field and from which they could not escape—but they greatly enjoyed and apparently profited by having smaller and less visually exciting crib decorations. The reverse is true for children in Head Start programs; age four is a late start for looking at picture books, naming objects around them, and asking, "Why?"

In summary, then, the first variable which distinguishes one child from another is his biological inheritance; and for every child this is different. The second variable is the effect of that particular child's environment, physical or social, upon a multitude of inherited qualities—among which one must include his sensitivity to environmental pressures. The third variable is timing; the developmental point at which such pressures have maximum impact. Out of all this there can come no "average" children, only specific and highly individual ones.

Let us now consider children's individual modes of learning, and then their equally individual modes of utilizing that learning.

The term "cognitive style" has in recent years been adopted by many psychologists to describe the stable preference shown by any one person for a particular way of organizing and categorizing what he perceives. Jerome Kagan says, "Some are splitters, others are lumpers"—by which he means that of two individuals of equal intelligence whose social background is similar, one will characteristically analyze the subelements of a scene or situation whereas the other will categorize the scene or situation as a whole.

Given a picture of two native Polynesian adults and a child, the splitters will describe them as "people with no shoes on" whereas the lumpers will describe them as "a family." Label a photograph full of detail as a DEP, a ROV, or some other nonsense syllable, then show it again with some of the detail missing: analytic-style children will do better at recall because they have a greater tendency to associate DEP or ROV with some of the details and are thus more likely to notice their absence.

The Fels Research Institute (as you will remember from the work of Lester Sontag that was reported in Chapter 16) has kept long-time records of the same individuals. A few years ago, Jerome Kagan and an associate, Howard Moss, were engaged in a follow-up study of seventy-one Fels Institute children who had grown up. Kagan interviewed and tested them, and Moss went back over their childhood records. Both investigators were interested in a variety of dimensions of ability and personality. When they finished their separate tasks and compared their results they were surprised to discover a correlation between Moss's ratings on the degree to which these adults had been physically active as children and Kagan's ratings on the degree to which these adults were now interested in and motivated to pursue and persist in intellectual tasks. It turned out that childhood *hyper*-activity was predictive of future avoidance of intellectual activities.

Then, with the assistance of Irving Sigel, the psychologists launched a study of children currently on the Fels Institute roster—checking both their general behavior and their techniques for remembering things and solving problems. These findings were compared to the childhood records of the adults whose examination had started the project. There was great consistency among the case histories of those who, as adults, used a particular cognitive style and of those who, as children, were obviously working their way into it. Here, for example, are case histories of two boys who were matched as to intelligence and background—but how different they are!

JOHN (*IQ, 133*)

Age 3: Plays quietly, sits looking at books, or watches the other children. Very long attention span. Obeys the teacher if she speaks directly to him but ignores her if she gives a general order. Can play cooperatively and occasionally initiates games with the other children, but is quite content to be alone.

Age 4½: Curious about everything. Tells himself stories with lots of expression and imagination. Plays contentedly without noticing the children who mill around him. Prefers to play alone.

Age 5½: Outstanding ability to concentrate. Full of inventive play ideas. Sense of humor. Quick to retreat if play gets rough, but not afraid of physical activity; in fact, likes to climb and jump from high levels.

CHRIS (*IQ, 130*)

Age 3½: Active, lively, full of enthusiasm. Shows little interest in toys; colors or pastes only when someone is doing it with him. Reckless on tricycle; highest accident rate of any child in his nursery school group. Talks a lot. Never sticks long at one activity.

Age 4½: Friendly and affectionate. Rarely plays by himself. Occasionally destructive. Doesn't stick long with one activity; gives up quickly if a puzzle proves too difficult.

Age 5½: Flits from one activity to another; never sits down and works at anything. Talks all the time. Constantly seeks approval and attention from adults. Likes to kick objects around and tease the girls. Keeps falling over things because he doesn't notice them.

"The contrast between the two children is striking," Kagan says. "They are of equal intelligence, and there is no difference in the quality of their language. The major dimensions that differentiate them involve hyperkinetic impulsive behavior, reflectiveness, withdrawal from social situations, and task involvement."

How did they develop as they have? Kagan and his associates suggest that hyperactivity is one class of behavior that might have a constitutional foundation—that is, be of genetic origin. They think it possible, too, that John (and children like him) may experience less conflict and tension in relations with parents. The more relaxed one is, of course, the more likely one is to be reflective in one's approach to problems. Other psychologists (among them, those whose work was reported in the preceding chapter) have found correlations between the amount of freedom that parents allow young children and both the children's motivation and mastery of intellectual tasks. Herman A. Witkin (Chapter 13) has noted that restricted and overprotected children tend to be field-dependent; this trait, you remember, reduces the child's awareness of details and makes him susceptible to the impact of a total situation rather than alert to the significance of its various parts.

A preschool pile-up of these several influences, some biological, some cultural, could bring a child to school unable to sit still long enough to attend to lessons. Consequently he would become less able than others to observe, to discriminate differences ("dog" from "bag," say, in his basal reader), to categorize, and therefore to remember. With a poorer base to build on, each of the successive tasks of the school years would be done more laboriously and less effectively, and at least on the dimension of intellectual mastery children like Chris would be less competent than those like John.

This does not mean that their intelligence would be less; in fact, the analytic-style adults in the Kagan and Moss study had IQ's only a shade higher than those who were more impulsive and less intellectual. Nor does it mean that their "success" in life would be less. But it does mean that their responses to life situations would differ. The Johns would characteristically reflect and analyze and *enjoy* challenging intellectual problems; the Chrises would feel more comfortable and perform better in situations requiring direct and immediate action.

Now, what about the *use* that children make of what they have learned about the world around them? Again, each of us seems to fall somewhere on a continuum between the two modes described by Jacob W. Getzels and Philip W. Jackson as follows: "In one mode, individuals retain the known, learn the predetermined, and conserve what is; in the other, they revise the known, explore the undetermined, and construct what might be. A person for whom the first mode is primary tends toward the usual and expected; a person for whom the second mode is primary tends toward the novel and speculative. The one favors certainty, the other risk."

Asked to give as many uses as possible for, say, a brick, the one kind of person may say, "Bricks are used for building purposes.

You can build a wall, a sidewalk, or a fireplace with brick." The other kind of person may say, "Bricks can be used for building. You can also use them as paperweights or doorstops. You can heat a brick and use it as a bed warmer. You can throw one as a weapon. You can hollow out the center of a brick and make an ashtray."

For another example, the person who uses his knowledge pretty much in the form that he got it will tell a quite different story about the scene in FIGURE 34 than the person who characteristically recombines what he has learned. The first type says:

"Mr. Smith is on his way home from a successful business trip. He is very happy and he is thinking about his wonderful family and how glad he will be to see them again. He can picture it, about an hour from now, his plane landing at the airport and Mrs. Smith and their three children all there welcoming him home again."

The other type of person tells this tale:

"This man is flying back from Reno where he has just won a divorce from his wife. He couldn't stand to live with her any more, he told the judge, because she wore so much cold cream on her face at night that her head would skid across the pillow and hit him in the head. He is now contemplating a new skid-proof face cream."

And two more contrasting examples, this time of the scene shown in FIGURE 35. The one:

"There's ambitious Bob, down at the office at 6:30 in the morning. He's trying to show his boss how energetic he is. Now, thinks Bob, maybe the boss will give me a raise for all my extra work. The trouble is that Bob has been doing this for the last three years, and the boss still hasn't given him a raise. He'll come in at 9:00, not even noticing that Bob had been there so long, and poor Bob won't get his raise."

The other:

"This man has just broken into the office of a new cereal company. He is a private eye employed by a competitor firm to find out the formula that makes the cereal bend, sag, and sway. After a thorough search of the office he comes upon what he thinks is the formula. He is now copying it. It turns out that it is the wrong formula and the competitor's factory blows up. Poetic justice!"

Skid-proof face cream, indeed! And cereal that "bends, sags, and sways"! You are surely aware by now that the second example in each of these parallels was the brainchild of a youngster who

FIGURE 34

FIGURE 35

had been rated as "highly creative." All the above quotations come from a classic study of gifted students that was published in 1962 by Getzels and Jackson, who are educational psychologists at the University of Chicago. They undertook their study because they felt that "gifted" was coming to be synonymous with the possession of an extra-high rating on an IQ test but that giftedness can express itself in other ways as well.

They say, "Whereas common observation insists on distinguishing between knowing and discovering, between the ability to remember and the ability to invent, between being 'intelligent' and being 'creative,' it is this distinction that seems largely to have been lost sight of in the rush to apply the intelligence test or some derivative of it to everything from grouping children in kindergarten to choosing executives in business."

And they recommend that more people should "accept the notion, however provisionally, that the number of words an individual can define or his ability to memorize digits backwards may tell us very little about his ability to produce new forms and restructure stereotyped situations."

Getzels and Jackson began their study by administering some forty tests—among them, of course, some that were particularly intended to measure creativity—to some five hundred pupils in the sixth through twelfth grades at a private school which caters to bright youngsters. The average IQ of the group, in fact, was 132. Teachers were asked to rate the children along a variety of dimensions; the children were asked to rate each other; and their parents responded to questionnaires or were interviewed.

Then, twenty-six pupils who had scored especially high on the creativity tests but were below the school average on IQ and twenty-eight pupils who had exceptionally high IQ's but had scored low on the creativity tests were compared to each other and to the school population in general. Here are some of the findings:

▶ Despite their lower IQ's, the creative children did just as well on academic subject-matter tests as the highly intelligent children. Both groups were equally superior to the general school population in this regard.

▶ They also performed at the same level on tests measuring strength of motivation for achieving school goals or those to which they aspired in adulthood.

► And they agreed with each other when asked to evaluate the qualities in students that teachers are likely to prefer and the qualities that are likely to bring success in life. *However,* the high IQ pupils accepted these qualities as desirable for themselves, whereas the creative children did not.

► The creative children were much more likely than the high IQ children to exhibit humor and playfulness in their responses. (Asked to draw a picture appropriate to the title "Playing Tag in the School Yard," one of the creative children added ". . . During a Blizzard" to the title and handed in an otherwise blank sheet of paper.)

► The creative children enjoyed incongruity, mocked conventional values, told stories in which there was more violence. They tended to use pictures such as we have shown merely as departure points, whereas the high IQ children restricted themselves to the situations as shown.

► Asked to pick (from the entire school population) the pupils they most enjoyed having in the classroom, it was the high IQ children rather than the creative children whom the teachers picked. And this despite the fact (see the first point above) that the creative children scored higher on academic achievement tests *relative to their IQ's* than the high IQ children, a situation that theoretically should delight a pedagogue.

(Teachers are, in general, conservators of knowledge. Is it too unsettling to them to try to cope with minds that can dream up skid-proof face cream? Do they see that blizzard "picture" as nothing but the stunt of a smart-aleck?)

► Insofar as parental occupation was related to the child's kind of giftedness, there was a correlation between high IQ children and fathers who are university professors, researchers, or editors. There was also a correlation between creative children and fathers who are businessmen. But the physicians' and attorneys' children in this particular group were almost equally divided between the creative and high IQ types.

► As for the mothers, those of the high IQ children tended to be full-time housewives, rather conventional in their own standards of behavior and in their aspirations for their children. They were extremely child-centered, and kept close tabs on their youngsters' activity. Said one, "We expect a daily report at dinner time. We have always shared her school life."

The mothers of the creative children, on the other hand, were employed full or part time; were less vigilant in overseeing their children's activities; and were more relaxed about life in general. "He got bored with school," one such mother said of her child, "so I sometimes let him stay home." Asked if she tried to keep up with his school activity, she replied, "Yes. But I didn't like to pry."

Getzels and Jackson sum up by saying, "Both high intelligence and high creativity are valuable, and we do not wish to give the impression of one group as somehow representing 'good guys' and the other 'bad guys.' Both the 'conservative' and the 'constructive' aspects of cognition and social behavior are socially valuable."

And finally, out of all that he has inherited from his forebears—biologically or culturally—and out of his own life experience, each child constructs his dearest psychological possession, his concept of self. It may or may not be accurate (in the view of others, and insofar as they can discover it), but it is *his*, he cherishes it, and he defends it.

In an early chapter, I mentioned homeostasis, the compulsion of an organism to maintain itself in a state of physical and chemical equilibrium. There is a psychological equivalent: we all order our behavior and attempt to control our environment in such a way as to protect our self-concept. If we believe that we are intelligent, honest, and industrious, we behave in ways intended to maintain and enhance that picture; conversely, if we believe that we are stupid, untrustworthy, and lazy, we will strive just as hard to maintain and enhance *that* picture. Such behavior may be thoroughly self-defeating in school, job, or social situations, but because it arises from a source as deeply imbedded in its owner's psychological organization as the lungs and heart are imbedded in his physiological organization, it must be equally protected.

The University of Michigan's Nathan S. Caplan and Jeffery M. Paige, in a study of ghetto rioters, have found that it was not the poorest of the poor, not the hard-core unemployed, not the least educated, and not the newcomers from the South who were most active in the Detroit and Newark riots of 1967. The typical rioter was a young Negro who had managed to free himself from the stereotype of black people as shiftless, incompetent, less intelligent than whites—in fact, inferior in every way—and had developed some pride in being black.

As Mary Ellen Goodman pointed out (Chapter 18), the majority of Negroes accept this no-good evaluation which originated with whites, and having accepted it as part of their self-concept they build various psychological defenses to preserve it. However, once a young Negro comes to believe that his blackness does not in itself make him inferior to whites, such defenses are useless to him. If he is then denied a dwelling that he can afford to rent or a job that he is capable of doing, and he lacks the psychological supports that enable other Negroes to adjust to such discrimination, he will be as dangerously out of psychic equilibrium as a man who is dying of thirst is out of chemical equilibrium. In the latter case, the man shrivels; in the former, he explodes.

The first self-knowledge that babies acquire is of their own bodies, and indeed one's body-image is an important part of one's self-concept throughout life. How we perceive our bodies is in part a matter of how well they function and whether we enjoy the sensations they provide us, but also the comments and actions of others play a large role. A mother who changes diapers with great distaste or who is harsh about toilet training can create in a child the belief that there is something wrong with his body and therefore with *him*. A mother who occasionally praises a little girl because she "walks like a ballerina" and a father who occasionally admires his son's budding biceps or praises his endurance on a hike are likely to raise children who have positive feelings about their own bodies.

The psychiatrist Erik Erikson, whose first "crisis" of psychosocial development was mentioned in Chapter 6 (the infant's need to develop trust in himself and his environment), goes on to describe others. The second such developmental crisis, he says, spans the period from about fifteen months to about four years. This is the time that children become fully mobile, want to do quantities of things that they are physically incapable of doing or that would be harmful to them, and sensitive parents must walk a chalk line between imposing too much and too little control.

The child should come out of this period feeling, and being, self-reliant—but he must still be willing to accept and use the guidance

of others. If he has had too few opportunities to make choices, if his
efforts to do things have too often been frustrated by overprotec-
tive or impatient parents; or, conversely, if he has had no control
whatsoever and has repeatedly failed or been hurt by what he has
attempted—he will develop a sense of self-doubt that may haunt
him through life.

The third crisis of development is triggered, Erikson says, by
the child's emerging conscience. He wants to and should be free
to explore and discover a physical world that he is increasingly able
to cope with. But during the years between four and six his behavior is guided to an ever-increasing extent by concepts of "right"
and "wrong"; in fact, he often feels guilty for his thoughts as well
as for his actions. If his parents punish him too severely for curiosity
about the sexual anatomy of the little girl next door, if they repeatedly tell him that it's wrong to grab a playmate's toys, if they
expect him to love his baby brother as much as they do (although
he is in fact eaten up with jealousy), he may emerge from this period
with an oppressive burden of guilt as his future companion.

The fourth period, which Erikson names the "crisis of industry
versus inferiority" coincides with the years from six to twelve. The
stage is wider now; in addition to parental help or hindrance in
meeting the challenges of his life, the child is interacting with
teachers, playmates, their parents, the cop on the corner, and the
clerk at the store where his mother sends him for a loaf of bread
she forgot to buy.

But the emphasis is on school, on the mastery of intellectual and
socially useful tasks. If the child can master these tasks, he will
consider himself a success (see FIGURE 36); if he cannot, he will
consider himself a failure. Him*self*—the total, inner being. To relate such failure only to his performance in the school context is too
subtle a distinction for young children to grasp, especially if failure
is chronic and the sense of inferiority is reinforced in other contexts.
("Go 'way, nigger boy. No one wants you 'round here." Or: "*Catch*
it, Jerry. My God, Edith, the kid is all thumbs. Almost eight years
old and he can't catch a ball!")

Erikson's crises continue through life, but I will cease their recital at this point. My concern has been with the young child's
mind, and especially with that of the very young child. If there is
one overriding "message" in these pages, it is that of the first chapter
title: children are never too young to learn. But I have tried to

FIGURE 36

School entrance may signal the beginning of formal instruction
but not of learning; in fact, by age six, the average child has
already mastered one third of the intellectual skills he will
eventually possess, and has acquired the personality traits upon
which a large part of his success in life will depend.

make the point that "learning" does not mean (although it includes) such specifics as using language or acquiring the ability to count. It means the changes in overall behavior that result from each child's interaction with his environment: changes that vary greatly from child to child because each child's inheritance and experiences are unique; changes that may be "good" or "bad" in either a personal or a social sense—but that will be woven into the fabric of the self with equal permanence.

I hope, therefore, that no one will close this book with a resolve to buy one of those mail-order courses that promise to teach four-year-olds to read. In the homes of most of you, children are adequately exposed to the language arts from infancy. What you might consider, though, is the emotional and intellectual climate in which each of your children is being reared. How sensitive are you to their characteristic reactions to sound and color and motion, to social contact, to freedom and restraint? How capable are you of establishing limits for each child that allow him room to grow but at the same time protect him from his own immaturity? Do your children like themselves?

And beyond your own four walls, what of the children less fortunate than yours: the children of the poor, whose dull eyes may bespeak malnutrition instead of low innate intelligence, whose toys are beer cans retrieved from a gutter, whose fumbling use of language may reflect a home in which no one talks to them? These are the children whose first years of school often *reduce* such abilities to achieve as they brought with them on opening day. What is your responsibility as a citizen and as a human being to such children? Should *they* grow up to like themselves?

Society would benefit immeasurably if every child could have a good beginning.

REFERENCES

(Notes: Sources of short descriptive quotations are not included in this list. Whenever several papers by the same investigator are cited, the chapter number in which the work is mentioned follows the reference. Whenever conclusions or remarks from two papers are combined, the references appear as one entry.)

ADORNO, T. W., et al. *The Authoritarian Personality.* New York: Harper, 1950

AGRANOFF, BERNARD W. (1967) "Memory and Protein Synthesis." *Scientific American,* 216, 115–22. Also: "Agents that Block Memory," in *The Neurosciences* (Eds., G. C. Quarton, T. Melnechuk, F. O. Schmitt). New York: Rockefeller University Press, 1967

AINSWORTH, MARY. (1962) "Deprivation of Maternal Care, a Reassessment of Its Effects." *World Health Organization* (Geneva), Public Health Papers No. 14, 97–165

ALBERT, D. J. (1966) "Memory in Mammals: Evidence for a System Involving Nuclear Ribonucleic Acid." *Neuropsychologica,* 4, 79–92

ALLPORT, GORDON W., and KRAMER, BERNARD. (1946) "Some Roots of Prejudice." *Journal of Psychology,* 22, 9–39

ALMY, MILLIE, with CHITTENDEN, EDWARD, and MILLER, PAULA. *Young Children's Thinking: Studies of Some Aspects of Piaget's Theory.* New York: Teachers College Press, Columbia University, 1966

AMBROSE, JOHN A. "The Development of the Smiling Response in Early Infancy," in *Determinants of Infant Behavior*. New York: Wiley, 1961. Also: "The Concept of a Critical Period for the Development of Social Responsiveness in Early Human Infancy," in *Determinants of Infant Behavior II*. London: Methuen, 1963

ASHBY, W. ROSS. Comment (p. 42) in *Prospects in Psychiatric Research* (Proceedings of the Oxford Conference of the Mental Health Research Fund). Oxford: Blackwell Scientific Publications, 1953

BALDWIN, ALFRED L. (1948) "Socialization and the Parent-Child Relationship." *Child Development*, 19, 127–36

BENDER, LAURETTA. *A Visual Motor Gestalt Test and Its Clinical Use*. New York: American Orthopsychiatric Association, 1938

BENNETT, EDWARD L., DIAMOND, MARIAN C., KRECH, DAVID, AND ROSENZWEIG, MARK R. (1964) "Chemical and Anatomical Plasticity of the Brain." *Science*, 146, 610–19

BERNARD, JACK, and SONTAG, LESTER. (1947) "Fetal Reactivity to Tonal Stimulation." *Journal of Genetic Psychology*, 70, 205–10

BERNSTEIN, BASIL. (1961) "Aspects of Language and Learning in the Genesis of the Social Process." *Journal of Child Psychology and Pyschiatry*, 1, 313–24

BETTELHEIM, BRUNO. *The Empty Fortess*. New York: The Free Press, 1966

BIRCH, HERBERT G. (1945) "The Role of Motivational Factors in Insightful Problem Solving." *Journal of Comparative Psychology*, 38, 295–317 (Ch. 9)

———. "Field Measurement in Nutrition, Learning, and Behavior," in *Malnutrition, Learning, and Behavior* (Eds., Nevin Scrimshaw and John E. Gordon). Cambridge: Massachusetts Institute of Technology Press, 1968. (Ch. 16)

BLOOM, BENJAMIN S. *Stability and Change in Human Characteristics*. New York: Wiley, 1964

BOND, GUY, and DYKSTRA, ROBERT. (1967) "The Cooperative Research Program in First-Grade Reading Instruction." *Reading Research Quarterly*, 2, No. 4 (Summer)

BOWER, T. G. R. (1966) "The Visual World of Infants." *Scientific American*, 215, 80–92

BOWLBY, JOHN. (1951) "Maternal Care and Mental Health." *World Health Organization* (Geneva), Monograph Series No. 2. (Ch. 5 and Ch. 10)

———. (1952) Comment (p. 80) in *Prospects in Psychiatric Research* (Proceedings of the Oxford Conference of the Mental Health Research Fund). Oxford: Blackwell Scientific Publications, 1953. (Ch. 6)

BRIDGES, KATHARINE. (1932) "Emotional Development in Early Infancy." *Child Development*, 3, 324–41

BROWN, ROGER W. *Words and Things.* Glencoe: The Free Press, 1958

BRUNER, JEROME S. (1956) "Freud and the Image of Man." *The American Psychologist*, 11, 463–66. (Ch. 10)

BRUNER, JEROME S., and GOODMAN, CECILE. (1947) "Value and Need as Organizing Factors in Perception." *Journal of Abnormal and Social Psychology*, 42, 33–44. (Ch. 13)

BRUNER, JEROME S., and OLVER, ROSE S. (1963) "Development of Equivalence Transformations in Children." *Monographs of the Society for Research in Child Development*, Serial 83, Vol. 28, 125–41. (Ch. 15)

BUTLER, R. A. (1953) "Discrimination Learning by Rhesus Monkeys to Visual Exploration Motivation." *Journal of Comparative and Physiological Psychology*, 46, 95–98

CAPLAN, NATHAN S., and PAIGE, JEFFERY M. (1968) "A Study of Ghetto Rioters." *Scientific American*, 219, 15–21

CARMICHAEL, LEONARD. (1926) "The Development of Behavior in Vertebrates Experimentally Removed from the Influence of External Stimulation." *Psychological Review*, 22, 51–58

CARR, E. A., et al. (1959) "The Effect of Maternal Thyroid Function on Fetal Thyroid Function and Development." *Journal of Clinical Endocrinology*, 19, 1–18

CASEY, M. D., et al. (1966) "Sex Chromosome Abnormalities in Two State Hospitals for Patients Requiring Special Security." *Nature*, 209, 641–42

CHASE, WILTON P. (1937) "Color Vision in Infants." *Journal of Experimental Psychology*, 20, 203–22

CLARK, KENNETH B., and CLARK, MAMIE P. (1939) "The Development of Consciousness of Self and the Emergence of Racial Identification in

Negro Pre-School Children." *Journal of Social Psychology,* 10, 591–99. Also: (1940) "Skin Color as a Factor in Racial Identification of Negro Pre-School Children." *Journal of Social Psychology,* 11, 159–69

CLARKE, A. D. B., and CLARKE, ANN M. (1960–61) "Some Recent Advances in the Study of Early Deprivation." *Journal of Child Psychology and Psychiatry,* 1, 26–36

CLAY, MARIE. "Emergent Reading Behavior." Unpublished doctoral dissertation, University of Auckland, 1966

COBB, STANLEY. *Borderlands of Psychiatry.* Cambridge: Harvard University Press, 1943

COLEMAN, JAMES S., et al. *Equality of Educational Opportunity.* Washington, D.C.: National Center for Educational Statistics, U. S. Government Printing Office, 1966

DAVIDSON, HELEN P. (1934) "A Study of Reversals in Young Children." *Journal of Genetic Psychology,* 45, 542–65. (Ch. 13)

———. (1931) "An Experimental Study of Bright, Average, and Dull Children at the Four-Year Mental Level." *Genetic Psychology Monographs,* 9, 119–289. (Ch. 16)

DENNIS, WAYNE. (1941) "Infant Development Under Conditions of Restricted Practice and of Minimum Social Stimulation." *Genetic Psychology Monographs,* 23, 143–91. (Ch. 3)

———. (1960) "Causes of Retardation Among Institutional Children: Iran." *Journal of Genetic Psychology,* 96, 47–59. (Ch. 3)

———. (1957) "A Cross-Cultural Study of the Reinforcement of Child Behavior." *Child Development,* 28, 431–38. (Ch. 17)

DEUTSCH, J. A. *The Structural Basis of Behavior.* Chicago: University of Chicago Press, 1960

DEVRIES, RHETA. "Conservation of Generic Identity in the Years Three to Six." Unpublished doctoral dissertation, University of Chicago, 1967

DIAMOND, MILTON. (1965) "A Critical Evaluation of the Ontogeny of Human Sexual Behavior." *The Quarterly Review of Biology,* 40, 147–75

DIZMANG, LARRY H. "Observations on Suicidal Behavior Among the Shoshone-Bannock Indians": paper read at the First Annual National Conference on Suicidology, Chicago, March 20, 1968

EAYRS, J. T. "Effects of Thyroid Hormones on Brain Differentiation," in *Brain-Thyroid Relationships* (Ciba Foundation Study Group No. 18). Boston: Little, Brown, 1964

EIBL-EIBESFELDT, IRENÄUS. "Concepts of Ethology and Their Significance in the Study of Human Behavior," in *Early Behavior: Comparative and Developmental Approaches* (Eds., Harold Stevenson, Eckhard Hess, Harriet Rheingold). New York: Wiley, 1967

EISENBERG, LEON. "The Development of Intelligence," in *Child Care in Health and Disease* (Ed., Albert Dorfman). Chicago: Year Book Medical Publishers, Inc., 1968

EPSTEIN, W. A. (1962) "The Influence of Syntactical Structure on Learning." *American Journal of Psychology,* 74, 80–85

ERIKSON, ERIK H. *Childhood and Society.* New York: Norton, 1950

FANTZ, ROBERT L. "Visual Perception and Experience in Early Infancy," in *Early Behavior: Comparative and Developmental Approaches* (Eds., Harold Stevenson, Eckhard Hess, Harriet Rheingold). New York: Wiley, 1967

FISCHER, LISELOTTE. (1952). "Hospitalism in Six Month Old Infants." *American Journal of Orthopsychiatry,* 22, 522–33

FLAVELL, JOHN H. *Developmental Psychology of Jean Piaget.* Princeton: Van Nostrand, 1963

FLEXNER, L. B., and FLEXNER, J. B. (1966) "Effect of Acetoxycycloheximide and of an Acetoxycycloheximide-puromycin Mixture on Cerebral Protein Synthesis and Memory in Mice." *Proceedings of the National Academy of Sciences,* 55, 369–74

FULLER, JOHN L. (1967) "Experiential Deprivation and Later Behavior." *Science,* 158, 1645–52

FUNKENSTEIN, DANIEL H. (1955) "The Physiology of Fear and Anger." *Scientific American,* 192, 74–82

GALAMBOS, ROBERT. "Brain Correlates of Learning," in *The Neurosciences* (Eds., G. C. Quarton, T. Melnechuk, F. O. Schmitt). New York: Rockefeller University Press, 1967

GEBER, MARCELLE. (1958) "The Psycho-Motor Development of African Children in the First Year, and the Influence of Maternal Behavior." *Journal of Social Psychology,* 47, 185–95

GELLERMAN, LOUIS W. (1933) "Form Discrimination in Chimpanzees and Two Year Old Children." *Journal of Genetic Psychology*, 42, 3–48

GESELL, ARNOLD, and AMES, LOUISE B. (1947) "The Development of Handedness." *Journal of Genetic Psychology*, 70, 155–75. (Ch. 7)

————. (1946) "The Development of Directionality in Drawing." *Journal of Genetic Psychology*, 68, 45–61. (Ch. 13)

GETZELS, JACOB W., and JACKSON, PHILIP. *Creativity and Intelligence*. New York: Wiley, 1962

GIBSON, ELEANOR J. (1963) "Development of Perception: Discrimination of Depth Compared with Discrimination of Graphic Symbols." *Monographs of the Society for Research in Child Development*, Serial No. 86, Vol. 28, 5–24. (Ch. 13)

GIBSON, ELEANOR J., and WALK, RICHARD. (1956) "The Effect of Prolonged Exposure to Visually Presented Patterns on Learning to Discriminate Them." *Journal of Comparative and Physiological Psychology*, 49, 239–42. (Ch. 1)

GINSBURG, BENSON E. "Genetics and Personality," in *Concepts of Personality* (Eds., J. Wepman and R. Heine). Chicago: Aldine, 1963. (Ch. 2)

————. (1966) "All Mice Are Not Created Equal: Recent Findings on Genes and Behavior." *The Social Service Review*, 40, 121–34. (Ch. 20)

GOLDFARB, WILLIAM. (1943) "The Effects of Early Institutional Care on Adolescent Personality." *Journal of Experimental Education*, 12, 106–29

GOODGLASS, HAROLD, and QUADFASEL, F. A. (1954) "Language Laterality in Left-Handed Aphasics." *Brain*, 77, 521–48

GOODMAN, MARY ELLEN. *Race Awareness in Young Children*. Cambridge: Addison-Wesley, 1952; revised and published in paperback in 1964 by Crowell-Collier

GRAY, PHILIP H. (1958) "Theory and Evidence of Imprinting in Human Infants." *Journal of Psychology*, 46, 155–66

GREENSPOON, JOEL. (1955) "The Reinforcing Effect of Two Spoken Sounds on the Frequency of Two Responses." *American Journal of Psychology*, 68, 409–16

GUILFORD, J. P. (1956) "The Structure of Intellect." *Psychological Bulletin*, 53, 267–93

HALL, C. S. (1938) "The Inheritance of Emotionality." *Sigma Chi Quarterly*, 26, 17–27

HARLOW, HARRY. (1959) "Love in Infant Monkeys." *Scientific American*, 200, 68–74. Also: "Motivation in Monkeys—and Men," in *Psychology and Life* (Ed., Floyd L. Ruch), 6th ed. Chicago: Scott Foresman, 1963. (Ch. 5)

———. (1949) "The Formation of Learning Sets." *Psychological Review*, 56, 51–65. (Ch. 15)

HARLOW, HARRY, and MCCLEARN, G. E. (1954) "Object Discrimination Learned by Monkeys on the Basis of Manipulation Motives." *Journal of Comparative and Physiological Psychology*, 47, 73–76. (Ch. 9)

HARRELL, RUTH F., WOODYARD, E. R., and GATES, A. I. *The Effects of Mothers' Diets on the Intelligence of Offspring*. New York: Bureau of Publications, Teachers College, 1955

HARTLEY, EUGENE L., ROSENBAUM, MAX, and SCHWARTZ, SHEPARD. (1948) "Children's Use of Ethnic Frames of Reference." *Journal of Psychology*, 26, 367–86

HAYES, KEITH J., and HAYES, CATHERINE. (1951) "The Intellectual Development of a Home-Raised Chimpanzee." *Proceedings of the American Philosophical Society*, 95, 105–9

HEBB, D. O. *The Organization of Behavior*. New York: Wiley, 1949

HENRY, SIBYL. (1947) "Children's Audiograms in Relation to Reading Attainment: II." *Journal of Genetic Psychology*, 71, 3–49

HERNÁNDEZ-PEÓN, RAÚL, SCHERRER, HARALD, and JOUVET, MICHEL. (1956) "Modification of Electric Activity in Cochlear Nucleus During 'Attention' in Unanesthetized Cats." *Science*, 123, 331–32

HESS, ECKHARD. (1958) "Imprinting in Animals." *Scientific American*, 198, 81–90

HESS, ROBERT D., and SHIPMAN, VIRGINIA. (1965) "Early Experience and the Socialization of Cognitive Modes in Children." *Child Development*, 36, 869–86

HOCKETT, CHARLES F., and ASCHER, ROBERT. "The Human Revolution," in *Man in Adaptation, the Biosocial Background* (Ed., Y. A. Cohen). Chicago: Aldine, 1968

HOEFNAGEL, DICK, et al. (1965) "Hereditary Choreoathetosis, Self-Mutilation and Hyperuricemia in Young Males." *New England Journal of Medicine*, 273, 130–35

HOFSTAETTER, PETER R. (1954) "The Changing Composition of 'Intelligence': a Study in T-Technique." *Journal of Genetic Psychology*, 85, 158–64

HOROWITZ, EUGENE L., and HOROWITZ, RUTH. (1938) "Development of Social Attitudes in Children." *Sociometry*, 1, 301–38

HUSÉN, TORSTEN. "Talent, Opportunity and Career—a 26 Year Follow Up." Lecture delivered at University of Chicago, May 8, 1967

HYDÉN, HOLGER. "RNA in Brain Cells"; also "Biochemical Changes Accompanying Learning." Both in *The Neurosciences* (Eds., G. C. Quarton, T. Melnechuk, and F. O. Schmitt). New York: Rockefeller University Press, 1967

INGRAM, T. T. S. (1963) "Delayed Development of Speech with Special Reference to Dyslexia." *Proceedings of the Royal Society of Medicine*, 56, 199–203

IRWIN, O. C., and CHEN, H. P. (1948) "Infant Speech: Vowel and Consonant Frequency." *Journal of Speech and Hearing Disorders*, 13, 31–34

JACOBS, PATRICIA, et al. (1965) "Aggressive Behavior, Mental Subnormality and the XYY Male." *Nature*, 208, 1351–52

JACOBSON, ALLAN L., FRIED, CLIFFORD, and HOROWITZ, SHELDON D. (1966) "Planarians and Memory." *Nature*, 209, 599–601

JAHODA, GUSTAV. (1964) "Social Class Differentials in Vocabulary Expansion." *British Journal of Educational Psychology*, 34, 321–23

JENSEN, ARTHUR R. (1968) "Social Class, Race, and Genetics: Implications for Education." *American Educational Research Journal*, 5, 1–42. Also: (1969) "How Much Can We Boost IQ and Scholastic Achievement?" *Harvard Educational Review*, 39, 1–123

JERNE, N. K. "Antibodies and Learning: Selection Versus Instruction," in *The Neurosciences* (Eds., G. C. Quarton, T. Melnechuk, and F. O. Schmitt). New York: Rockefeller University Press, 1967

JOHN, E. ROY, et al. (1968) "Observation Learning in Cats." *Science*, 159, 1489–91

JOHNSON, EDWARD E. (1953) "The Role of Motivational Strength in Latent Learning." *Journal of Comparative and Physiological Psychology*, 45, 526–30

KAGAN, JEROME, MOSS, HOWARD A., and SIGEL, IRVING. (1963) "Psychological Significance of Styles of Conceptualization." *Monographs of the Society for Research in Child Development*, Serial No. 86, Vol. 28, 73–111

KATONA, GEORGE. *Organizing and Memorizing: Studies in the Psychology of Learning and Teaching*. New York: Columbia University Press, 1940

KENDLER, TRACY S., KENDLER, HOWARD H., and WELLS, DORIS. (1960) "Reversal and Nonreversal Shifts in Nursery School Children." *Journal of Comparative and Physiological Psychology*, 53, 83–88

KLINGHAMMER, ERICH. "Factors Influencing Choice of Mate in Altricial Birds," in *Early Behavior: Comparative and Developmental Approaches* (Eds., Harold Stevenson, Eckhard Hess, Harriet Rheingold). New York: Wiley, 1967

KNOBLOCH, HILDA, and PASAMANICK, BENJAMIN. (1962) "Mental Subnormality." *New England Journal of Medicine*, 266, 1092–96

KOHLBERG, LAWRENCE. (1966) "Cognitive Stages and Preschool Education." *Human Development*, 9, 5–17

KOOISTRA, W. H. "Developmental Trends in the Attainment of Conservation, Transivity, and Relativism in the Thinking of Children." Unpublished doctoral dissertation, Wayne State University, 1963

KUO, Z. Y. (1930) "The Genesis of the Cat's Response to the Rat." *Journal of Comparative Psychology*, 11, 1–36

LANSDELL, H. (1962) "A Sex Difference in Effect of Temporal-Lobe Neurosurgery on Design Preference." *Nature*, 194, 852–54

LASHLEY, K. S. (1938) "An Experimental Analysis of Instinctive Behavior." *Psychological Review*, 45, 445–72

LEE, E. S. (1951) "Negro Intelligence and Selective Migration." *American Sociological Review*, 16, 227–33

LENNEBERG, ERIC H. "The Capacity for Language Acquisition," in *Man in Adaptation, the Biosocial Background* (Ed., Y. A. Cohen). Chicago: Aldine, 1968

LESSER, GERALD S., FIFER, GORDON, and CLARK, DONALD H. (1965) "Mental Abilities of Children from Different Social-Class and Cultural Groups." *Monographs of the Society for Research in Child Development*, Vol. 30, No. 4

LIDDELL, HOWARD S. (1954) "Conditioning and Emotions." *Scientific American*, 190, 48–58

LIPSITT, LEWIS P. "Learning in the Human Infant," in *Early Behavior: Comparative and Developmental Approaches* (Eds., Harold Stevenson, Eckhard Hess, Harriet Rheingold). New York: Wiley, 1967

LURIA, ALEXANDER R. *The Role of Speech in the Regulation of Normal and Abnormal Behavior.* New York: Liveright, 1961

MARCHBANKS, GABRIELLE, and LEVIN, HARRY. (1965) "Cues by Which Children Recognize Words." *Journal of Educational Psychology*, 56, 57–61

MC CARTHY, DOROTHEA. (1930) "Language Development of the Preschool Child." *Institute of Child Welfare Monograph Series*, No. IV. Minneapolis: University of Minnesota Press

MC CLELLAND, DAVID C., et al. *The Achievement Motive.* New York: Appleton-Century-Crofts, 1953

MC CONNELL, J. V. (1962) "Memory Transfer Through Cannibalism in Planarians." *Journal of Neuropsychiatry*, Suppl. 1, Vol. 3, S42–S48

MC GINNIES, ELLIOTT, and ADORNETTO, JOSEPH. (1952) "Perceptual Defense in Normal and Schizophrenic Observers." *Journal of Abnormal and Social Psychology*, 47, 833–37. (Ch. 13)

MC GINNIES, ELLIOTT, and SHERMAN, HOWARD. (1952) "Generalization of Perceptual Defenses." *Journal of Abnormal and Social Psychology.* 47, 81–85. (Ch. 13)

MELZACK, RONALD. (1954) "The Genesis of Emotional Behavior: an Experimental Study of the Dog." *Journal of Comparative and Physiological Psychology*, 47, 166–68

MESSERSCHMIDT, RAMONA. (1933) "The Suggestibility of Boys and Girls Between the Ages of Six and Sixteen." *Journal of Genetic Psychology*, 43, 422–37

MILLER, GEORGE A. (1956) "The Magical Number Seven, Plus or Minus Two: Some Limits in Our Capacity for Processing Information." *Psychological Review*, 63, 81–97. Also: (1956) "Information and Memory," *Scientific American*, 195, 42–46. (Ch. 15)

MILLER, GEORGE A., and NICELY, P. E. (1955) "An Analysis of Perceptual Confusions Among English Consonants." *Journal of the Acoustical Society of America*, 27, 338–52. (Ch. 14)

MILLER, WILLIAM A. (1938) "What Children See in Pictures." *Elementary School Journal,* 39, 280–88

MILNER, ESTHER. (1951) "A Study of the Relationship Between Reading Readiness in Grade One School Children and Patterns of Parent-Child Interaction." *Child Development,* 22, 95–112

MONEY, JOHN, and ALEXANDER, DUANE. (1966) "Turner's Syndrome: Further Demonstration of the Presence of Specific Congenital Deficiencies." *Journal of Medical Genetics,* 3, 47–48. (Ch. 2)

MONEY, JOHN, HAMPSON, JOAN, and HAMPSON, JOHN. (1957) "Imprinting and the Establishment of Gender Role." *Archives of Neurology and Psychiatry,* 77, 333–36. (Ch. 11)

MONEY, JOHN, and LEWIS, VIOLA. (1966) "IQ, Genetics, and Accelerated Growth: Adrenogenital Syndrome." *Bulletin Johns Hopkins Hospital,* 118, 365–73. (Ch. 2)

———. "Longitudinal Study of Intelligence Quotient in Treated Congenital Hypothyroidism," in *Brain-Thyroid Relationships* (Ciba Study Group No. 18). Boston: Little Brown, 1964. (Ch. 16)

MOORHEAD, P. S., MELLMAN, W. J., and WENAR, CHARLES. (1961) "A Familial Chromosome Translocation Associated with Speech and Mental Retardation." *American Journal of Human Genetics,* 13, 32–46

MORTON, N. E. "The Components of Genetic Variability," in *The Genetics of Migrant and Isolate Populations* (Ed., E. Goldschmidt). Baltimore: Williams and Witkins, 1963

MYERS, ARLO K., and MILLER, N. E. (1954) "Failure to Find a Learned Drive Based on Hunger; Evidence for Learning Motivated by 'Exploration.'" *Journal of Comparative and Physiological Psychology,* 47, 428–36

NICHOLS, R. C. (1965) "The Inheritance of General and Specific Ability." *National Merit Scholarship Corporation Research Report,* 1, 1–9

OLDS, JAMES, and MILNER, PETER. (1954) "Positive Reinforcement Produced by Electrical Stimulation of Septal Area and Other Regions of Rat Brain." *Journal of Comparative and Physiological Psychology,* 47, 419–27

OSLER, SONIA F., and FIVEL, MYRNA WEISS. (1961) "Concept Attainment: I. The Role of Age and Intelligence in Concept Attainment by Induction." *Journal of Experimental Psychology,* 62, 1–8

PENFIELD, WILDER, and ROBERTS, LAMAR. *Speech and Brain Mechanisms.* Princeton: Princeton University Press, 1959

PIAGET, JEAN. (1957) "The Child and Modern Physics." *Scientific American,* 196, 46–51

PRICE, W. H., and WHATMORE, P. B. (1967) "Behavior Disorders and Pattern of Crime Among XYY Males Identified at a Maximum Security Hospital." *British Medical Journal,* 1, 533–36

PRICE-WILLIAMS, D. G. (1961) "A Study Concerning Concepts of Conservation of Quantitatives Among Primitive Children. *Acta Psychologica,* 18, 297–305

PRINGLE, KELLMER, and BOSSIO, Y. (1960–61) "Early Prolonged Separation and Emotional Maladjustment. *Journal of Child Psychology and Psychiatry,* 1, 37–48

QUARTON, GARDNER C. "The Enhancement of Learning by Drugs and the Transfer of Learning by Macromolecules," in *The Neurosciences* (Eds., G. C. Quarton, T. Melnechuk, and F. O. Schmitt). New York: Rockefeller University Press, 1967

RADKE, MARIAN, TRAGER, HELEN G., and DAVIS, HADASSAH. (1949) "Social Perceptions and Attitudes of Children." *Genetic Psychology Monographs,* 40, 327–447

RIMLAND, BERNARD. *Infantile Autism.* New York: Appleton-Century-Crofts, 1964

ROBERTSON, JOYCE. (1962) "Mothering as an Influence on Early Development," *Psychoanalytic Study of the Child,* Vol. 17

ROCK, IRVIN. (1958) "Repetition and Learning." *Scientific American,* 198, 68–72

ROSENBLUM, LEONARD A., and CROSS, HENRY A. (1963) "Performance of Neonatal Monkeys in the Visual Cliff Situation." *American Journal of Psychology,* 76, 318–23

SCHAFFER, H. R. (1958) "Objective Observations of Personality Development in Early Infancy. *British Journal of Medical Psychology,* 31, 174–83

SHUEY, AUDREY M. *The Testing of Negro Intelligence* (second edition). New York: Social Science Press, 1966

SKEELS, HAROLD M. (1966) "Adult Status of Children with Contrasting Early Life Experiences." *Monographs of the Society for Research in Child Development,* Serial No. 105, Vol. 31, No. 3

SKINNER, B. F. (1960) "Pigeons in a Pelican." *American Psychologist,* 15, 28–37

SMITH, MADORAH E. (1926) "An Investigation of the Development of the Sentence and the Extent of Vocabulary in Young Children." *University of Iowa Studies in Child Welfare,* Vol. 3, No. 5

SMITH, MARY KATHERINE. (1941) "Measurements of the Size of General English Vocabulary Through the Elementary Grades and High School." *Genetic Psychology Monographs,* 24, 313–45

SONTAG, LESTER W., BAKER, CHARLES T., and NELSON, VIRGINIA L. (1958) "Mental Growth and Personality Development: a Longitudinal Study." *Monographs of the Society for Research in Child Development,* Serial No. 68, Vol. 23, No. 2

SPELT, DAVID K. (1948) "The Conditioning of the Human Fetus in Utero." *Journal of Experimental Psychology,* 38, 338–46

SPERRY, ROGER W. (1964) "The Great Cerebral Commissure." *Scientific American,* 210, 42–52

SPITZ, RENÉ. (1945) "Hospitalism: an Inquiry into the Genesis of Psychiatric Conditions in Early Childhood." *Psychoanalytic Study of the Child,* 1, 53–74. (Ch. 6)

SPITZ, RENÉ, and WOLF, K. M. (1946) "The Smiling Response: a Contribution to the Ontogenesis of Social Relations." *Genetic Psychology Monographs,* 34, 57–125. (Ch. 3)

SPUHLER, JAMES N., and LINDZEY, GARDNER. "Racial Differences in Behavior," in *Behavior-Genetics Analysis* (Ed., Jerry Hirsch). New York: McGraw-Hill, 1967

STERN, CURT. "Genes and People," the National Foundation-March of Dimes Public Lecture for the Third International Congress of Human Genetics meeting in Chicago, September 9, 1966

STOCH, MAVIS, and SMYTHE, P. M. "Undernutrition During Infancy and Subsequent Brain Growth and Intellectual Development," in *Malnutrition, Learning, and Behavior* (Eds., Nevin Scrimshaw and John E. Gordon). Cambridge: Massachusetts Institute of Technology Press, 1968

TEMPLIN, MILDRED C. (1957) "Certain Language Skills in Children." *Institute of Child Welfare Monographs,* No. 26. Minneapolis: University of Minnesota Press

TERMAN, LEWIS M. *Genetic Studies of Genius.* (Vol. I, 1925; Vol. V, 1959). Stanford: Stanford University Press

THOMPSON, WILLIAM R., and HERON, WOODBURN. (1954) "The Effects of Restricting Early Experience on the Problem-Solving Capacity of Dogs." *Canadian Journal of Psychology*, 8, 17–31

TOLMAN, EDWARD C. (1948) "Cognitive Maps in Rats and Men." *Psychological Review*, 55, 189–208

VERNON, PHILIP E. (1954) "Symposium on the Effects of Coaching and Practice in Intelligence Tests" (Summary). *British Journal of Educational Psychology*, 24 (Part 2), 57–63

WALK, RICHARD D., and GIBSON, ELEANOR J. (1961) "A Comparative and Analytical Study of Visual Depth Perception." *Psychological Monographs*, 75, No. 15

WALLACH, MICHAEL A. "Research on Children's Thinking," in *Child Psychology*, the 62nd Yearbook of the National Society for the Study of Education (Part I). Chicago: University of Chicago Press, 1963

WATSON, JOHN B. *Psychologies of 1925.* Worcester: Clark University Press, 1926. (Ch. 4)

——. *Behaviorism.* New York: Norton, 1924. (Ch. 15)

WHEELER, LESTER R. (1942) "A Comparative Study of the Intelligence of East Tennessee Mountain Children." *Journal of Educational Psychology*, 33, 321–34

WHITE, BURTON L., and HELD, RICHARD. "Plasticity of Sensorimotor Development in the Human Infant," in *The Causes of Behavior* (Eds., Judy Rosenblith and Wesley Allensmith), 2nd ed. Boston: Allyn and Bacon, 1966

WHITE, ROBERT W. (1959) "Motivation Reconsidered: the Concept of Competence." *Psychological Review*, 66, 297–333

WHITE, SHELDON H., and PLUM, GERALD. (1964) "Eye Movement Photography During Children's Discrimination Learning." *Journal of Experimental Child Psychology*, 1, 327–38

WILLIAMS, JESSIE M. (1961) "Children Who Break Down in Foster Homes: a Psychological Study of Patterns of Personality Growth in Grossly Deprived Children." *Journal of Child Psychology and Psychiatry*, 2, 5–20

WILLIAMS, ROGER J. *You Are Extraordinary*. New York: Random House, 1967

WINDLE, C. D. (1956) Technical Report No. 29 for George Washington University's Human Resources Research Office

WINICK, MYRON. (1969) "Malnutrition and Brain Development." *Journal of Pediatrics*, 74, 667–79

WINICK, MYRON, and ROSSO, PEDRO. (1969) "The Effect of Severe Early Malnutrition on Cellular Growth of Human Brain." *Pediatric Research*, 3, 181–84

WINTERBOTTOM, MARION R. "The Relation of Childhood Training in Independence to Achievement Motivation." Unpublished doctoral dissertation, University of Michigan, 1953. (Cited by McClelland in *The Achievement Motive*.)

WITKIN, HERMAN A., et al. *Personality Through Perception*. New York: Harper, 1954

WOHLWILL, JOACHIM F. (1960) "Developmental Studies of Perception." *Psychological Bulletin*, 57, 249–88

WOLF, R. M. "The Identification and Measurement of Environmental Process Variables Related to Intelligence." Ph.D. dissertation in progress, University of Chicago, 1963. (Cited by Bloom in *Stability and Change in Human Characteristics*.)

WOLFENSTEIN, MARTHA. (1951) "The Emergence of Fun Morality." *Journal of Social Issues*, 7, 15–25

WOLFF, PETER H. "Observations on the Early Development of Smiling," in *Determinants of Infant Behavior II*. London: Methuen, 1963. (Ch. 3)

WOLFF, PETER H. and WHITE, BURTON L. (1965) "Visual Pursuit and Attention in Young Infants." *Journal of Child Psychiatry*, 4, 473–84. (Ch. 4)

WOOLDRIDGE, DEAN E. *Mechanical Man, the Physical Basis of Intelligent Life*. New York: McGraw-Hill, 1968

YERKES, ROBERT M., and DODSON, JOHN D. (1908) "The Relation of Strength of Stimulus to Rapidity of Habit Formation." *Journal of Comparative Neurology*, 18, 459–82

INDEX